Maya Lords and Lordship

MAYA LORDS AND LORDSHIP
The Formation of
Colonial Society in Yucatán, 1350–1600

by
Sergio Quezada

Translated
by
Terry Rugeley

UNIVERSITY OF OKLAHOMA PRESS : NORMAN

Also by Sergio Quezada

Bibliografía comentada sobre la cuestión étnica y la Guerra de Castas de Yucatán, 1821–1910 (Mexico, 1986)
Relación documental para la historia de la provincia de Yucatán 1520–1844 (Mexico, 1992)
Pueblos y caciques yucatecos, 1550–1580 (Mexico, 1993)
Documentos de indios Yucatecos, 1822–1847 (Mexico, 1995)
Los pies de la República: Los mayas peninsulares, 1550–1750 (Mexico, 1997)
Breve historia de Yucatán (Mexico, 2001)
Mujer maya: Siglos tejiendo una identidad (Mexico, 2001)
Papeles de los Xiu de Yaxá, Yucatán (with Tsubasa Okoshi Harada) (Mexico, 2001)
Las Encrucijadas de la ciudadanía y la democracia: Yucatán, 1812–2004 (Mexico, 2005)
Yucatán en la ruta del liberalismo mexicano, siglo XIX (with Inés Ortiz Yam) (Mexico, 2008)
Visita de Diego García de Palacio a Yucatán, 1583 (with Inés Ortiz Yam) (Mexico, 2009)

Library of Congress Cataloging-in-Publication Data

Quezada, Sergio.
 [Pueblos y caciques yucatecos, 1550–1580. English]
 Maya lords and lordship : the formation of colonial society in Yucatán, 1350–1600 / by Sergio Quezada ; translated by Terry Rugeley.
  p. cm.
 Includes bibliographical references and index.
  ISBN 978-0-8061-4422-1 (hardcover) ISBN 978-0-8061-9414-1 (paper)   1. Mayas—Politics and government.   2. Mayas—Kings and rulers.   3. Yacatán (Mexico : State)—History—16th century.   I. Title.
 F1435.3.P7Q4913 2014
 323.1197'427—dc23

2013019099

The paper in this book meets the guidelines for permanence and durability of the Committee on Production Guidelines for Book Longevity of the Council on Library Resources, Inc. ∞

Copyright © 2014 by the University of Oklahoma Press, Norman, Publishing Division of the University. Paperback published 2024. Manufactured in the U.S.A.

All rights reserved. No part of this publication may be reproduced, stored in a retrieval system, or transmitted, in any form or by any means, electronic, mechanical, photocopying, recording, or otherwise—except as permitted under Section 107 or 108 of the United States Copyright Act—without the prior written permission of the University of Oklahoma Press. To request permission to reproduce selections from this book, write to Permissions, University of Oklahoma Press, 2800 Venture Drive, Norman OK 73069, or email rights.oupress@ou.edu.

A Cuquis

Contents

List of Illustrations	ix
List of Tables	xi
Preface	xiii
Introduction	3
1. Personal Ties and Maya Political Organization	6
2. From Lordship to Early Colonial Pueblo	38
3. Gobernadores and Indian Cabildos	76
4. Decline of the Caciques	100
Conclusion	123
Appendix A: The Cúuchcabalob of the Mid-Sixteenth Century	125
Appendix B: Lineages, Caciques, and Gobernadores	141
Sources for Appendices A and B	170
Appendix C: Major Spanish Urban Centers and Their Jurisdictions	175
Appendix D: Sixteenth-Century Governors of Yucatán: Names, Titles, and Tenure	179
Notes	181
Glossary	227
Bibliography	235
Index	245

Illustrations

FIGURES

1. Page 14 of the Calkiní Codex	10
2. The Cocom Lineage and Its Cúuchabal	25
3. The Cupul Lineage and Its Cúuchabal	26
4. The Virgen of the Purísima Concepción of Izamal	53
5. Franciscan Church and Convent of San Antonio de Padua of Izamal	54
6. Franciscan Church and Convent of Santa Clara of Dzidzantún	55
7. Church of San Luis Obispo of Calkiní	67

MAPS

1. Spatial Distribution of the Batabilob or Lordships	19
2. Maya Political Organization, ca. 1545	28
3. The Perimeter of Yaxkukul Village, According to *Documento Núm. 1*, 1552	62
4. Reducciones of Pueblos into a Single Location; The Cúuchcabal of Maní, 1565–1582	72

Tables

2.1.	Reducciones into a Single Location, 1565	64
2.2.	Reducciones into a Single Location, 1582	73
A.1.	The Cúuchcabal of Calkiní (Campeche)	126
A.2.	The Cúuchcabal of Calotmul (Mérida)	127
A.3.	The Cúuchcabal of Chancenote (Valladolid)	128
A.4.	The Cúuchcabal of Chichén Itzá (Valladolid)	129
A.5.	The Cúuchcabal of Dzidzantún (Mérida)	130
A.6.	The Cúuchcabal of Hocabá (Mérida)	132
A.7.	The Cúuchcabal of Maní (Mérida)	133
A.8.	The Cúuchcabal of Motul (Mérida)	134
A.9.	The Cúuchcabal of Sací, 1 and 2 (Valladolid)	135
A.10.	The Cúuchcabal of Sotuta (Mérida)	136
A.11.	The Cúuchcabal of Tihosuco (Valladolid)	137
A.12.	Independent Batabilob	138

Preface

The original Spanish version of this book grew from "Pueblos y caciques yucatecos, 1550–1580," my 1990 doctoral dissertation in History at the Centro de Estudios Históricos de El Colegio de México. Three years later that same institution published it under the same name, and without substantive changes. Now, following many years of reflection on the historical evolution of power in Maya political organization, and working with the University of Oklahoma Press, I am pleased to offer a new interpretation and a substantially modified book, one that I have entitled *Maya Lords and Lordship: The Formation of Colonial Society in Yucatán, 1350–1600*.

As with the original version, the analysis presented here grew from a meditation on the nature of indigenous political authority. The story begins somewhere in the fourteenth century, when the *batab*, a figure of murky origins, emerged as the link to thousands of family chieftains living dispersed throughout the Yucatecan forests. Building on his own power and prestige, each batab started to construct and consolidate his own lordship, that is, a complicated network of supporters based on ties of mutual obligation. This new interpretation discards the now familiar model of political organization based on supposed "pre-Hispanic provinces." Correlatively, it rejects the idea of a territorial fragmentation during the early colonial years, since such fragmentation would have been meaningless for political units based on the principle of personal association. The originality of the interpretation of Yucatec Maya society presented here lies precisely in this distinction: the batab (at diverse times also called *cacique*, or lord) maintained his power through personal, and not territorial, associations. This way of seeing things flies in the face of what I had assumed in 1990, and what Mayanists have always held.

In fact, much of what we associate with Last Postclassic Maya society only came later. As I argue in the following pages, the notion that the Maya operated through some sort of territorial association was a Spanish invention and a colonial imposition that began when the Crown initiated the practice of concentrating or "reducing" a population to the place of its lord's residence. To reduce the batab's power, they began to lay out the boundaries of the early colonial villages. Along with the campaign to restrict that power to defined spaces came a policy of organizing a *república* or *cabildo* (that is, a governing council), in each of the villages. While caciques and prominent Maya opposed the process, the cabildo inevitably weakened those personal ties that bound the lords to their subject population. Spaniards intended these redesigned villages, along with their repúblicas, to be the new basis of allegiance for Maya peoples.

The book concludes with the history of surviving caciques' decline. During the second half of the sixteenth century, the Spanish conquest and the conflicts associated with Europeans' initial presence wrought profoundly negative effects on Maya society. Despite the privileges that Spaniards authorized for the caciques, and despite designating them *gobernadores* of their villages, colonial policy nevertheless aimed at limiting their ancient privileges and prerogatives, and at excluding them from control of their lordships. This growing exclusion, together with the mid-century demographic crisis, played a decisive role in the lords' decline, since the web of personal ties that sustained those lords began to break apart, weakening indigenous nobility and allowing Spaniards to insert more malleable replacements in village governance. The book ends in 1600, by which point Yucatec Maya lordships had become little more than relics of the past.

Maya Lords and Lordships draws from sources that can hardly be described as new. Ralph L. Roys, France V. Scholes, and Robert S. Chamberlain consulted them decades ago when writing their masterworks, and many other accomplished Mayanists have followed suit. Still, original documents, and particularly documents as important as those generated by the Yucatecan conquest, will always continue to speak anew. It is also important to recognize John V. Murra and Bernardo García Martínez, two men whose scholarship helped inspire this new interpretation concerning the personal nature of the batab's political ties with his vassals.

Needless to say, many people have contributed to the evolution of this work. The first two chapters profited from a careful reading by Bernardo García Martínez; his comments and suggestions proved enormously useful in clarifying the interpretation about the personal nature that characterized political ties in Yucatec Maya society. I am indebted to my friend and colleague Tsubasa Okoshi Harada who, for many long years, has shown unconditional support for my studies of the Yucatec Maya. I also owe much to Inés Ortiz Yam. It was she who prompted me to see pre-Hispanic Maya political organization in a fundamentally new way. Moreover, her patience in reading early drafts of the text was unflagging. Special thanks go to Yanni Yannakakis and John Chuchiak IV for their encouraging readings of and thoughtful suggestions for the manuscript. Alessandra Jacobi and Kathleen Kelly of the University of Oklahoma Press have my eternal gratitude for the unwavering support they showed for this project, and for their sagacious advice at critical moments in the process. So too, my debt to Terry Rugeley is large: first, for encouraging and motivating me to publish this work in English; second, for his patience in waiting for me to produce a new version, something that required no small amount of time; and third, for his meticulous translation. Above all, I cannot fail to mention how much I owe to my wife Cuquis, who always gave me her unconditional support while I completed this book, and who was a never-ending source of understanding, patience, love, and inspiration.

Maya Lords and Lordship

Introduction

Interest in understanding the lords and lordships of indigenous Mesoamerica is as old as the conquest itself. The long list of individuals contributing to this elusive field of knowledge includes Spaniards: conquistadors, tribute-holders, friars, and royal functionaries who composed chronicles, memoirs, accounts, orders, and vocabulary lists, among other documents. So, too, there were the Indian peoples themselves: those nobles or commoners who by means of their colonial codices, books, lawsuits, and legal depositions left testimony of their ancestors and their ancient privileges. Many years later, in the contemporary period, a veritable army of researchers has concerned itself with studying indigenous lords through the theories and methods of their specific disciplines, creating in the process an impressive and almost overwhelming body of articles, monographs, and primary sources.

Despite the abundance of material, a consensus holds that indigenous *señoríos*, or lordships, shared three common characteristics. First, the lordship was the fundamental building block of the pre-Hispanic political system. Second, lords were the most prominent individuals in their particular señoríos, and they were in some way responsible for the destinies of their vassals. And third, lords found support for their authority in elaborate networks of personal ties. While key distinctions do exist relative to different languages, religions, ideologies, geographical settings, and spatial arrangements of peoples, these three characteristics emerge time and again throughout all Mesoamerican cultures.

For example, the Nahuas of central Mexico called the basic unit of their society the *altepetl* (plural, *altepeme*), a unit simultaneously political and territorial. Unlike the modern state, with its key powers located in a capital city, the altepetl's political center resided in the person and lineage of a lord known as the *tlahtoani* (plural, *tlhatoque*). Significantly, no evidence indicates that this center took a spatial form equivalent to that of the head town or modern capital.[1] The Yucatec Maya, for their part, called their basic unit the *batabil* (plural, *batabilob*), and it was a unit of jurisdiction or authority, not of territory. Its leader was a lord known as the *batab* (plural, *batabob*). While his vassals might live dispersed throughout this rural world, often alongside vassals of other lords, the batab's place of residence became the fixed point to which his subjects gathered when summoned for celebrations or wars or when matters of governance or justice required attention.

The territorial aspect of the altepetl did not imply a precise demarcation of boundaries. Indeed, some altepeme territories overlapped, and two tlahtoque shared a single territory, in which instance the houses of their vassals stood beside one another.[2] Whatever the exact circumstances, the tlahtoque's exercise of power was based on the principle of personal association and remained circumscribed within the territory of their respective altepeme. The situation was different for a batabil, which lacked territory; instead, the batab's political influence was delimited by the presence or absence of individuals who shared ties of personal association with him.[3]

The altepetl, in turn, was composed of a conjunction of semi-independent units. In the region of Tlaxcala, Puebla, and the Valley of Mexico these were called such Náhuatl terms as *calpolli*, *tlaxilacalli*, *teccalli*, and *tecpan*, all denoting the idea of a "seignorial house."[4] The tlahtoani thus headed his own seignorial house, while directly under him stood the *teuctli*, persons of lesser rank. In economic terms, each seignorial house was a corporation, and some were richer and more powerful than others, owing to the fact that their domain included more extensive lands and, in some cases, a greater number of tenants.

Unlike the altepetl, the batabil was not subdivided into seignorial houses; nor did the Yucatec Maya language contain terms for the equivalent of calpolli, tlaxilacalli, teccalli, or tecpan. Indeed, no documentary evidence proves or even suggests that either the batab or the Maya nobility were landowners, or whether they had a greater number of tenants on those lands under their control. The most we can say is that some batabob were richer than others, owing to the number of vassals who recognized the formers' authority, cultivated their milpas, and offered them personal service. Put another way, the batab's rights were limited to exploiting the human energy of his subject population.

Realizing that altepetl and batabil were the basic units of Mesoamerican political organization, the Spanish referred to them as *pueblos de indios* or simply *pueblos*. But these terms carried connotations more social than territorial.[5] It was upon the individuals who led these organizations—the tlahtoani in the Náhuatl world, and the batab among the Yucatec Maya—that the conquistadors began to construct their colonial system. With this point in mind, *Maya Lords and Lordship* offers a history of the batabilob from their precontact origins and practices to their conversion to pueblos de indios situated in the northwest region of the Yucatán peninsula. The pages that follow analyze the nature of the batabob's political power, the way in which the Spanish imposed territorial limits on the batabob's domains, the impact of imposing Spanish-sanctioned indigenous town councils over and above the batab's personal ties, and finally, the political and demographic causes that brought about the decline and eventual disappearance of the indigenous lords who survived European conquest.

CHAPTER 1

Personal Ties and Maya Political Organization

A broad scholarly consensus attributes our knowledge of Yucatec Maya political organization at the moment of Spanish conquest to the studies of Ralph L. Roys. This author began to outline his thinking in 1933, when he explained the differences between the *halach uinic*, or "overlord," and the batab, meaning "lord" or "cacique." Roys elaborated his ideas about the political structure of Maya pueblos, or villages, in 1939–1940, and three years later published *The Indian Background of Colonial Yucatan*, his definitive statement on the institutions and social hierarchies that defined peninsular life.[1]

Roys's model held that when the Spanish came to Yucatán, the peninsula was divided into "provinces," each falling into one of three types of political organization. The first was characterized by centralized power personified by the halach uinic, who ruled each of his subordinate pueblos through a batab, or village headman. The second type consisted of a confederation of batabob drawn from the same lineage, a group of individuals with a common ancestor and distinguished by their shared patronymic. Still a third variety consisted of an alliance of batabob, unrelated by lineage, who joined forces to avoid submission to some better-organized neighbors.[2] Roys considered the "prehispanic provinces" to be continuous territories regardless of their style of political integration. He assumed that like modern states, Maya power extended over a specific area at the time of the Spanish invasion, and he tentatively proposed boundaries for these supposed provinces.[3]

Maya scholars of the Preclassic, Classic, and Postclassic period have followed suit. Regardless of the type of source they use—whether archaeological record, epigraphic information, anthropological theory, or ethnography—they also begin with the concept of power exercised over continuous territory when propounding models of a regional, unified state composed of well-defined segments or geographic subdivisions. Correlatively, these scholars share the idea that power was exercised by control over spatial territory. One conspicuous example of this way of understanding the relationship between power and territory appears in the 2004 work of Suhler et al. In attempting to determine how far the dominion of Chichén Itzá reached between 900 and 1000 A.D., they write: "Itza territory at this time was marked on the northwest by the trading port of Isla Cerritos, extending along the coast for ca. sixty kilometers to the east. On the eastern interior, the boundary seems to have been in the vicinity of Ichmul de Morley, while the western boundary was probably somewhere east of Izamal. . . . The initial southern Itza boundary was some unknown distance to the north of Yaxuna, perhaps somewhere near the modern village of Popola, ten kilometers away. With their internal social integration complete and their core polity secure, the Itza set forth on the road to conquest and empire."[4]

Beyond this particular case, innumerable Maya scholars have labored to demonstrate territorial limits by means of graphic representations, while others, more ambitious, have even tried to calculate in square kilometers the territory that a political center dominated.[5] Regardless of the individual author, then, the paradigm of spatially defined power has dominated our understanding of precontact Yucatec Maya society for nearly seventy years.

PERSONAL TIES

Unquestionably, these investigators' proposals and explanations have provided an impressive body of knowledge concerning the historical, political, and cultural developments of the Maya from Pre- to Postclassic times. But they have also unearthed clues for an entirely different perspective: that Maya use of power was more personal than territorial. Indeed, advances in epigraphy demonstrate that hierarchical relations in Maya society were expressed in terms of possession. Then as now, the Maya prefix "*u-*" signifies "his" or "her." When further identification is necessary, the possessive noun comes last in the phrase. For example, *u cahal* means "his village," while *u cahal Juan* means "Juan's village." For that reason, a *sahal*—a ceremonial office assumed by certain members of the dominant nobility—could become *usuhal*, or literally, "the noble of," when used to link a specific lord with his king. This way of establishing hierarchical relationships can be seen in the monarchical status of *ahau* when, by military triumph, family connections, protection, or some asymmetrical alliance, this word changed to *u yahau*, meaning "king of another king."[6] Both cases point to some form of hierarchical subordination.

The opening generated by this epigraphic study widens when read against Maya sources from the early colonial period. Scholars have traditionally used the term *cuchteel* exactly as Ralph L. Roys defined it in 1957: that is, to refer to "the smallest organized political unit [which] seems to have been the ward, or barrio, of a town." The dictionaries give its Maya name as "cuchteel."[7] In accordance with this definition, Roys thought that pre-Hispanic pueblos were divided into barrios or districts identified by separate toponyms.[8]

Nevertheless, Okoshi Harada points out that "cuchteel" designated the "functionaries who belonged to the governing body under the command of a *batab* or cacique."[9] If this interpretation does indeed point toward the idea that political ties among the ruling elites were of a personal and not a territorial nature, then we need to analyze a bit more deeply the nuances of the Maya word "cuchteel" and the context in which it appears in the indigenous documents in order to understand its original meaning.

The word "cuchteel" has four meanings, all with the common denominator of expressing the idea of dependence between persons, but in each case, dependence of a different nature. In one instance "cuchteel" designates an individual subordinated to someone else when the concept of territory does not apply: "subject or vassal under the rule or governance of another." In a second meaning, this subordination has a social quality: "family or people whom one has in his household."[10] The third meaning of cuchteel was roughly equivalent to "parishioner." While this noun bears spatial implications, insofar as a person is bound within a particular parish, we must remember that "parishioner" (*feligrés*) is also used to describe the worshiper's spiritual subordination to his parish priest. The fourth meaning of "cuchteel" is "*parcialidad*, part of the pueblo under one's charge." This definition carries a sense of social rather than territorial subordination, since the word "parcialidad" was used to designate "a group of many who form a family," and who, as a group, stood in a dependent relationship to another.[11] Whichever of the four meanings we invoke, the term "cuchteel" expresses the idea of a person or persons hierarchically subordinated to someone else. It does *not* refer to territory.

Maya scribes used the word "cuchteel," and occasionally its synonym *cuchul*, to designate one Indian politically subordinated to another, but not to refer to a "barrio."[12] In Maya phrasing, cuchteel appears with its plural suffix (*-ob* or *-oob*) and is preceded by the name of a lord, then *yetel u* (a phrase indicating possession by that lord). In *Documento núm. 1*, an indigenous-language text brought to light by the seminal Maya linguist Alfredo Barrera Vásquez, we read: "*Cacathil in bin yetel in dzin Nachan Pech yetel u kuchteilob*." Translated, this reads, "I was accompanied by my younger brother Nachan Pech and his subjects."[13] Similar evidence comes from the *Calkiní Codex*, a collection of Maya-language texts gathered in the late sixteenth century that narrates the history of the Canul and Canché lineages through the Spanish invasion. Here the Maya scribe writes, "*u benel tun chacah canul siho yetel u cuchteelob*": "Then [Ah] Chacah Canul went to Siho with his subjects."[14] So too, in the "Crónica de Chac-Xulub-Chen," a chronicle of the Spanish conquest, Ah Nakuk Pech, the lord of that place, wrote, "*Macan Pech, don Pedro Pech, yetel u cuchteelob*": "Macan Pech, don Pedro Pech and his subjects."[15]

Multiple factors may have led one Maya to accept another's lordship—or, in the words of friar and linguistic scholar Antonio de Ciudad Real, to decide to become his "vassal." Such factors included protection, kinship, convenience, war, or the simple quest for recognition of a title. In this sense, dependency was constructed from the ground up, and for that reason the tie of subordination did not bind the individual to his lord for life; nor was it hereditary, and it could

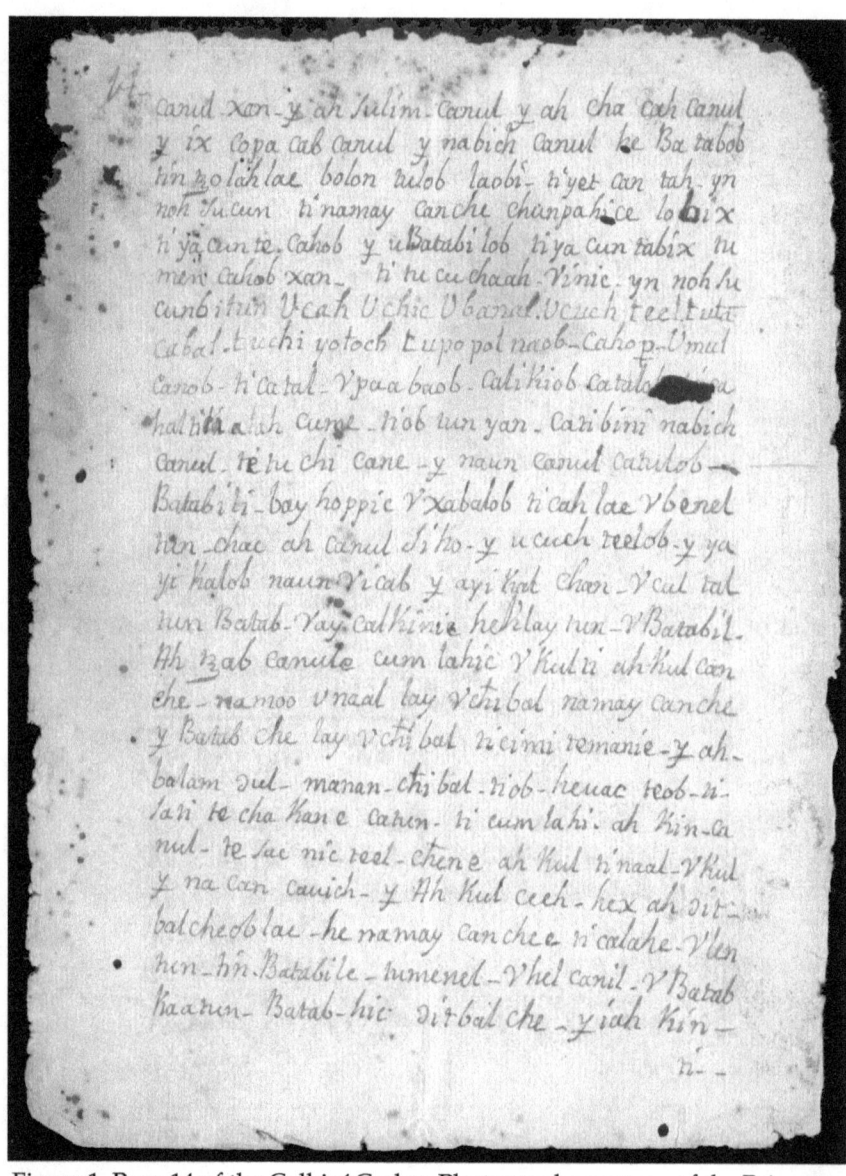

Figure 1. Page 14 of the Calkiní Codex. Photograph courtesy of the Princeton University Library.

be made or unmade according to circumstances. The Maya thus used the terms "cuchteel" or "cuchul" to express the lord-vassal relationship, without reference to a territorial designation for one or the other.

It was the Western World, rather than the Mayas themselves, that interpreted that hierarchical bond of lord-vassal as something imposed from the top down, a relationship initially lifelong and eventually hereditary. Observers from the conquistadors onward have failed to conceive of that relationship as jurisdictional. They consistently missed its meaning as "authority, power, or dominion over another"; and instead read it as the "boundary or limit of one place or another in which one's authority is circumscribed."[16] It is this latter meaning that has usually informed our understanding of Maya political organization.

But was this really the Maya way? The idea, derived from both indigenous and Spanish-language colonial sources, that the Maya forged political organization by links based on personal ties opens a new perspective for understanding how a pyramidal network of hierarchical links was constructed from the tenth century onward. However, these same sources are so threadbare, confusing, and contradictory that Mayanists typically accept them when they coincide with material evidence, and reject them when they clash. But, despite the limitations of the evidence, these document sources offer a vision of how a vast network of personal ties could be woven and then unraveled. This vision, in turn, offers us a new way of reconstructing the political history of the Maya of Yucatán's northern lowlands.

THE HEGEMONY OF CHICHÉN ITZÁ

Up to the moment of the Spanish invasion, Maya ruling organization had resulted not from an autonomous evolution, but rather through a process informed by invading groups entering the peninsula during the tenth century. Our ability to reconstruct these invasions is limited by the chronological lacunas in sources of that period. Nor do those sources always explain the identity and origin of the groups involved. Moreover, archaeological evidence appears to contradict historical information, at times directly. These limitations have generated an intense polemic regarding ethnic origins, the dates of invasions, and the places through which invaders came to Yucatán. Nevertheless, a prevailing concensus holds that from the second half of the ninth century onward, the northern lowlands reveal definitive evidence of conquering groups arriving from "the west."[17]

A certain amount of evidence on this point comes from the traditional accounts incorporated into the various versions of the *Book of Chilam Balam*, a compilation of Maya-language texts chronicling all phases of the precolonial and colonial Maya history. According to this narrative, a people known as the Itzá conquered Chichén Itzá sometime between 968 and 987 A.D.[18] Later, between 987 and 1007, a group called the Xiu, imposed their rule over Uxmal, and somewhat later, still another group of invaders, known as the Cocom, overwhelmed Mayapán.[19] Once these various new lords cemented their authority, they expropriated the title of halach uinic, or "overlord," in order to legitemize themselves. And, since this was a conquest of men and not of territory, each one sustained his authority through preexisting hierarchies.[20]

Meanwhile, the overlord of the Itzá continued his campaign of conquest.[21] Historical sources tell of how he subjugated all the lords of the peninsula, and how his influence reached as far as Chiapas and Guatemala.[22] By the late twelfth or early thirteenth century, he had already overcome the halach uinicob of Uxmal and Mayapán, and held the rank of *ah tepal* (sovereign) atop a pyramid of personal relationships.[23] In other words, he ruled with absolute dominion over his vassals—the overlords of Uxmal, Mayapán, and others—and there was no one above him.[24] By means of these campaigns of domination and personal consolidation, Chichén Itzá became the center of all forms of power in the peninsular north, and took the name *chuccabal Chichén Itzá*: roughly, "Chichén Itzá, conquerer of lordships."[25] Similtaneously, the ah tepal began to organize a complex and state-like command structure to govern Yucatán's northern lowlands.[26]

A similar process transpired with the Cocom and Xiu. When they made their respective conquests of Mayapán and Uxmal, the halach uinic of each center built his state over a preexisting network of personal ties. In this way the halach uinicob of the two centers, now as vassals to another sovereign, maintained their jurisdiction over their subordinate Maya lords. The ah tepal may have elevated some conquered Maya lords to the rank of halach uinic, in the process transferring to them a variety of powers to use over the vassals whom they, in turn, recognized as lords. Personal loyalty to one's superior thus played a decisive role in reproducing and reaffirming the political order of the ah tepal, and helped assure that those promoted to higher ranks could maintain their power.[27]

Tribute also played a role in the matter. The Early Postclassic world operated on an immense volume of tributary goods and labor, and the need to collect and direct these resources in the most efficient way possible inevitably led to administrative centralization.[28] Because of its hegemonic position in this process, Chichén Itzá assumed an architectural and monumental splendor; indeed, it became one of the largest cities of the entire Maya region and ranked among the most prosperous in all of Mesoamerica.[29]

As an inextricable component of these changes, the Early Postclassic conquests brought new gods to the Yucatecan pantheon and introduced new rituals.[30] According to indigenous testimonies, these new rites and deities smacked of idolatry. Without question, the cult of Kukulkán acquired the greatest splendor in terms of religious ceremony.[32] One indigenous testimony states: "It is said that Chichén Itzá's people were not idolaters until the Mexican leader Kukulkán came to these parts; he brought them idolatry, or, as they say, necessity taught them to worship false gods."[31] The classic Maya priesthood presumably adapted itself to the beliefs brought by these invaders.

But the new order was not to last. By the middle of the thirteenth century, disagreements between Hunac Ceel, halach uinic of Mayapán, and Chac Xib Chac, ah tepal of Chichén Itzá, initiated a period of internecine warfare. The ensuing struggles in turn brought about the collapse of the pyramid of personal ties that the sovereign had constructed through the overlords and their respective vassals. The ah tepal vanished as a source of sovereignty, and Chichén Itzá declined as northern Yucatán's leading political center.[33]

The most critical change at this point was the resurgence of lineages, or clans of nobility, as social institutions. Heretofore, they had played a secondary role in constructing the network of personal ties, functioning almost as silent institutions that people understood, but of which they seldom spoke. However, with the fall of the ah tepal the lineages showed new signs of life, taking their place along with personal ties as the entities upon which political structure would be built in the second half of the thirteenth century.

THE FRAGILITY OF THE MAYAPÁN *MULTEPAL*

The consequences of this renewed vitality soon became apparent. The great lords of the Cocom, Xiu, Chel, Tzeh, Canul, Cupul, Iuit, Pech, and Cochuah lineages dedicated themselves to the task of reorganizing the northern lowlands around the *multepal*, a form of government in which the overlords made decisions in common.[34] Mayapán did serve as the place of residence for the Cocom halach uinic, for as the great Franciscan evangelist and chronicler friar Diego de Landa wrote, "for the republic to continue, the house of Cocom would have to have the principal voice, for it was the oldest and richest, and its head was the bravest." Nevertheless, everything indicates that the Mayapán leader lacked sufficient power to be considered a *primus inter pares*.[35] Unlike the ah tepal, participation in the multepal was limited to certain prominent lords of the peninsular northwest.[36]

The institution was certainly innovative. It centralized political decisions to a degree unprecedented in the history of Maya governance.[37] Decisions on matters of politics, religion, or administration now came to depend on mutual recognition of authority, and on precarious alliances among prominent lords—all in the interest of maintaining equilibrium and unity. Although creative the multepal was thus born with an inherent fragility.[38]

Despite the intrinsic weakness of the multepal, it had its beneficiaries. The halach uinicob, sustained by tradition, and using the preeminence of their lineages, threw themselves into the task of reorganizing their own sets of personal bonds.[39] In this process, however, it was actually the batab who played the leading role. He enjoyed a privileged position, close to thousands of family chieftains who lived with their relatives in dispersed groups throughout the forests of Yucatán.⁴⁰ This allowed him to forge an elaborate web of personal ties, whether through kinship or by offering protection or recognition; in turn, he could bind and solidify relationships within these ties. The batab's newfound prestige and authority thus made him the arbiter of the lives of his cuchteelob; and during the second half of the fourteenth century, his lordship became the building block of any political arrangement. In reality, beginning with the multepal, the overlords began to envy the batabob, and one of the formers' main objectives was to convert as many of the latter as possible into cuchteelob, or vassals.

The overlords' task of reordering their networks of personal ties came about in an atmosphere of uncertainty and instability. For, with the fall of the ah tepal, innumerable family chiefs, following the traditional Maya reaction in moments of crisis, began to emigrate in search of more powerful lords.⁴¹ Many of these lords, even those with a larger subject population, nevertheless felt themselves vulnerable, and thus willingly subordinated themselves to other, more powerful lords or overlords. Some did so based on the historical rights of vassalage—that is, on the idea that protection previously extended to one's ancestor established a precedent for continued protection—while others appealed to the fact that they belonged to the same lineage. In the first instance, the tie was strictly political, but in the second, it was reinforced by kinship. One way or another, as a result of the multepal's rise, the halach uinicob managed to sustain their power through affiliations with those batabob who recognized them. The batabob, in turn, traded on personal connections with the family chieftains.⁴²

In the early fifteenth century, however, those alliances took an ugly turn. The Cocom overlord "became greedy for wealth"; he allied himself with the lords of "Tabasco, brought more Mexicas into the city [of Mayapán], and began to tyrannize and enslave the commoners." With the equilibrium shattered, the overlords of the other lineages, led by those of the Xiu, "agreed to assassinate the Cocom, and so they did, even killing all his children, leaving only one who happened to be away."⁴³ Mayapán was destroyed in the mid-1400s, and the league fell apart.

BATABIL AND SEIGNEURIAL JURISDICTION

During the century prior to the Spanish invasion, the peninsula was home to myriad dispersed groups of family chieftains, including those groups headed by a batab.[44] Martín de Palomar, one of Mérida's first Spanish settlers, working with Maya interpreter and informant Gaspar Antonio Chi, described the dispersed nature of settlements thus: "Because the people . . . were accustomed to dividing into six or eight pueblos, and as they were scattered throughout all the land . . . so they held it."[45] One factor that determined their exact location included direct access to water sources, whether artificial wells or the natural limestone sinkholes known as cenotes, or else rain-fed seasonal wetlands known as *aguadas*. Another critical resource was the availability of dense woods; indeed, the settlements were invariably surrounded vegetation.[46] It comes as no surprise, then, that residential clusters were frequently identified by the toponym of the cenote, savanna, aguada, or forest where they had settled.[47]

Within these settlements, each chieftain and his kinsmen—including the nobility—constituted an extended family of both blood and affinity.[48] In 1548 friar Lorenzo de Bienvenida described the composition of these households: "In this land there is hardly any home with only a single resident; rather, each one has two, three, four, six, and even more."[49] Residential government was patrilocal, and this characteristic fostered a bond of blood kin traced through the paternal line. Both descent and succession followed patriarchal lines.[50]

Naturally, the issue of land usage was critical. No evidence indicates that the family chieftains worried about marking off lands where they farmed or hunted or where they gathered firewood, wax, and honey. Demarcation of these lands seemed pointless from their perspective, since membership in the residential cluster legitimized possession, and for that reason recognition by the other family chieftains, along with historical memory, determined the natural resources over which each family chieftain maintained control.[51] The system of place names served to identify the woods, savannas, cenotes, aguadas, caves, and salt flats over which each family chieftain and his kin, by custom, enjoyed usufruct.[52]

Because *monte*, or woods, surrounded the residential cluster, the heads of families had little need to travel outward to cultivate their slash-and-burn cornfields known as *milpas*.⁵³ As is well known, the Maya region presented unfavorable conditions for agriculture. Even today, common wisdom regards the land as the source of fertility and the basis of milpa, when in reality the monte itself is responsible.⁵⁴ That is to say, it is only the overgrowth and its eventual burning off that render the soil fertile enough for cultivation. Over the course of millennia the native peoples developed a specialized knowledge in making effective use of the monte, the types of soil, and the varieties of corn, cotton, and other crops. In this way, "to make milpa," far from some primitive activity, was the core of a complex agricultural system.⁵⁵

Once he selected a stretch of land, the intending cultivator would call out for the *kuil-kaxob* (guardians of the monte) for some time so that they would know that the was a friend.⁵⁶ A *milpero* (milpa farmer) would have to clear only enough land to satisfy his needs, for it would be a transgression to use more than the gods allowed. He was not to fell the luxuriant trees indiscriminately. He was to leave stumps so that the forest could regenerate itself, and would prepare his milpa in unconnected patches to facilitate rapid reforestation.⁵⁷ After burning off the vegetation, family groups planted the first milpa (known as *milpa roza*); a year later they would burn the stubble to make a second milpa (the *milpa caña*). After these two cycles, the soil, now devoid of ashes and nutrients, could no longer produce, and the milpero would abandon these plots for some twenty-five years to allow the monte to regrow, moving on to surrounding monte to start the cycle all over again.

Key to the productive process was *mulmenyah*, or collective labor. Family chieftains organized these group labor drafts for weaving cloth, building homes, or extracting salt.⁵⁸ The Maya conducted their most taxing labors of the milpa—slashing and burning the monte—with sons, brothers, or sons-in-law. A family lacking sufficient members, or as Diego de Landa put it, "those who do not have their own people to do it," would organize groups of twenty men, and "all would participate in the common labor according to their ability, and would not stop until everything was finished."⁵⁹ The women, for their part, used mulmenyah in order to weave cotton. Groups of Indian women gathered to spin the cotton that each of them had previously combed. Landa reports, "They have the custom of helping one another to spin the fabric."[60] Similarly, in the construction of homes, it was "custom to provide mutual assistance."[61] For hunting, groups of fifty men would set out with bows and arrows, accompanied by their dogs.[62]

The mulmenyah system implied reciprocity. When one family group collaborated with another "to make milpa," the former knew that it could count on the latter in times of need. When one woman helped another to spin cotton, she would immediately receive the same help in return. When constructing homes, the participants expected the same assistance when it was their turn. And everyone received meals when performing a turn of labor.

The Spanish called this system of labor rotation *rueda* (wheel), or *tanda* (turn). In the *Calepino maya*, a Maya-Spanish dictionary compiled by friar Antonio de Ciudad Real between 1584 and 1610, we find different terms to capture this idea. The term *saplam saplam* referred to the process in which the women distributed "cotton already prepared by one Indian woman among them. . . . And when the cotton was finished . . . they spun the cotton of one and then of another." The word *xoth* referred to the groups that were to "spin among many Indian women the cotton already prepared by one of them; and afterwards, the cotton of another woman, until the *rueda* was complete, yielding for each one of them a yard and half of cotton cloth."[63]

But unity had its limits. Even though blood and marriage ties, together with mulmenyah, allowed a high degree of cohesion among family chieftains, the members of a residential cluster did not necessarily bear ties to the same batab. Rather, evidence suggests that divided allegience penetrated even to this level.[64] In Kulá, for example, three family heads lived with their respective offspring. Two of these heads, Ah Chuuac Kauil and Ah Cot Balam Kauil, recognized the batab of Tikom, but Napuc Yah held to the lord of the Xiu lineage, resident in Cuncunul. As another example, in a place called Tubuluichba, a residential cluster made up of nine family chieftains, Nachan Chay and Namay Pot were cuchteelob of the Xiu lineage's lord; Napuc Uitizil, Nachan Dzul, Nachan Batun, and Dzulub Batun were cuchteelob to the batab of Tekom; and Nacam Ucan, Nachan Coyí, and Namay Poy were vassals of the batab of the Kauil lineage of Tixcacal.[65]

In this way, the batabob's power extended to those family chieftains who recognized them, regardless of either's place of residence.

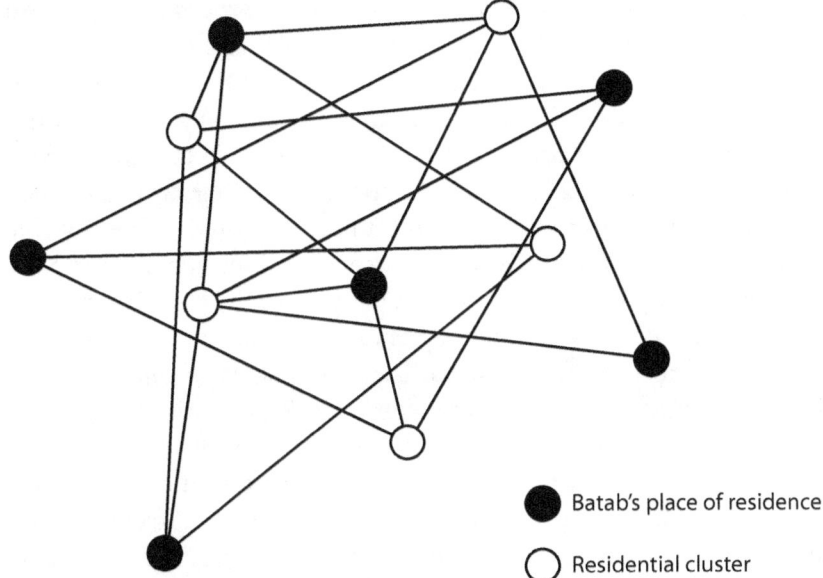

Map 1. Spatial Distribution of the Batabilob or Lordships. Drawn by Tom Jonas.

Their association formed a web interwoven throughout the length and breadth of the peninsula. In other words, Yucatec Maya lordship remained jurisdictional, not territorial. The name of this intermeshing of personal ties was "batabil," a Maya word composed of two morphemes. The first is "batab," which, as previously noted, designates "lord" or "cacique." Second, "-il" is a suffix indicating the state of belonging. Together, they express the idea that the batab was integrated into a socially preeminent group, and that such a lord exercised power or command.[66] The *Calepino maya* provides a more explicitly political definition, equating "batabil" with the more familiar term *cacicazgo*, understood as "the dignity of [being] cacique or lord of the Indians," and not of territory.[67]

Diego de Landa tells us that the batab, in his capacity as lord of the Indians, "organized and directed the affairs of their respective republics." He handled litigations in matters of justice; and when claims involved vassals of other lordships, the batab of the agressor made his vassal satisfy the aggrieved party.[68] His most important constituency comsisted of the Maya nobles called *almehenob* or occasionally *chuntanob*, but known to the Spanish as *principales* or "leading citizens."[69] These individuals carried out his orders and decisions. In terms of administration, an official known as the *ah cuch cab* was responsible for organizing Indians to cultivate the lords' and overlords' milpas, to erect these lords' homes, to edify and conserve public and ceremonial buildings, and to bring the people together for war, fiestas, and banquets.[70] In sum, the batab, whether he wasvassal of some overlord or not, spoke for and unified hundreds of family chieftains and their kin who lived dispersed in the monte. Above all, he was the link that joined his subject peoples to the halach uinic.[71]

In matters of jurisdiction, the batabob and halach uinicob had the right to impose a variety of obligations. The *encomendero* (tribute holder) of Hocabá said that the overlords "hold the Indians in such a thrall that the latter served the former without reward." Diego de Landa wrote more explicitly, "Commoners constructed the lord's homes at their own cost . . . [and] besides the home, the entire village managed the lord's plantings, and gave him as much as he wanted for himself and his household from their own homes."[72] Vassals were subject to levies. The same encomendero of Hocabá reported that the halach uinic was "so obeyed and feared by the naturales [indigenous peoples] that they dared not anger him, but rather preferred to serve him in war without recompense."[73] Martín de Palomar expressed the matter most clearly when he wrote, "The dominion that these lords and caciques had over their vassals was such that they obeyed him and held him in the highest regard; giving him whatever was necessary in times of peace, and lending him their persons in times of war . . . in recognition of his sovereignty."[74]

The Indians also rendered tribute to their lords and overlords. But Spanish encomenderos without exception emphasized the small quantities and lack of compulsion involved in the actual goods delivered.[75] In other words, the most important prerogative of the lords and overlords was their ability to deploy their vassals' labor.[76] Toward the mid-sixteenth century, the Indians used mulmenyah so that the demands for service made by the batab and halach uinic did not interfere with their own work and, by extension, their livelihoods.[77] That is to say, vassals measured the time they dedicated to supporting themselves in order to be able to meet their tributary obligations.

But this obligation had limits. In times of drought, locust plague, hurricane, epidemics, or crop-loss, neither the batab nor the halach uinic could demand goods that vassals needed for their families. Indeed, the vassal's obligation ended the moment he had finished harvesting the lord's or overlord's milpa and filling his granary. The labor a vassal dedicated to the nobles thus appears to have been separate from the time and space reserved for his family.

Given that land ownership was not a part of Maya culture, the Yucatecan lord's most important perogative was his use of human energy. It would have been incomprehensible and alien to Yucatec reality to speak of the lands of the halach uinic, of the batab, of the *ah kin* (sun priest), of the almehenob, or of the lineages themselves. Neither the Spanish nor the indigenous documents of the colonial period indicate that the pre-Hispanic nobility had direct dominion over the land; nor was land the corporate property of the multepal or the batabil. Simply put, the contact-era Maya lacked a concept of private land-ownership. To the Indian mind, the land served as the sacred mother of life, and was not a resource over which one could exercise direct dominion for either sale or purchase; it was inalienable.[78] For this reason, in the Yucatec Maya language there is no equivalent for the term "property" as exclusive rights over some object. This symbolic and cultural context explains why the halach uinic, the batab, and the nobility lacked territorial definition, and why they failed to develop a system of rents. This state of affairs so deeply struck friar Francisco de Toral, bishop of Yucatán, that in 1563 he wrote, "The Indians . . . do not pay rent to their principales as in New Spain."[79] Commoners paid no land usage fee, but rather contributed by recognizing the sovereignty of the lords and overlords.

FRAGMENTATION OF THE MULTEPAL AND THE CREATION OF THE CÚUCHCABAL

With the collapse of Mayapán and the subsequent decline of the multepal around 1450, Maya society once more fell into a prolonged period of instability and political confusion.[80] The hierarchical pyramid of personal ties constructed so patiently since the mid-1300s, now disintegrated. No one had the power to forge new alliances that might somehow centralize political life in the peninsular northeast. In a closely related change, lineages composed of more than six lords, including overlords, showed signs of weakness and exhaustion. The halach uinicob proved incapable of arresting this heart-rending phenomenon, since the batabilob could function independently of any overlord.

In such an atmosphere, the fabric of the lineages' personal ties began to fray. Countless batabob—of unknown but distinct lineages—began to emigrate with their vassals to the peninsula's southern base. One group settled in a region known as the Cehache, a territory extending from the southern Campeche lagoons of Mocú and Civiltuk to the northern Guatemala Petén villages of Chuntunqui and Yaxuncabil. Another went to Dzuluinicob, an area bordered by the Nuevo and Macal rivers south of the Maya city of Chetumal, but east of the Petén Itzaes (that is, the northern and central portions of modern-day Belize). Evidence suggests that none of these lords subordinated himself to a halach uinic. Political organization was now limited to the personal ties between each lord and his cuchteelob or vassals.[81]

At this same time, the Canul lineage split. Some of its lords settled in the Petén, while others headed to the peninsula's west coast, putting down roots close to their overlord's home in Calkiní.[82] The overlords of the Xiu and Cupul also proved unable to maintain cohesion in their now-divided lineages. The Xiu splintered in two, the Cupul in four, and each new group elevated one of its lords to the rank of halach uinic.[83] One branch of the Xiu made their home in Maní, the other in Calotmul. Of the now-divided Cupul, one overlord went to Popolá, a second to Ekbalam, a third to Chichén Itzá, and two others to Sací.[84] Meanwhile, the Cocom lineage also sundered. The only one of their chieftains to survive the great massacre at Mayapán relocated with his vassals and kinsmen to Tibolón. When three of his lords deserted, thereby diminishing his ranks, he moved again, this time opting for Sotuta.[85] The lineage as an integrating institution, then, was plunged deep into crisis; in turn, the halach uinic's power fell into doubt, since it became evident that blood kinship gave no guarantee of protection or security to those who continued as his cuchteelob. Thus, while this fragmentation continued, the remaining overlords abandoned Mayapán. The halach uinic Ah Chel made Tecoh his home, but later changed to Dzidzantún. Kaual Op Tzeh headed northeastward for Chancenote.[86] And Noh Cabal Pech, a relative of the Mayapán lord, settled in Motul.[87] The diaspora from Mayapán was now complete.

It was in this setting that a new institution was born: the *cúuchcabal* consisted of the political alliance that the halach uinic—in his place of residence—enjoyed with the group of lords that still accepted him.[88] An exploration of this term's meaning will help understand the institution at the moment of Spanish invasion. The word consists of three morphemes. The first of these, "cúuch," means "something's natural place or location," and normally refers to the site where some natural object stands.[89] By extension it can also designate the site of political or religious power. The second morpheme, "cab," is translated in the *Calepino maya* as "village or region"; but indigenous sources use it more in a social or political sense than a territorial one. It most commonly denoted those groups of persons who organized under the authority of a batab and carried out their daily activities in a particular place.[90] The suffix "-al" joins to a noun, in this case a toponym of an overlord's place of residence.[91] Read thus, "cúuchcabal" can refer to groups of lords that accept the dominion of a halach uinic, who resides in a specific place (indicated by a toponym) that I will refer to as the capital. In this way of thinking, the jurisdiction of the overlord remained conditioned by the presence or absence of batabob who participated in these associations. Personal ties thus undergirded and sustained the cúuchcabal.[92]

Once the overlords had founded their capitals, they began the work of reconstructing their ties with the lords, in order to place as many as possible in the cúuchcabal. This proved no simple matter. The lords were in disarray owing to the crisis of the lineages, which kept the family chieftains in constant turmoil. For one thing, they feared being captured in the wars that lords and overlords so incessantly waged. Nor did they fear in vain. Many Indians fell prisoner during these engagements; captured commoners found themselves sold as slaves, while nobles were sacrificed.[93] Second, a succession of natural disasters struck the northern lowlands. In 1470 torrential rains decimated crops. Between 1480 and 1500 an epidemic scourged the population with "pestilent fevers that lasted twenty-four hours, and once they ended, [the victims] swelled up and were filled with worms." Finally, somewhere around the 1520s the devastating smallpox plague that had flattened the Indians of central Mexico reached Yucatán.[94]

In this context of general crisis, hundreds of family chieftains fled with their relatives in search of shelter from war, or of food in times of famine. They settled in other residential clusters, or else founded new ones as soon as the social convulsions had abated. Occasionally these new settlements became permanent; in other instances, the settlers returned to their original homes. Whether the move was temporary or lasting, innumerable family chieftains now faced the challenge of finding someone to offer them shelter and protection. During these turbulent times, the personalist networks of lords and cuchteelob remained in flux, since vassalage was neither lifelong nor hereditary. The lords, also prisoner to this unsettled state of affairs, sometimes saw their authority increase, but at other times diminish and even disappear altogether.

The lords who managed to survive followed different paths. Whether from distrust or simple convenience, countless batabob of all lineages kept themselves independent, and tried to consolidate their authority among the people who still recognized them despite all the dislocations. Others opted to maintain blood ties with an overlord; still others, whether or not they were tied by kinship to a halah uinic, accepted vassalage under an overlord of a different lineage. At the same time, some halach uinicob braved these adverse circumstances and used alliances independent of lineage to form and consolidate cúuchcabal, thereby preventing Yucatán's complete political fragmentation.

The splintered history of the Xiu gives some indication of how lords and overlords formed cross-lineage alliances. At some point during the second quarter of the sixteenth century, Ix Kaual Xiu, daughter of Ah Tzulub Xiu and descendent of Ah Xupan Xiu, founder of Maní's cúuchcabal, married the governor of the lordships of Oxkutzcab and Muna, who was a member of the Pacab lineage.[95] By the time the Spanish arrived in Yucatán, Ah Mochan Xiu, the halach uinic, had organized his cúuchcabal with seven other batabob of his lineage, and through matrimonial alliances with the two aforementioned lordships. Recognition, protection, and possibly even conquest brought in seven other lords: two of the Che lineage, and one each of the Ku, Nauat, Uz, Uluac, and Chan families.

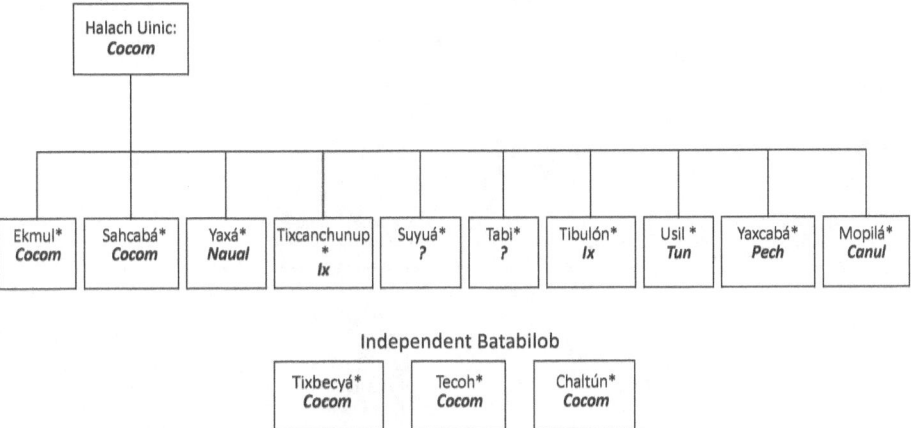

Figure 2. The Cocom Lineage and Its Cúuchabal. Drawn by Tom Jonas.

With the lineages in crisis and the halach uinic's power questioned, overlords found their ability to offer protection and security to their lords weakened, and their old vassals could scarcely organize their cúuchcabalob. For example, when the Spanish invaded the Canul lineage, based in Calkiní, consisted of twenty-six lords and their halach uinic. Lacking political strength, the halach uinic had only been able to organize a cúuchcabal with two Canul lords, to which he added one Euán and one Tayú lord. Twenty-two other Canul lords were independent, and one was a vassal of Nachí Cocom. A similar fate befell the Cupul lineage, which consisted of five overlords and fourteen lords. Five of the lords recognized four halach uinicob of the same lineage; one was a vassal of Na Mox Chel, the overlord of Dzidzantún; and eight others were independent. By the mid-sixteenth century six lordships governed the Cocom lineage. They included that of Sotuta, the capital from which halach uinic Nachí Cocom had organized his own cúuchcabal with eleven lords. Two of these—from Ekmul and Sahcabá— were Cocom, two were Ix, and seven others came from separate lineages.[96] The Cocom lords of Tecoh, Chaltún, and Tixbeyá remained independent.

The cases of the Pech and Chel lineages constitute a noteworthy exception. At the moment of contact, the Pech governed thirty-one lordships; their halach uinic, working through blood ties, had

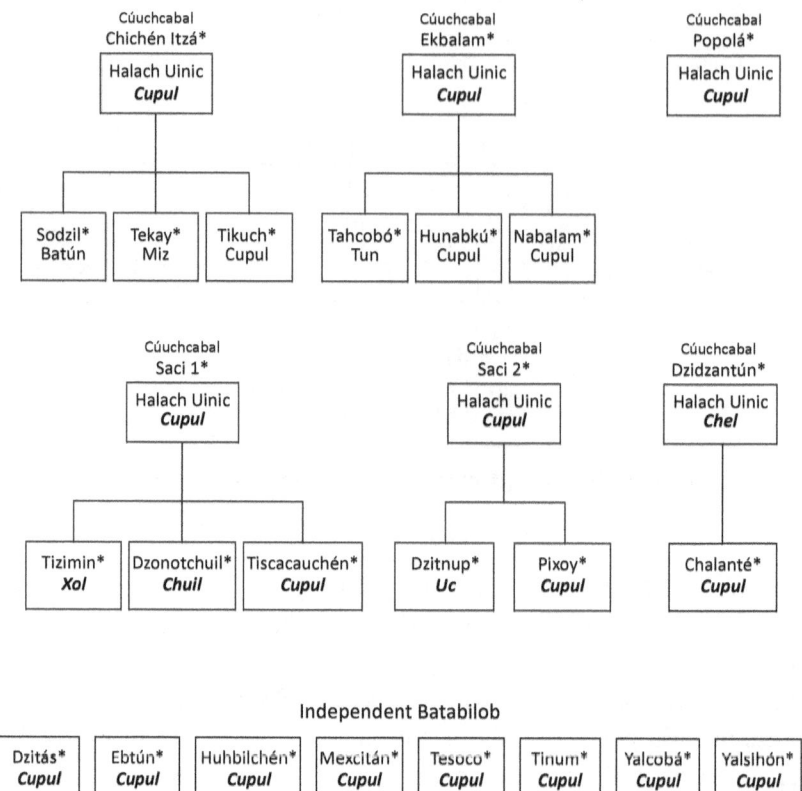

Figure 3. The Cupul Lineage and Its Cúuchcabal. Drawn by Tom Jonas.

effectively halted further disintegration of his lords. His successor, Naum Pech, managed to organize the Motul cúuchcabal with twenty-eight lords, twenty-four of whom hailed from his own lineage. Of the remainder, two belonged to the Canché lineage: one from Oxté, and one from the Ek. Seven other Pech lords broke away. Two became vassals of Namox Chel, overlord of Dzidzantún; one attached himself to Nachí Cocom, overlord of Sotuta. The last four remained independent. Namox Chel himself had a lineage made up of three other lords. Using political alliance, matrimony, war, or simple recognition, he put together a cúuchcabal of twenty-eight lords, twenty of which were from different lineages.[97]

Whatever the exact means, by 1526 a vast number of lords had managed to elude vassalage and to remain independent. They tended to cluster in the Dzuluinicob, the Cehache, the northwest corner, and the Tizimín area. Simultaneously there were eighteen halach uinicob that forged somewhat reduced cúuchcabalob by drawing upon batabob of both their own and other lineages. Map 2 and Appendix A illustrate these relationships.

The capitals in which the overlords made their residence held populations that integrated activities of various señoríos, or lordships. For that reason, the halach uinic's presence centralized decision making, including for matters of religion. For example, during the month of *xul* (a Maya calendric designation without exact correspondence to the European annual calendar), Maní became the scene of festivities in memory of Kukulkán and while Indians came to Sací to adore the divinity known as Ah Zaciual.[98] While there is no evidence to suggest that the overlords controlled a military organization or religious hierarchy everything points to the presence of an ah kin in every lordship. The ah kin was a religious dignitary whom the Indians greatly respected for managing the calendar and religious rites.[99] To conclude on the matter of capitals, the following is a list of places thus far identifiedas such:[100] Chauac-há, Chancenote,[101] Motul,[102] Calkiní,[103] Tihosuco,[104] Popolá,[105] Chetumal,[106] Sací, Chichén Itzá,[107] Ekbalam,[108] Maní, Sotuta, Hocabá, Dzidzantún,[109] Cozumel, Can Pech,[110] and Calotmul.[111]

LINEAGE GOVERNORS

When the Spanish invaded the Maya lowlands, they found a decayed but ancient social class whose members styled themselves *almehenob*. The Spanish translated the term *almehen* as "hidalgo, noble, a gentleman distinguished by his lineage, and the lord and principal of his pueblo."[112] Behind this social and political characterization, Maya nobles considered themselves as differentiated from one another by their membership in separate lineages. Anxious to establish proof of the legitimacy of their power, they authored a series of texts, in some cases "copies" of pre-Hispanic codices or else transcriptions of oral history, concerning their own origin myths.[113] These documents contain narratives of the "relevant events" both before and after the Spanish invasion, and support the origin stories of the lineages. Unlike western

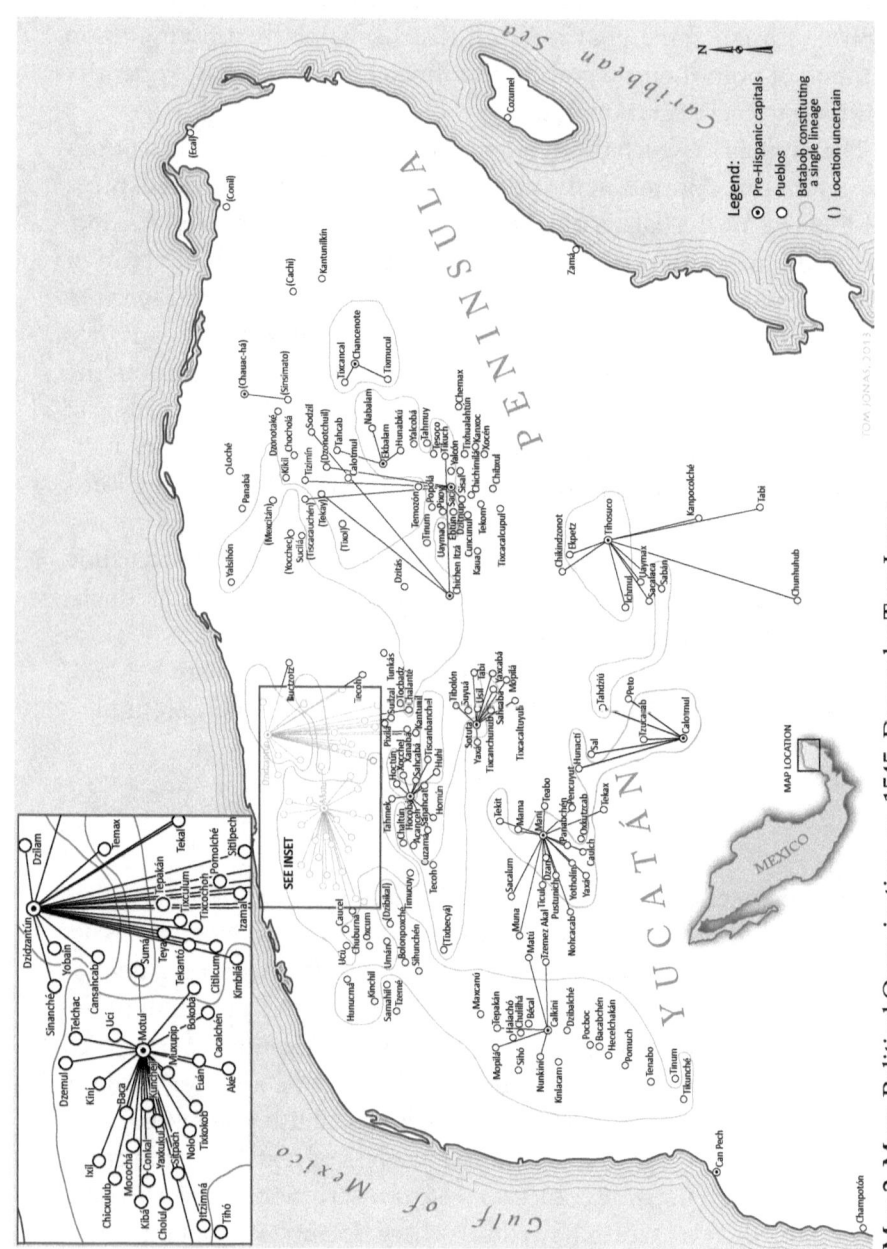

Map 2. Maya Political Organization, ca. 1545. Drawn by Tom Jonas.

culture's linear concept of time, Maya scribes paid little heed to chronological sequence or causal relation in those events; rather, their own particular cosmovision informed the way the narrative was structured. The Maya conceived of time as recurring within certain large recurring cycles, the most important of which was the *katún*, a period equal to twenty solar years. Accordinly, the goal was to demonstrate to contemporaries and successors in each katún the cosmic legitimacy of the established power in their political and ceremonial centers.[114] Following the Spanish invasion, the Maya lineages used their origin myths as tools to protect their social statuses and heirarchical ranking before the newcomers. Management of cyclical time in the narrative allowed them to manipulate chronologies, events, and the interpretation of those events to their own advantage—or, better said, to their enemies' detriment.[115] Indeed, despite sharing a common political tradition, they continued to harbor resentments about the roles they had played in the shared government—and the fall—of Mayapán. The Cocom accused the Xiu of being foreigners and traitors for having assassinated their rightful lord. The Xiu, for their part, framed themselves as liberators who had brought down a tyrant. Similarly, the Chel lord based claims for the nobility of his lineage on the fact that he was the grandson of the highest priest of Mayapán.[116]

Maya lords recognized themselves as such because they descended directly from a known common ancestor. Indigenous traditions recorded by the conquistadors demonstrate this fact. Juan Cueva Santillán, encomendero of Izamal, wrote, "Kinich Kabá, Kinich Kakmó, and Cit Ah Cutz referred to themselves as the first inhabitants of [Izamal], from whom descended the Xoles, Moes, and Coyes, Indians distinguished in this province [of Yucatán] by these ancestors and surnames." The encomendero Juan Botes also encountered this tradition in the following form: "and so in the present there are many Indians who boast of the lineage of that pueblo, such as the Nahuates, Chulines, Euanes, Chunabes, and others in that village, who according to them descend directly from the ancient lords that were in this land."[117]

Not surprisingly, some of these nobles preened themselves on being descendants of the Early Postclassic conquistadors. One member of the Kauil lineage claimed that this ancestors had come from the Kingdom of Mexico, and as "principales and lords . . . [they] had peopled

[Yucatán] and ruled in this land."[118] Other nobles insisted that they were descendants of one of the multepal's governing lineages. Diego de Landa wrote that "it greatly mattered to them to know their lineage origins, especially if they descended from some house of Mayapán; and they learn this from the priests, it being one of their realms of knowledge, and they boast greatly of the distinguished men who have come from their lineage."[119]

In reality, the matter of lineage origins remains rather murky. Members clearly turned the "exploits of war and journey" of their ancestors into historical traditions in order to reaffirm their own authority and prestige. In this way, the Xiu lineage left a record of the fact that their presence in Yucatán dated back to the ninth century, when their ancestors, led by one Holón Chan Tepeu, arrived from Tulapan Chiconahthan-Nonoual, reaching a place to the west of Suyuá, where they settled for some eighty years (849–928 A.D.).[120] In the time cycle known as Katún 8 Ahau (928–948), the narratives tell, the Xiu abandoned that region for the northern Yucatán peninsula; and at this moment, it seems, they split into two groups. In Katún 2 Ahau (987–1007) one group, led by Ah Mekat Tutul Xiu, reached Chacnabitón, where they remained until the early twelfth century. The later history of this group remains shrouded in mystery. The other group, headed by Ah Zuytok Tutul Xiu, spent Katún 2 Ahau far differently, initiating a four-decade period of wandering through uninhabited parts of the Yucatán until they finally conquered Uxmal.[121] There, according to Landa, "they began to people, and to raise excellent buildings in many places."[122] Quite possibly, this Ah Zuytok Tutul Xiu was Hun Uitzil Chac, founder of the lineage that appears in the often-reproduced drawing of the Xiu genealogical tree, a unique colonial document that narrates in illustrated form the lineage from that founder until don Juan Xiu Cimé, who died in the late eighteenth century.[123] In other words, the Xiu left testimony that they were not Yucatec Maya, and disdained to consider themselves as such. Well into the 1650s the Spanish who collected accounts insisted that, with regard to origins, "they were natives of Mexico."[124]

The Kauil lineage, for its part, claimed that its ancestors had been "brave and warlike people" who hailed from the "kingdom of Mexico," and who came to people Chichén Itzá, Bacalar, and the northern coast. They also claimed that one of their lords, a certain Tumispolchicbul, was a relative of Moctezuma, the ruler of one of the Mexican kingdoms. But, unlike the Xiu, the Kauil prided themselves on the claim that Cuhuikakcamalcacalpuc, one of the Mexican lords, was a close relative, and that a Kauil had bound himself to the Cupul clan through matrimony.[125]

The Pech lineage, to the contrary, originated in Yucatán. Its members legitimized themselves through their ancestors' military feats. Martín de Palomar writes of their narratives thus:

> The pueblo of Mutul [Motul] takes its name from a lord who settled it a long time ago; his name was Sacmutul, meaning white man... this individual was a captain and he came from the west looking for a place to make his home. Where he came from is a mystery, but he was an indio. He settled in the location of Motul pueblo and filled it with his people, and he and his descendents reigned for 140 years, until Kak U Pacal arrived with his own warriors to slay them and lay waste to the pueblo. After many years another lord and captain, named Noh Cabal Pech, a close relative of the overlord of Mayapán, now settled Motul with his own people, and since then the señorío has belonged to this Noh Cabal Pech and his descendants.[126]

The histories and traditions of other lineages—families such as the Chel, Tzeh, and Cochuah—possibly emerged during the twelfth and thirteenth centuries, since they tell of no events prior to those years, while those of the Pot, Caamal, Che, and others may date from the fall of Mayapán.

We know from early colonial sources that only some noble lineages ruled—that is to say, occupied the ranks of halach uinicob and batabob. As cuchteelob, members of other lineages held secondary positions within the power structure, and formed part of the lords' and overlords' retinues. On this point, Landa writes, "and when the lords went out of the pueblo, they took much company with them, just as when they left their homes."[127] These accompanying nobles made up a group called the chuntanob, people whom the Spanish characterized as principales.[128] Strictly speaking, those members who held the ranks of lord and overlord comprised a sort of closed, corporate elite who used a protocol of linguistic formulas known as Suyuá (not to be confused with a pueblo of the same name) to exclude parvenus.[129] It consisted of a series of riddles that served to examine successors in order to see if they were truly worthy of lordship; or if they were really descendents of a batab or halach uinic.[130] In other words, the formulas of Suyuá passed from generation to generation, rendering titles patrimonial.[131]

We do not know for certain which criteria the lineage rulers used when selecting one or more descendants to learn Suyuá. It seems to have been the batab's or halach uinic's prerogative to choose a successor—usually through primogeniture—to educate and train in the knowledge of the riddles. Once in power, at the beginning of every twenty-year-long katún, the halach uinic conducted an examination.[132] An individual who failed, even if he were a descendent, was hanged, or had his tongue and eyes cut out.[133]

At times succession suffered interruptions. When a descendent was too young, an adult paternal uncle would ascend to power. He would be the oldest or the most "self-assured," that is, the man with the greatest capacity to discharge the office, and would hold that office for life. The nephew, meanwhile, was educated in the matters of "customs and celebrations"; and quite possibly, some halach uinic or batab might teach him the Suyuá formulary. If the break was definitive—when there was no son or paternal uncle—the priests and principales met to deliberate and decide how to fill the power vacuum. In these deliberations, the quality of "sufficiency" most strongly affected selection. In sum, the new individual had to demonstrate ability, knowledge, and intelligence, all basic requisites to such a rank.[134]

THE CONQUEST OF YUCATÁN

Spain's prolonged and arduous campaign to take Yucatán is now the stuff of legend.[135] Francisco Hernández de Córdoba discovered the peninsula in 1517, but it was not until 1526, after Hernán Cortés had already conquered Tenochtitlán, that Francisco de Montejo signed the Capitulaciones de Granada on December 8, 1520 in which Spain's

King Charles V authorized him to organize the conquest of the Yucatec Maya. Unlike the Mexican altiplano, where an organization that centralized political life allowed the Spanish soldiers an astonishingly rapid victory (1519–1521), Yucatec Maya society had suffered a profound fragmentation; and for that reason, Montejo's signing marked the beginning of a prolonged and grueling campaign. The Spanish only triumphed in 1546, after two decades, and after barely putting down an indigenous rebellion.

Spanish forces unsuccessfully attempted to subdue the Maya on two separate occasions. The first began at the end of 1527 when conquistadors entered the peninsula via the southeast coast, and within a few days founded Salamanca de Xel-há. The invaders later relocated to Xamanhá (today Playa del Carmen), since don Francisco de Montejo, also known as Adelantado (roughly, "trailblazer" or "pioneer") thought that port offered better advantages for a prolonged occupation. During this first expedition they crossed the entire east coast of the peninsula. But skirmishes with the Maya, climate-related illnesses, and shortages of supplies left the Spanish decimated. Given these circumstances, Montejo had no choice but to abandon his enterprise in the summer of 1528. The invasion had only lasted six months.

One year later, in March or April of 1529, Montejo launched a second campaign of conquest. This time his expedition began on the Campeche coast, and he remained in Yucatán for five years. During that time the Spanish managed to found four large settlements. In 1531 they created Salamanca de Campeche and the Villa Real de Chetumal; in 1533, the Ciudad Real de Chichén Itzá; and one year later, the Ciudad Real de Dzilam. Their intention was to use these points as springboards to colonization, but the war proved tough going. In the end the Spanish, discouraged by their fortunes, abandoned the peninsula around late 1534 or early 1535.

Various circumstances converged to thwart this attempt as well. Unquestionably, the most important was Maya society's lack of a political center; the existence of nearly two dozen halach uinicob and innumerable independent batabob frustrated the Adelantado's enterprise. The submission of an overlord did not necessarily mean the acquiescence of his dependent batabob, or of nearby halach uinicob or independent batabob. Nor did attempted alliances with the native lords bring better results. Rather, the pacts of obedience that Maya governing elites formed with Montejo turned out to be more performative than real.

Moreover, the Adelantado committed strategic errors. His attempt to conquer simultaneously all of this territory occupied by a politically fragmented society led him to divide his three hundred–man army in two. He sent one expedition, led by Alonso Dávila, to Chetumal, where Dávila founded the Ciudad Real. Indigenous forces conclusively expelled them in 1532. The other expedition, under the leadership of Francisco de Montejo the Son, also known as "El Mozo," headed north and founded the Ciudad Real de Chichén Itzá. All seemed to be proceeding smoothly; but within a short time the Maya began to lay siege, and soon drove the Spanish to the north coast. Although the conquistadors proclaimed the Ciudad Real de Dzilam in 1534, with the aim of reinvigorating the conquest, the news of vast wealth in Peru caused many soldiers to desert, thus ending the second conquest altogether.

Without doubt, however, the Adelantado gleaned both experience and knowledge from the two previous expeditions, and in 1537 launched a third and definitive campaign. The key lessons were to avoid a division of forces and to work the Roman strategy of taking small regions, establishing control, and continuing until all territory lay in one's hands. On this occasion Montejo restricted himself to administrative affairs, delegating the actual conquest to his son, who had been governing Tabasco. In compliance with his father's instructions, in 1537 El Mozo sent a group of soldiers from the Usumacinta to Champotón to establish a beachhead. For the center of operations he chose Xicalango, a pre-Hispanic trading center on the westernmost peninsula separating Lagúna de Términos from the Gulf of Mexico.

The Adelantado now counted on the support of his nephew (also named Francisco de Montejo), who had joined the conquistadors and now assumed control of the new settlement of San Pedro de Champotón, subsequently known as Salamanca. El Mozo reached Champotón shortly afterward to take charge of the army, and in late 1540 moved the encampment to Campeche. One year later he established the Villa de San Francisco in this same place with some thirty soldiers.

The conquistadors kept advancing northward, and established a base in the lordship of Tuchicán, between the pre-Hispanic capital of Calkiní and the independent batabil of Maxcanú. There he learned that Ah Kin Chuy, a priest of the Pebá señorío, was preaching a war of extermination against the Spanish and had formed an alliance with Nachí Cocom, the halach uinic of Sotuta. Warned in advance by Maya allies, Montejo the Nephew led an attack and captured the priest in avictory, which raised morale. Bouyed up by fresh arms and reinforcements from the Adelantado, Montejo the Son, along with some three hundred soldiers, was able to advance to Tihó by mid-1541. Here he founded the city of Mérida on January 6, 1542.

Confronted with the Spanish onslaught, the Maya now organized themselves. Led by Nachí Cocom, various contingents laid siege to the recently founded Mérida. Spaniards counterattacked and dispersed them. At this point a significant part of the independent batabilob located in the city's vicinity, along with dependent lordships of the pre-Hispanic capitals of Hocabá, Motul, and Dzidzantún, fell under Spanish control. With this advance, Montejo the Son launched the conquest of the peninsula's central and eastern territory, and led a campaign against Nachí Cocom. Once defeated, Cocom had to accept Spanish dominion. Montejo the Son subsequently advanced to the pre-Hispanic capital of Tihosuco, while his cousin battled for the peninsular northeast. There, in May of 1543, Montejo the Nephew founded Valladolid over the pre-Hispanic capital of Chauac-há. The cúuchcabalob of Sací, Tihosuco, Popolá, Ekbalam, and Chancenote launched an uprising, but Captain Francisco López de Cieza caught them by surprise and seized Sací, capturing the leaders and suffocating the intended revolt.

By 1544 the only remaining Maya lordships left to conquer were located in the Dzuluinicob region, and those dependents of the pre-Hispanic capital of Chetumal. Responsibility for their conquest fell to one Gaspar Pacheco and his son Melchor. Their war against the Maya stood out for its cruelty, violence, and recourse to extermination tactics. Exhausted and nearly depopulated, the people of this region had to accept the Spanish presence. The Pachecos pushed all the way to eastern Guatemala's Golfo Dulce (today known as Lake Izabal), but the protests of Dominican friars forced them to withdraw. In the same year, Melchor Pacheco founded the villa of Salamanca de Bacalar in an area near a lagoon of the same name.[136]

After so many long years, the conquest of the Mayas seemed to be over. But appearances deceived. Demands for tribute and personal service proved so oppressive that Mayas soon tired of the abuse and mistreatment. Moreover, latent resistance to Spanish rule persisted, as did the cohesive force of religion, all of which fed the spirit of indigenous rebellion. On the Maya calendar date of 5 Cimí (death) 19 Xul (end), a date that Indians interpreted to mean the death of the Spanish and the end of colonial rule (in the European calendar, November 9, 1546), the Maya launched a huge rebellion that engulfed the entire east and south of the peninsula. The uprising began in Valladolid, and was singularly bloody. Captured Spaniards, including women and children, were crucified, shot through with arrows, ceremonially burned in place of the indigenous *copal* incense, or used as victims for heart sacrifice. As symbols of victory, the rebels sent the severed limbs of the Spanish cadavers to other pueblos in order to incite them to join the revolt.

Maya repudiation of Spanish rule went beyond slaughter and sacrifice. They also destroyed the domesticated plants and animals the conquistadors had brought from Europe. Nor were Indians who served in Spanish homes spared; rather, the rebels executed them as traitors to their gods and customs. The uprising lasted four months, during which time the Spanish struggled desperately to regain the upper hand. In March 1547 they overran the last rebel village and killed the caciques and priests who had led the affair, at times even burning them alive.[137]

Once the revolt was put down, the peninsula remained divided into two large regions. One extended from the Puuc (a low hill range running from Campeche to Peto) all the way to what is today the Petén district of northern Guatemala. This region became a zone of refuge where the Maya escaped from colonial rule. The second was the northwest, where the indigenous population was concentrated, and where Hispanic colonization had made its greatest advances. Diego de Landa described the regional division as follows: "This range [the Puuc] divides Yucatán into two parts. The southern half, reaching to Lacandón and Taiza, is thinly peopled owing to a lack of water, which disappears altogether except when it rains. The other is the north, which is populated."[138]

Landa erred regarding southern demography: after all, the region was inhabited prior to Mayapán's collapse in 1450. However, numbers increased significantly following the Spanish conquest, when thousands of family chieftains fled with their kin to remote locations throughout the peninsula. They constructed an impressive network of personal ties with their lords, based on batabilob, and could function in an independent manner, regardless of whether or not those batabob were cuchteelob of an overlord.

To recapitulate: since it first appeared in the Maya landscape in the mid-fourteenth century, jursidictional lordship had constituted the basic unit of Maya political organization. The halach uinicob used these reciprocal interpersonal relationships in building the multepal. These lordships had sufficient strength to survive the changes spinning out of Mayapán's fall, just as they weathered the multifaceted crises of the century preceding Spanish invasion. In the course of that century, overlords depended on them to construct their cúuchcabalob. And with the establishment of the colonial order, jurisdictional leadership entered a new phase of its history.

CHAPTER 2

From Lordship to Early Colonial Pueblo

When the Spanish ended their Yucatecan conquest in the mid-sixteenth century, only a hundred years had passed since the destruction of Mayapán and the multepal's fragmentation. The wars and crises of that century had initiated a long, complicated period of reaccommodation, a time of social and political rebuilding. The halach uinicob of lineages such as the Cupul, Xiu, and Cocom still commanded the wherewithal to consolidate their cúuchacabalob via recognition of their lords, and at the moment of invasion, this political entity continued to bind together dozens of batabob throughout the northern lowlands.

But there were lords who did not desire or else did not accept the role of cuchteel to some overlord. Rather, they remained independent, and their señoríos covered a significant part of Yucatecan territory. This was especially true in the peninsula's northwest corner. Meanwhile, if somewhat outside the scope of this study, independent señoríos also characterized the region of the Dzuluinicob and the Cehache, at the peninsula's southern base.

Colonization brought with it a mix of political, economic, and religious factors that began to erode the bonds joining the batab and the halach uinic. In some cases the Spaniards intentionally caused the division; in other instances, they respected the Maya's social bonds, but ended up weakening them anyway, either partially or completely. Isolated from their lords, the halach uinic and his cúuchcabal became easy prey to the pressures of the new order, and soon disappeared altogether from the indigenous political landscape.

The decay spread from two sources. One was the awarding of *encomiendas*, or tributary rights to Spanish conquistadors, since the Maya lords were assigned to various encomiendas independent of the conquistadors' personal ties to the overlords. The other was the religious and political apparatus which the Spanish Crown had designed to administer its territory. Even though, in some cases, the new entities—the political district and the Franciscan *guardianía*—were juxtaposed over the cúuchcabal, they nevertheless brought new authorities, such as the *tenientes de alcalde* (secular officials appointed for villages) and the *guardián* (leaders in religious towns), respectively. These individuals, in turn, bore powers delegated by the colonial authorities. From the beginning, they began to compete with the overlords' power within their respective areas, ultimately displacing that power.

Key to colonization was the Crown's project of concentrating the population in territorially defined settlements in which the batabob or caciques would wield authority. This population transfer did not immediately weaken the lordship's integrity, however, since it failed to sever the batab's personal ties with his vassals. Moreover, his political functions continued, at least during the initial years of Spanish presence. Nevertheless, the process of concentrating the population made clear to the lords that the transition to the colonial world had begun.

With the military phase of the conquest now concluded, the peninsula witnessed the emergence of diverse factions of Spaniards, which strained the remaining bonds between lords and overlords. At first these new factions did not have equal importance, nor could they necessarily work together as organized groups. But events followed so rapidly that, shortly after the century's midpoint, they had already become stable corporate bodies capable of defending their own interests. They demand close attention, since their actions so powerfully shaped colonial Yucatecan society and so dramatically modified indigenous political organization.

Two primary factions emerged. The first group initially consisted of seven Franciscans. They were the weaker in terms of armed force, but at the same time their corporate spirit made them the most stable.[1] The other group consisted of the conquistadors, whose numbers and military might initially awarded them the greater importance. They became encomenderos, and were the first to establish themselves; beyond that, their leader, Francisco de Montejo, served as the first governor of Yucatán.[2] In reality, friars and conquistadors practically marched arm-in-arm from 1540 until 1548, when the Crown stripped the military of its power. Royal authority emerged thereafter as a third political force in the region, and through the *audiencias*, or courts, it began to appoint administrative officials.[3]

But this first wave of Spaniards, the very individuals who worked to destroy the cúuchcabal, drew the line when it came to the batab. Whether they were royal authorities, encomenderos, or clergy, the Spanish depended on the batab for matters of sheer practicality. Indeed, he served as the fulcrum for justice and administration for thousands of families who lived in the monte.[4] During the colony's first years, the batab's retention remained a fundamental priority. When the Franciscans began to concentrate villages, the batab proved crucial, for he knew the identities and locations of his vassals, information critical for gathering together subject peoples and relocating them to his place of residence. With his assistance, the colonial system could impose territorial limits over a hitherto jurisdictional señorío. Moreover, both friars and secular Spaniards needed the batab to oversee the production of tribute, the collection of alms, and the mobilization of personal service. The batab was therefore *the* indispensable man of indigenous politics, and for that reason the Spanish depended on him for many features of their daily lives; indeed, he became the foundation of the whole colonial system.

THE SPANISH VISION OF INDIGENOUS POLITICAL ORGANIZATION

During the first attempt to invade the Maya area (1527–1529), the Spanish had tremendous difficulty gathering precise information about indigenous political organization, since their incursion was limited to the peninsula's eastern coast. More than anything, Spanish chronicles of this adventure reflect a concern for describing the places they visited in the course of their expedition. Places such as Chauac-há, Chetumal, Belmá, Conil, Cachi, Sinsimató, and Dzonotaké represented rich settlements ripe for exploitation. Newcomers failed to perceive that the former two were pre-Hispanic capitals, and that the latter five lordships, in fact, belonged to different cúuchcabalob. The failure to grasp the pueblos' political alignment doubtless stemmed from the fact that Maya personal ties remained too intangible and too invisible for the Spanish to discern. Even the most observant soldier could hardly determine whether the lordships he visited were aligned with particular cúuchcabalob, or whether they maintained their independence. But unlike the first invasion, the second attempt (1529–1535) allowed Europeans to come to know practically the entire peninsula, and they developed considerably more sophisticated ideas regarding indigenous political organization. Perhaps the most important Spanish insight was understanding that, despite ethnic and cultural homogeneity, the Yucatec Maya were politically fragmented. That is, there was no central political authority that might have unified the 150,000 square kilometers they occupied.

By 1546, with the military phase of the conquest over, Spanish understanding of their new colony continued to improve, and they began to use a set of territorially based categories drawn from their own culture to characterize and understand indigenous political entities such as cúuchcabalob or independent batabilob. Most conspicuously, they soon began to use the term "province" in at least two contexts. The term could refer to the entire territory of Yucatán, but might also indicate presumed pre-Hispanic territorial divisions. A comment by an encomendero nicely captured this double usage: "We found this province divided into many provinces."[5] Regarding the second context, the conquistadors used the word "province" in at least three ways. The first referred to a territory defined by natural features and containing groups of independent batabilob. The second referred to the patronymic of a halach uinic, or rather to designate a group of batabilob belonging to the same lineage. The third applied to the place name of the halach uinic's residence.[6] To avoid confusion, this study uses the word "province" exclusively in the sense of the entire Yucatecan colony.

Spatially oriented language inserted itself in other ways as well. Within Yucatán, the Spanish indiscriminately employed words such as pueblo, *colación, estancia, anexo,* and *milpería* to designate a residential cluster: that is, a place inhabited by a group of family chieftains.[7] Of these, the most common was *pueblo*. For example, encomendero Iñigo Nieto said of two lordships, "The pueblos of Citilcum and Cauich, both part of my encomienda . . . are inhabited, and scattered in seven or eight pueblos."[8] This generalized deployment of the term "pueblo" was not entirely fortuitous. Indeed, the Spanish usually had in mind the territory where a particular social body lived, and not the social body itself. Its use in a certain way did reflect the existence of that body's political dependence on a batab; but it failed to note that the family chiefs found therein might be subjects of different lords.

But the word "pueblo" had other usages. The Spanish also deployed it to mean the equivalent of New Spain's altepeme, that is, the plural form of the altepetl, a term referring to Indian social bodies, and not to places where Spaniards lived. In Yucatán, too, the word was applied to much the same end. Mérida, the capital and seat of political and religious power, bore the rank of *ciudad* (city), while the urban settlements of San Francisco de Campeche, Valladolid, and Salamanca de Bacalar, all carried the secondary status of *villa*.[9] In the Spanish order, ciudads and villas enjoyed town councils known as ayuntamientos, while pueblos were administered or supervised by an appointed teniente de alcalde. Henceforth this study uses the term "pueblo," which came to mean "batabil" or "señorío," the fundamental building block of indigenous political organization.

Eventually, the process of concentration populations brought linguistic change. The terms estancia, anexo, colación, and milpería fell into disuse, since virtually all families came to be congregated in their batab's place of residence. The resulting subdivisions acquired the names parcialidades or barrios.[10]

Spaniards in Yucatán used the term *cabecera* indiscriminately to refer to the place of residence of either the batab or halach uinic. This study uses "capital" to refer to the overlord's home base, and reserves "cabecera" for that of the batab. For conquistadors, the term *sujeto* referred to one of two subordinate relationships in the hierarchy. In the first instance, it denoted a pueblo dependent on some pre-Hispanic capital, a usage this study avoids. The other use designated residential clusters subordinate to a batab, without recognizing that the family chieftains within often answered to different lords or caciques.[11]

This hierarchical context explains why Spaniards generally employed the word to establish subordinate relations that the vast colonial reorganization created for all pueblos in relation to the city of Mérida and its three subject villas, and to the various *cabeceras de doctrina*, or Franciscan-supervised communities where a guardián lived and where a convent had been erected.

Regarding the halach uinic and batab, Spaniards lumped them all together under the rubric of *señores*, or lords, without any consistent understanding of the distinctions between these ranks.[12] As is well known, the Crown, in its quest for centralized power, had prohibited the use of the word "señor" in reference to an indigenous ruler from 1538 onward.[13] And while Spaniards in Yucatán, like their counterparts in central Mexico, continued to violate this prohibition until the eighteenth century, the usage of "señor" referred more to that individual's social rank in the colonial order than to his precontact status.[14] The term cacique, which similarly could mean "batab" or "halach uinic," enjoyed tremendous popularity.[15] Moreover, its use carried less political implication than "señor," and did not require the existence of hierarchies, since the term was far too generic. In 1562, for example, don Lorenzo Cocom was recognized as "cacique-gobernador of the pueblo of Sotuta." Similarly, don Juan Ix, batab of Tibolón and a dependent of don Lorenzo, was styled "cacique-gobernador."[16]

ENCOMIENDA AND ENCOMENDEROS

Encomienda, or the process of tributary payment to conquistadors, had a long tradition in America by the time of the Maya conquest. Literally, the word meant "a trust" or "entrusting" in the sense that Indians were "entrusted" to a Spanish conquistador's oversight for Christianization, and in exchange provided him with goods or services. Spaniards who received such privileges were called "encomenderos." First in the Antillas and later in central Mexico, the practices associated with this institution could substitute for political structure, and constituted the starting point of the colonizing process.[17] The encomienda's application in Yucatán did not deviate from this model. Here, the Spanish respected lordship as the fundamental element of indigenous political organization when assigning a cacique, along with his respective subject population, to a conquistador.[18] The lord's personal influence was so great that when he was assigned in encomienda to two or more Spaniards, they did not break up his señorío, but rather respected his dominion over his subjects.[19] A Spaniard might hold rights to various encomiendas at the same time, as was the case with the brothers Melchor and Francisco Pacheco, who jointly controlled the lords of Hocabá, Hoctún, Huhí, Sanahcat, Tahmek, and Tiscanbanchel. Claims on encomienda thus actually outnumbered available caciques, a fact that occasionally required caciques to divide their responsibility among multiple encomenderos. Around 1565 there were 180 caciques entrusted to some 125 Spaniards in Yucatán.[20] If this new network of ties emerging among caciques and encomenderos respected the Maya señoríos, the same did not hold true for its effect on relations between batab and halach uinic. The encomienda distinctly favored the batab, enhancing his base of authority over his subjects so that tribute and personal services flowed to the conquistadors without complication.

One notable if relatively brief exception was the vast encomienda of don Francisco de Montejo the Elder. At the start of the third and final conquest of Yucatán, he ordered his son to secure for him control of the capital of Maní and all its dependent pueblos.[21] The younger Montejo carried out these instructions shortly after founding Mérida (1542). But the Adelantado only enjoyed his privileges until 1548, the year in which a series of stringent colonial reforms known as the New Laws prohibited colonial governors from holding encomiendas.[22] One year later the encomienda rights to the halach uinic and one of his batabob passed to the Crown, while fourteen caciques were distributed among an equal number of Spaniards.[23]

In the early days—until at least 1549—the encomenderos virtually owned their pueblos, and made them their places of residence.[24] It was not until the rebellion of 1546 that they learned the wisdom of keeping to Mérida and its three subordinate villas. This bitter experience notwithstanding, ambition ruled the colonials in their relations with the native peoples in the initial years. Encomenderos determined the quantities and timetables for tribute, as well as the ways and means for using Indian labor. Jorge Hernández provides an example. His tribute demands became notorious in Yucatán; acting every bit the colonial lord, he personally visited the pueblos to determine the size and number of cotton blankets the Indians would weave. Any protest on the part of the caciques was suppressed.[25] These and other excesses are well documented not only for Yucatán but for the entirety of colonial America.[26]

But this situation could not continue. Indeed, in 1532 the Crown largely ended the conquistadors' segnorial aspirations by declaring that the encomienda grant entailed no form of legal jurisdiction over the Indians; rather, it was nothing more than a ceding of part of the royal tribute as recompense for services the Indians rendered to the king.[27] In addition to setting these limits during the second audiencia (1531–1535), the Crown established regular tributary rates (*tasaciones*) for the entirety of New Spain, with the goals of curtailing excessive abuse and eliminating encomendero power. Finally, in 1549 the Crown abolished personal service as part of tribute; as José Miranda put it, this was a "key decision in the history of tribute."[28]

These decisions all came within a relatively short period. Doubtless the rapid redefinition of the Yucatecan encomienda and the role of encomendero owed much to the late conquest of the Maya (1541–1543), and also to the fact that Franciscan complaints of Spanish excess coincided with the Crown's own project of centralization.[29] Whatever the exact reason, though, the result was clear. After enormous struggles among Montejo, the encomenderos, missionaries, and the royal authorities who came to Yucatán with the goal of incorporating the peninsula into a larger colonizing project, don Francisco de Montejo the Adelantado was removed as governor, and in 1549 the Audiencia of Guatemala issued the first tasaciones for Yucatán's Indian villages.[30]

But the royal presence in Yucatán wobbled with fragility throughout the first half of the sixteenth century. The Crown was still unable to control the encomenderos, who continued to dominate the region's political and economic life through their *cabildos*, or town councils, in the four principal Spanish settlements.[31] Such was the state of affairs in 1552 when don Tomás Medel, the Guatemala audiencia's *oidor* (a magistrate assigned to hear and decide cases), made his *visita*, or inspection. His arrival marked the end of the turbulent early years.

For the encomenderos, it meant the end of their privileges and abuses; indeed, those who persisted in coercive practices toward indigenous society suffered the suspension of their tributary rights. One such case was the aformentioned Jorge Hernández. When don Tomás López Medel learned of these extortions, he suspended Hernández's encomienda rights. The oidor acted with such conviction that caciques later remembered him as the man "who stopped Spaniards from burning us, or having their dogs attack us."[32]

In the same fashion, don Tomás suppressed personal service and established the hiring of Indian labor as a means whereby Spaniards, encomenderos or otherwise, could obtain labor. This struck at the political and economic heart of encomendero power.[33] He also reduced tributes, but conversely added new products to existing tributary obligations.[34] This latter decision was probably designed to contain discontent. In any event, by the time his visita had ended, the institution of encomienda had come to consist entirely of goods, not services, and the tasaciones became a determining factor in tributary relations.

TENIENTES DE ALCALDÍA AND THE DISTRICTS

Before continuing this history of Yucatecan lords and their señoríos, it is worth pausing for a moment to analyze how colonial authorities and Franciscans organized the territory in order to establish their respective administrations efficiently over Maya society. In Yucatán, as elsewhere in the Americas, the Spanish raised their first settlements in those places that combined a variety of different factors necessary for the colonization process. The villa of Campeche was founded in 1541 on the pre-Hispanic capital of Can Pech, located on the peninsula's southwestern coast. When founding the city of Mérida in 1542, the Montejos selected the site of Tihó, an independent pueblo of the northwest, a densely populated area with relatively direct access to the coast. The villa of Valladolid was initially founded in 1543 on yet another pre-Hispanic capital, Chauac-há, east of Mérida near the north coast. However, its unhealthy surroundings forced the Spanish to relocate this settlement a year later to the pre-Hispanic capital of Sací, where it was to remain. Finally, in 1544 they established the villa of Bacalar on the western banks of a laguna of the same name, located in the peninsula's extreme southeast.[35]

The spatial layout of the city of Mérida and the villas of Campeche, Valladolid, and Bacalar divided the peninsula into four territories of roughly the same size. These territories were then termed *jurisdicciones* (jurisdictions) or *distritos* (districts), and each remained under the authority of one of the four settlements.[36] Even though colonial authorities never drew up formal boundaries, they clearly understood where the districts ended and which villages belonged to each district.[37] Appendix C provides a list of the pueblos according to their respective jurisdictions.

Nevertheless, the new order did not necessarily erase preexisting political orders. No dependent village was assigned to a district other than that of its pre-Hispanic capital. At most, the Spanish territorially based reorganization subordinated pueblos that had maintained their independence prior to European arrival. They were now assigned either to one of the four *cabeceras*, or head towns, places of Spanish residence and therefore home to *vecinos* (non-Indian town residents) who held encomienda rights over the caciques of their districts; cabeceras thus became centers for the collection of tribute and personal service. Under this system, however, the four Spanish cabildos had no legal authority over the pueblos of their districts.[38] Rather, supreme power lay in the hands of the royal representative in Mérida, Yucatán's new capital.

Once Montejo's governorship ended, these royal representatives arrived, bearing the title of *alcaldes mayores*. They were named by the audiencias of Guatemala or New Spain, depending on which of the two governed Yucatán at the moment.[39] Yet the presence of the alcaldes mayores proved entirely ephemeral, for they remained in office for only two years.[40] These functionaries either could not or would not create a political structure for exercising power in each of the districts that answered to their villas. Indeed, they seldom left Mérida. The conflicts that erupted among encomenderos, Indians, and Franciscans were settled according to the alliances these three groups established, and thus seldom reached the alcaldes mayores' attention. In the strictest sense, then, royal authority in Yucatán during these years made itself felt only with the visitas of the oidores—don Tomás Medel in 1552 and don Jofre de Loaysa in 1560.

A second phase, one which began with Loaysa's visita, was characterized by the Crown's renewed intervention in Yucatecan affairs. The Crown reclaimed the power it had once vested in the audiencia (in that moment, New Spain's) of appointing the alcalde mayor. Don Diego de Quijada was the first to be so chosen, and his administration lasted for six years. Apart from the political turbulence that characterized his period—turbulence stemming from his decisions favoring Crown interests—don Diego broke from his successor by extending the royal presence beyond Mérida. He now established *tenientes de alcaldes mayores* for each district in the villas of Campeche and Valladolid.[41] Hereafter the villages of each of these districts were subject to the cabeceras in which their respective tenientes held authority, while Campeche and Valladolid, as cabeceras, became subjects of Mérida. The tenientes de alcalde mayor stationed therein enjoyed both civil and criminal authority, since don Diego delegated them jurisdiction over villages geographically located within their districts.[42] In this way, when conflicts arose among Indians, the plaintiffs had to go to the teniente to obtain a ruling. By resolving disputes, Spanish functionaries thus began to displace what Ciudad Real's *Calepino maya* refers to as the "rule or dominion" of the Maya lords and overlords.[43]

FRANCISCANS AND GUARDIANS

One day in late 1544 or early 1545 seven humble Franciscans arrived in Yucatán. Three came from Guatemala, four from New Spain. Their intention was to evangelize, civilize, and colonize the gentiles of a land still in the throes of conquest.[44] They convened at the pre-Hispanic capital of Can Pech, where in 1541 Francisco de Montejo the Son had founded the villa of San Francisco Campeche. Using this point as a colonial cabecera, they built their first convent and threw themselves into the work of evangelization. It was no easy task. None of them had yet mastered the language, so they initially had to work through interpreters. While learning the Maya language, they dedicated themselves to baptizing their first converts and establishing a school for children.⁴⁵

Around 1546 they completed the organization of the Campeche mission. Five of the seven friars then proceeded to Mérida, the Yucatecan capital founded in 1542 over what had been Tihó, an independent village never integrated into any larger cúuchcabal. From here the friars made incursions into the peninsula's more densely populated regions. Montejo the Adelantado aided their work by ceding them a pre-Hispanic temple located on a hill—a site originally intended for a fortress, but which now came to serve as a second convent.⁴⁶

Toward the end of 1547, at the urging of don Francisco de Montejo the Adelantado, the friars launched an evangelizing campaign in the cúuchcabal of Maní, his grand encomienda. With the Adelantado's support they convened Maya lords and nobility in order to explain the reason for their visit and to ask for their help in constructing homes and a convent in Maní, which would be their third center of operations.⁴⁷ The friars also mustered forces for a campaign of evangelization in the population north of Mérida; and in Conkal, a village dependent on Motul, they built a fourth base. At this time they also came to Izamal, some seventy kilometers east of Mérida, and center of a densely populated area whose capital was Dzidzantún.⁴⁸ There the friars erected a fifth convent.

Consolidation followed. Within a few years of these initial efforts the Franciscans grew in both number and organizational strength, for in April 1549 friar Nicolás de Albalate returned to Yucatán with twelve more friars. And in the same year they created the *custodia* of San José. The term "custodia" was reserved for a group of convents that did not quite suffice to form its own independent *provincia* (mission territory); San José thus remained a dependency of the Franciscan province of Santo Evangelio, based in Mexico.⁴⁹ These pioneering missionaries soon celebrated their first governing junta, or *capítulo*, and with the presence of the general commissar of the order, friar Francisco de Bustamente, formalized the existence of the five convents thus far constructed.⁵⁰

The restless Franciscans soon scored additional triumphs. With their number strengthened and the great rebellion of 1546–1547 suppressed, the friars then headed for Valladolid. Here they founded a sixth convent and launched the evangelization of the eastern part of the peninsula. The vast majority of the Franciscans simultaneously worked to consolidate projects initiated to the north and northeast of Mérida. These enterprising Spaniards also continued to catechize and baptize the Indians, and founded schools in which children of the nobility could receive a Christian education.[51]

The Franciscans used three basic criteria to determine where to erect the first convents: political and administrative importance, pre-Hispanic religious significance, and density of Indian population. With regard to these, Campeche, Maní, and Sací were all pre-Hispanic capitals, places where the highest indigenous authorities lived, while Mérida, surrounded by a densely populated area, served as the capital of Yucatán. In placing a convent at Izamal, a dependency of Dzidzantún, the friars considered pre-Hispanic religious significance as well as surrounding population density. Conkal, to the contrary, met neither the administrative nor religious criteria; it was a dependent pueblo of the Motul province, and the creation of a Franciscan house here spoke mainly to the immense numbers of people living nearby.

This process, too, involved its own unique terminology. Sixteenth-century friars relied on the aforementioned criteria to select a group of pueblos which they termed cabeceras de doctrina. These served as hubs of religious administration and financing. Meanwhile, a secondary level of pueblos became *visitas* or *pueblos bajo campana* (literally, "villages under the bell"). A "visita" in this sense meant a pueblo catechized and supervised by periodic visits from a friar, and was not to be confused with a Spanish administrative inspection of the same name. The Franciscans referred to these new religious head towns and their concurrent visita villages as guardianías.

From the 1560s onward, the Franciscan order entered a period of vigorous expansion in Yucatán, and the cabeceras de doctrina proliferated among the Indian peoples. This contrasted sharply with central Mexico, where the Franciscan presence now entered a patent decline owing to the shortage of friars.[52] Indeed, between 1560 and 1561 sixteen more friars joined those already active in the peninsula, with twenty-one more arriving over the next decade.[53] By 1580 twenty-two convents had risen to govern 176 pueblos de visita.[54] This Franciscan expansion reorganized Yucatecan space in a pattern resembling small planetary systems, with smaller settlements in orbit around their larger and more powerful counterparts.[55]

In some cases the Franciscans took advantage of existing political arrangements in order to convert pre-Hispanic capitals into the cabeceras de doctrina of their dependent pueblos. In other instances they chose a dependent pueblo, and turned the surrounding villages into its visitas. For hubs of their new system the Franciscans also favored independent pueblos; in such instances, surrounding villages of the same status became the new cabecera's visitas, or satellites.

Whatever the individual dynamics, Yucatecan cabeceras de doctrina proliferated during the 1550s and 1560s. And in so doing, they quickened a process of centralizing numerous functions in the pueblos de visita. While not possessing the authority to do so, the guardianes intervened or imposed solutions when conflicts arose among Indians of the villages in their *guardianía* (mission district) without considering the existence of royal authorities—that is, tenientes de alcaldes mayores—and much less, of the lords and overlords.

The guardianes' purview was both broad and elastic. By means of the caciques in the guardianes' pueblos de visita, they summoned the Maya to come to the cabecera for fiestas to the patron saint, when the bishop conducted his pastoral visits, or when some important person wished to investigate matters among the Indians.[56] Similarly, the caciques supervised the collection of alms for the fiestas, and for the purchase of ornaments and other items necessary to maintain the divine cult. And they organized groups of Indians to work as basic laborers for building convents and churches.[57]

By the 1580s, then, the Franciscan guardianes had dominated the religious and economic landscapes of their respective pueblos de visita. Since their presence in the villages appeared to be permanent, they managed to construct within those guardianías broad networks of support (or perhaps better said, complicity) with the caciques. The Franciscans looked the other way in the caciques' and principales' administration of community revenues, in exchange for a veritable hemorrage of tributary goods, including cotton blankets and other products, from the common people. This arrangement allowed the friars to finance the purchase of silver ornaments for the divine cult, and to pay for masses, processions, silk capes, bells, and so forth; and it allowed the fiestas of the saints to achieve the desired splendor.[58]

Simultaneously, the cabeceras de doctrina became the real centers for most features of life in their pueblos de visita. This held true to such a degree that cabeceras began to compete with the power and prestige of the pre-Hispanic capitals. The cases of Izamal and Tizimín, dependent lordships of the pre-Hispanic capitals of Dzidzantún and Sací, respectively, illustrate this new rivalry.

Izamal had been a religious center prior to Spanish contact. Caravans of Maya pilgrims customarily trekked from the most remote corners of the peninsula in order to ask Itzamná, the father of all gods in the Maya pantheon, to cure their illnesses.[59] The Franciscans immediately perceived Izamal's role as sanctuary. Friar Diego de Landa persuaded the Indians of Santa María village to purchase an image of the Virgin Mary, and prompted them to collect alms for its acquisition. Once the money had been assembled, the friars donated the resources to buy another such image for the convent in Mérida. And since, in those days, the production of religious statues centered in Guatemala, Landa and a group of Indians sojourned to the convent of San Francisco de Guatemala (now known as Antigua, and at that time the provincial capital). The tradition maintains that, while returning, the caravan was overtaken by strong rainstorms, but "it never rained on the *imágenes* [images], nor on the Indians who carried them in crates, nor a few steps ahead of where they walked with these imágenes."[60]

From this miracle onward, the Virgin of la Purísima Concepción began to shower favors upon indigenous and Spaniards alike just as her Sun God predecessor had before her. Thus, it is said, Izamal's new patron saint began to make the lame walk, to make the dumb speak, to make the deaf hear, and even to restore the dead to life. The Virgin's fame spread, and with it Izamal reaffirmed its original role as sanctuary and became a key colonial religious center.[61] With the influx of pilgrims and their alms, the material wealth of the cabecera de doctrina shined in the construction of a magnificent convent that eclipsed not only that of the pre-Hispanic capital Dzidzantún, but all other colonial buildings of Yucatán as well.

Figure 4. The Virgen of the Purísima Concepción of Izamal. Photograph by Sergio Quezada.

Figure 5. Franciscan Church and Convent of San Antonio de Padua of Izamal. Photograph by Sergio Quezada.

Although lacking Izamal's grandeur and influence, Tizimín, too, illustrates how cabeceras de doctrina created from dependent villages could become centers for recruiting labor and Indian-produced resources. Tizimín was subordinate to the pre-Hispanic capital of Sací, and since well before 1526 was surrounded by a cluster of lordships, some dependent on other cúuchcabalob, and others independent. The Franciscans privileged Tizimín to such a degree that by 1580 its district contained twenty-two visitas.[62] With so many pueblos de visita, the available labor force was necessarily considerable, and permitted friar Francisco de Gadea to finish the convent in short order.[63] By the late 1580s friar Alonso Ponce wrote that this work was "completely finished, with its upper and lower cloister, cells and dormitories, all constructed of masonry, in a stout building."[64] At the same time, the alms and collections to purchase religious ornaments, which the caciques organized at the guardián's request, yielded such huge quantities that the convent assumed a material richness dwarfing that of its pueblos de visita.[65]

Figure 6. Franciscan Church and Convent of Santa Clara of Dzidzantún. Photograph by Sergio Quezada.

THE FORMATION OF THE INDIAN PUEBLOS

Thus far we have seen how the distribution of encomienda and the political and religious organization of Yucatecan territory tended to dissolve political ties binding Maya lords and overlords. We now turn once more to the señoríos, fundamental units of Maya political organization, in order to understand how the policy of *congregación*, or the reconcentration of indigenous populations, affected them.

For the conquistadors, the distribution of residential clusters throughout the monte was, as they put it, similar to the way wild beasts lived.[66] The colonial blueprint, then, demanded concentrating human beings in a single place that the Spanish called "pueblo." Such a place was to be planned and would have precisely defined limits; it would also allow its residents to enjoy order and peace, to adopt the Spanish way of life, and to be easily and efficiently Christianized. This process of concentrating people was variously called congregación, junta, and *reducción*.[67]

As in other parts of Mesoamerica, the Franciscans in Yucatán played the leading role in the reducción process. From the beginning, the priests who came to Campeche were convinced that the spacial layout of the lordships posed a serious obstacle to evangelization and the consolidation of their own presence in the indigenous world. Toward late 1545 or early 1546, for example, friar Luis de Villalpando, embued with apostolic fervor and the power of his own words, persuaded the Indians to form the first pueblos. The Franciscans began these early reducciones with the people living around Campeche villa, the main port leading to the outside world, and the place where the Franciscans had erected their first convent.[68]

While developing these initial congregaciones, the Franciscans lobbied the Crown to support their plan for concentrating the Indians into pueblos. In 1548 friar Nicolás de Albalate, who at the time was in Spain recruiting priests for the evangelization campaign, obtained a *cédula*, or royal decree, ordering Viceroy Antonio de Mendoza to take measures to facilitate the project. However, when Albalate reached Mérida in 1549, he found Yucatán convulsed by a period of political instability that caused him to postpone reducción.[69] The Adelantado had just been removed from the governorship, and the cabildos of the villas were now managing their own affairs while waiting for the audiencia to name a replacement. Furthermore, the wars of invasion and the Maya rebellion of 1546–1547 had traumatized the Indian population, while only some twenty Franciscans were available for what threatened to be a gargantuan task.

Two events of particular importance allowed the friars to launch reducciones in earnest. The first catalyst was the arrival of a new group of fifteen Franciscans. Second, the Audiencia of Guatemala sent Don Tomás López Medel to the peninsula in 1552. His visita answered the Crown's need to harmonize Yucatecan colonization with overall policy. The oidor arrived with sweeping powers, and during his two years of residence wielded unquestioned authority.[70] His presence constituted a watershed for Franciscan activities, for López Medel saw clearly that the old order posed a key obstacle to "the temporal and spiritual governance of the *naturales*."[71] With the *vistador's* unwavering support, the friars hazarded their great enterprise of congregating the Indians.[72]

From 1552 onward the process of reducción also began to transform the spacial distribution of indigenous society. The Franciscans would first visit the homes of the caciques, in order to determine which family chieftains would follow him, and whether the place was appropriate as a cabecera.[73] Once their inquiries were satisfied, the next step was to sketch out a plan for the village, which was to include the church, the *casa real* (the building that functioned as the center of government), streets, homes, and other structures. Macan Pech, batab of Yaxkukul, said, "[the Spaniards] put much effort into measuring the land where the Santa Iglesia Kuna [house of God] was to stand, and the community house and the lots [on which the Indians would construct their homes]." Once this had been done, the priests, with the help of the caciques, relocated the family chieftains and their relatives to the recently planned village.[74]

Still, enormous obstacles remained. Although the reducción process was built around the personal ties between the lords and their cuchteelob, it was no easy matter to convince people to leave their homes where they kept their beehives and domestic animals, or their orchards and milpas, or even the monte where they hunted. When the Maya refused to do so, the Franciscans resorted to violent means, forcing them into the new villages. Encomenderos have left us descriptions of some of the techniques thus employed. Juan de Urrutia said, "And on arriving to said village, [friar Francisco Aparicio] with much clamor ordered all the houses to be put to the torch. . . . in the same way, he commanded them to burn all the orchards in front of their homes."[75]

Indigenous resistance was not the only obstacle the Franciscans had to confront. At times the batab's residence proved not to be the ideal location to found a village, particularly if it was too inaccessible from a Spanish center of religion or politics. In such cases, the Franciscans and the cacique had to select a place in the monte where there was a source of water, then they would fell the woods, lay out the village, and finally bring in the people. The formation of Chocholá pueblo was one such case. Its encomendero, Juan Farfán, remarked, "Before this land was conquered, this village of Chocholá was not where it sits now, but rather one league to the east. . . . [now] it is situated on level land, with huge mountains of trees around it, and the only ground here without rock is where the village lies."[76]

The Franciscans invested long years in this project of geographically transforming the Maya señoríos, and by the mid-1560s could boast of having made some 190 villages.[77] Diverse circumstances informed their creation. The most critical of these was the fact that, generally speaking, the congregaciones followed the political alignments of the señoríos. However, no evidence suggests that the Crown waged a premeditated campaign to unravel the network of personal ties that the lords had spun with their vassals by moving the latter into different villages: that is, by turning them into subjects of other caciques.[78] Rather, this tended to happen as the unintended consequence of Franciscan practices with fundamentally different aims.

Linguistic and cultural homogeneity also contributed to success. For, unlike other regions of New Spain, ethnic conflicts were virtually absent here. Also important, and closely related, was the fact that Yucatán had a uniform climate, and was a vast open space without topographical obstacles and no irreducible technical-productive differences fragmented its indigenous society. Milpa formed the fundamental basis of agriculture everywhere.

Finally, and of the utmost importance, the Franciscans received Crown support in overcoming encomendero resistance. The encomenderos showed scant interest in the program, but later did not openly oppose it, either, but simply waited for their chance. When the Franciscans eventually disciplined Indians who resisted congregación, the encomenderos, former conquistadors who were hardly disinterested, denounced the friars. In the face of repression, the indigenous peoples began to flee to the dense monte of the deep south, thereby reducing tribute extractions. But the encomenderos' cause proved sterile and they were defeated. Take, for example, the case of Juan Cano and his accusations against the order. His complaint, couched in injured tones, ran as follows: "Considering the harms that friar [Hernando de Guevara] has done me in depopulating my encomienda [he had burned the houses of the Indians], I complained about him before licenciado Ortiz de Algueta, who was at that time alcalde mayor, and he condemned me to pay the costs. For said friar alleged that the *licenciado* Tomás López, oidor of the Royal Audiencia de Los Confines and visitador of these provinces, had ordered him to do it."[79]

If the encomenderos learned anything, it was that the Crown was determined to transform the spatial configuration of indigenous society, and that the Maya would be no exception. Moreover, at all moments the Franciscans enjoyed the support of colonial authorities and of the Audiencia of New Spain. Before the Indians, then, the order appeared as a powerful group determined to impose its concept of the pueblo. As if these advantages were not sufficient, no other religious order established a beachhead in Yucatán during the later 1500s, thus eliminating potential competition for control of the Maya.

FROM PERSONAL TO TERRITORIAL TIES

Once the population had been transferred to the lord's residence, the next step was to fix territorial limits on the new villages. Spanish authorities showed the greatest interest in defining the space over which caciques would exercise their power. To leave a formalized record of the matter, authorities drew maps that showed the new boundaries.[80] Only a few encomenderos participated as witnesses in these demarcations; rather, the majority kept a distance from the surveying process. Their aloofness owed to their hostility towards reducción, and even though encomenderos depended on cacique authority, encomendero interests were not necessarily jeopardized. Rather, the demarcations were a largely indigenous process, without the uncomfortable presence of the conquistadors. Hundreds of Maya were involved, including caciques, principales, witnesses, and family chiefs.

The Spanish conceptualized borders as lines that divide one political territory from another.[81] But these same Spaniards did not see borders as simply dividing lines, but also as paths or roads between the properties in question. Along those paths they placed *mojoneras* (boundary stones), as "permanent symbols to establish limits."[82] The opening of passes or roads through the monte and the creation of mojoneras as physical expressions of surveyed territory were not pre-Hispanic traditions. In reality, the Maya had no concept of boundary or mojonera, and for that reason their documents rely on descriptive phrases. For example, *u xoticob yetel u dzaicob u xul* expressed the action of "cutting down [monte] and placing a limit"; and *u tzolan u multunil*, the action of placing "in order a pile of stones" by hand, that is, the fact that someone constructed a mojonera.[83]

The agreements among caciques and principales to impose territoriality over their powers took place within the context of celebrations or *convites*, as the Spanish labeled these gatherings. Thus, when the batab of Mopilá met with his counterpart from Calkiní to settle their boundaries, they drank chocolate and *balché* (a mildly alcoholic ritual liquid composed of honeyed water fermented with the bark of a tree of the same name). These beverages flowed in abundance during ceremonial events.[84] But the convites could be more elaborate, according to the ranks of the individuals involved. In 1557, when don Francisco de Montejo Xiu met with the caciques of his cúuchcabal and their neighbors in order to mark boundaries, he gave each two thousand grains of cacao, five cotton blankets, a necklace of colored stones and another of malachite or green jade, and as they distributed these gifts they consumed three *arrobas* (roughly, seventeen quarts) of wine. Such presents helped don Francisco establish his authority, and legitimized the agreements in question.[85]

During demarcations the family chieftains played an essential role, for it was they who so intimately knew the montes, cenotes, aguadas, trees, *rejolladas* (natural stone basins), and savannas to which they claimed usage rights.[86] Simultaneously, these same chieftains created openings in the forest during the measurements and built the mojoneras; a carpenter who accompanied them constructed crosses to place atop the stone piles.[87] But during the survey the lords confronted the dilemma of how to determine their vassals' rights to natural resources, given the fact that residential clusters were interspersed irregularly across the land and, in some cases, now lay within another lord's territory. The family chieftains resolved these pitfalls first by determining access to monte, the key ingredient in milpa agriculture.[88] They also worked out agreements on water sources, since wells, cenotes, and aguadas (and secondarily, the trees and savannas) served as territorial markers.[89]

Beyond these critical decisions, the family chieftains also agreed to permit free access to territories that held resources indivisible by their very nature.⁹⁰ Once they came to a decision, they formalized the agreement in the presence of their batabob in order to prevent future conflicts. The boundary committees kept felling the monte in order to open the boundary and construct mojoneras as physical signs of the accord.⁹¹ They continued in this way until they traced out the perimeter of the new village.

Concentrating the Maya people in the cabeceras and impositing territorial limits on cacique power turned the lordships into pueblos, that is, into corporate entities to which the population belonged. From that moment on, the indigenous Yucatec world experienced the most important of Spanish interventions: with the delineation of frontiers, the power of the cacique became territorial instead of personal. The network of personal ties that the indigenous elite had constructed over the course of centuries to unite their political entities now entered its final phase. From the perspectives of family chieftains and their relatives, the personal loyalty that bound them to their lords now gave way to an identification with "nature and place of residence" ("*naturaleza y vecindad*")—that is, political ties acquired a territorial basis.

Meanwhile, congregación affected Indian society in many other ways. The most spectacular of these was the fact that Franciscans managed to congregate all of the family chieftains in their cabecera. No one remained physically separate from the cacique's residence except in isolated casesthat did so by accident and not design. Without doubt, the Franciscans' respect for the ties of personal association inadvertently made spatial reorganization more radical; and, in the end, the work of concentration succeeded despite all the opposition and conflict.⁹²

Reducing extended families into a single pueblo also helped to create barrios, each protected by its respective saint. Family groups now identified themselves principally with the new residential cluster. The Franciscan chronicler Diego López de Cogolludo wrote that, "to avoid confusion the pueblos are divided into barrios . . . each with the name of a saint, which is how they distinguish themselves."⁹³ As this took place, the original Maya place name of the incorporated barrio lost its importance; Franciscans substituted the cabecera's name (that is, the name of the cacique's residence), even though barrio inhabitants within the new villages still used their original indigenous name.⁹⁴

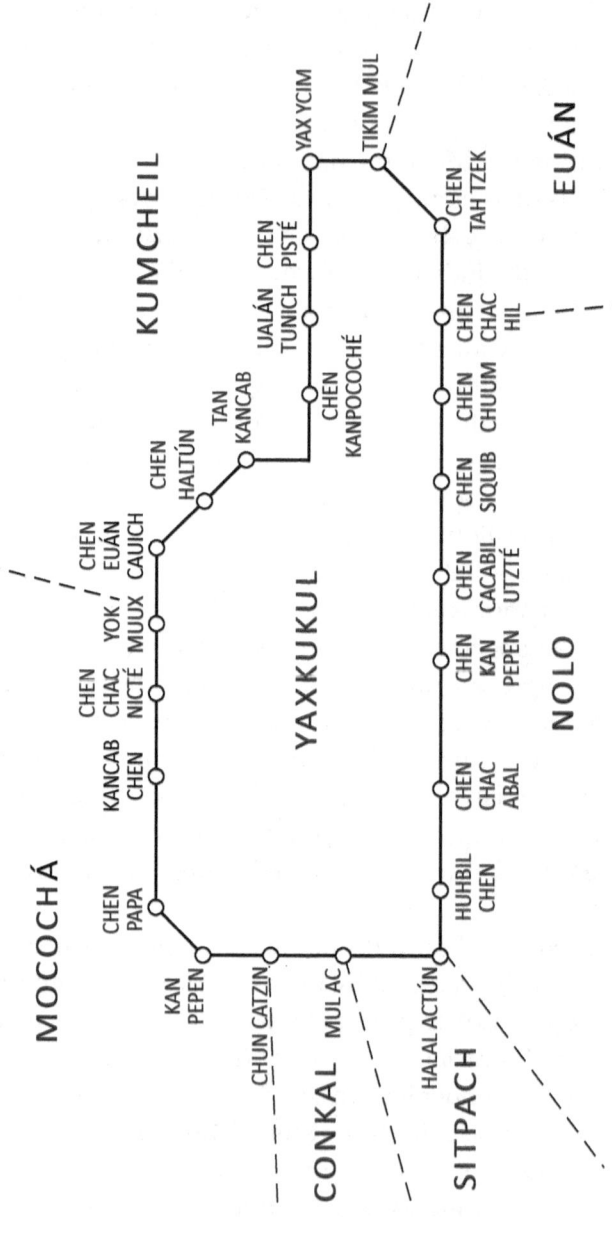

Map 3. The Perimeter of Yaxkukul Village, According to *Documento Núm. 1*, 1552. Drawn by Tom Jonas.

To complicate matters, these changes were accompanied by the friars' insistence on referring to the cabecera by the name of its patron saint and protector rather than its original Maya toponym.[95]

The Franciscans' strong-arm approach also prompted some of the Maya to flee to the remotest part of the peninsula. There they remained beyond Spanish control. When the initial furors of reducción calmed down, some returned to live in the recently formed villages, or else joined other ones. The upshot of all this was that, in one way or another, innumerable Maya lost their original social and political loyalties.[96]

Reducción also caused the virtual depopulation of Yucatán's northern coast. The reason for this was simple: Franciscans moved many of the coastal settlements (of fishermen, salt makers, etc.) further into the interior in order to maintain social control. Iñigo Nieto, encomendero of Citilcum, remarked on the matter as follows: "in some parts of this land, the native population has greatly declined, the cause being the removal of their villages. . . . The pueblos of the coast have suffered more loss than the others."[97]

REDUCCIONES AND SPATIAL REDISTRIBUTION

Among the most unique features of the Yucatecan reducciones was the tendency to join two or more caciques, along with their subjects, in the same village. This approach differed sharply from evangelization in other parts of New Spain, and it bore significant impact on indigenous society. In some cases, the friars exclusively gathered independent señoríos; in other cases, they joined señoríos that belonged to the same cúuchcabal. In these latter instances, the friars opted for grouping only dependent pueblos, or better said, for moving some of them to their pre-Hispanic capital. By the mid-1560s, there were seventeen reducciones of this sort, clustering seventy-one of the 190 villages that friars had originally formed in those same years.[98]

The Franciscans dedicated considerable thought to the physical layout of these reducciones. To each cacique they assigned a limited space in which his people could build their homes. The cacique of Citilcum, whose vassels were moved to the site of Kimbilá, described the boundaries thus: "[The two villages] are settled in such a way that

Table 2.1
Reducciones into a Single Location, 1565

Pre-Hispanic Entity	Pre-Hispanic Status	New Location, & Attached Pueblos
Calkiní	cúuchcabalob	CALKINÍ,[1+] together with: Halachó[IND] Kinlacam[IND] Kukab*[IND] Mopilá[C] Nunkiní[C] Panbilchén[IND] Sacalum*[IND] Sihó[IND] Tepakán[C]
Chancenote	cúuchcabalob	CHANCENOTE,* together with: Temaza* Tibatún* Tiholop* Tixmucul
Dzidzantún	cúuchcabalob	Citilcum,[2+] together with: Kimbilá Izamal,* together with: La Concepción* Pomolché Tekantó* Tecoh,[2] together with: Chaltunpuhuy* Sahcabá* Tocbadz Tunkás[1]
Maní	cúuchcabalob	MANÍ, together with: Cauich Dzan Mama Oxkutzcab Panabchén Pencuyut Pustunich Ticul Teabo Tekit Tikunché* Sacalum Yaxá
Sací	cúuchcabalob	Tizimín,[4] together with: Dzonotchuil[S]

Pre-Hispanic Entity	Pre-Hispanic Status	New Location, & Attached Pueblos
		Tekay[CH] Tiscacauché[S]

Sotuta	cúuchcabalob	SOTUTA, together with:
		  Ekmul*
		  Yaxá
		Suyhuá, together with:
		  Usil

Acanceh	independent pueblo	Acanceh,[3] together with:
		  Timucuy
		  Tixbecyá

Caucel	independent pueblo	Caucel,[5] together with: Ucú
Chichimilá	independent pueblo	Chichimilá, together with: Chibxul

Dzonotaké	independent pueblo	Dzonotaké, together with:
		  CHAUAC-HÁ
		  Polbalam*

Hunucmá	independent pueblo	Hunucmá,[5] together with:
		  Sihunchén
		  Yabacú*

Kinchil	independent pueblo	Kinchil, together with:
		  Bolonboxché
		  Tzemé

Panabá	independent pueblo	Panabá,[4] together with:
		  Mexcitán
		  Temul*

Umán	independent pueblo	Umán,[1] together with: Oxcum

Sources: "Residencia de ... Quijada (1565), in AGI, Justicia, legajo 245, ff. 1001–526; "Carta de don Guillén ... (25 de marzo de 1582)," in DHY, 2: 55-65; López Cogolludo, *Historia de Yucatán*, 232–39.

Note: Italicized names indicate new locations under reducción system; capital letters indicate pre-Hispanic capitals.

[1] Located on the camino real from Mérida to Campeche
[2] Located on the camino real from Mérida to Valladolid
[3] Located on the camino real from Mérida to Maní
[4] Located on the camino real from Valladolid to Río Lagartos
[5] Located on the camino real from Mérida to Sisal
* Unidentified pueblo
+ Cabeza de guardianía
[C] Dependent pueblo of the Calkiní cúuchcabal
[CH] Dependent pueblo of the Chichén Itzá cúuchcabal
[IND] Independent pueblo
[S] Dependent pueblo of the Sací cúuchcabal

the Indians' houses border upon one another." And, as Juan Cueva Santillán remarked concerning the space that his two encomienda villages occupied, "Santa María is in the same place as Izamal, with a street in between."[99]

Congregación led the Spanish to develop a varied terminology for physically joined pueblos. They would refer, for example, to the pueblo of "Mama settled in the site of Maní." Or, "Said pueblos of Ekmul and Yaxa are united and full and are located and settled in the place of said village of Sotuta." Or, in reference to the pueblo of Chibxul: "peopled in the same site and place of said village of Chichimilá." Or they might simply state that "such-and-such a village" was in a certain *asiento* (seat) or sitio (site), then add the name of the village to which it had been congregated.[100]

In some cases, the independent señoríos were priviliged over their neighbors (e.g., Umán, Kinchil, Hunucmá, and Panabá). In other cases, it was the dependent village of a pre-Hispanic capital (Izamal, Citilcum, and Tecoh, all part of Dzidzantún; or Tizimín, of Sací). In still other cases, the capital itself (Maní, Chancenote, and Calkiní) enjoyed the benefits of having the Franciscans gather various villages in their location. In all cases, congregación obeyed the Spanish idea of modifying the indigenous world by creating nodes for controlling all critical activities.[101] These nodes were intended to accelerate the colonization process in selected areas and lead the way in refiguring Yucatecan space.

Matters of travel, tribute, and trade also played a hand in the peninsular remapping. Congregaciones were organized at intermediate points along the *camino real* (main highways) linking Mérida with the villas, or on roads leading to ports. These were all strategic locations on large commercial routes defined during the administration of don Diego de Quijada (1561–1565).[102] In the final third of the sixteenth century, these congregaciones matured into centers into which flowed a vast quantity of people on matters of business. When conditions permitted, some of these same travelers settled down in order to nurture their nascent enterprises.

The history of Tizimín's congregación illustrates how new spatial alignments could bring prosperity to a village. The Franciscans had favored Tizimín's location by adding to it Dzonotchuil, Tekay, and

Figure 7. Church of San Luis Obispo of Calkiní. Photograph by Sergio Quezada.

Tiscacauchén.[103] In Yucatán as in other regions of the New Spanish and Peruvian viceroyalties, the Spanish, regardless of numerous royal prohibitions, took up residence in the pueblos with the intention of launching business activities. But not all villages experienced the colonial disruption with equal intensity. Those located far from the caminos reales only occasionally saw their encomenderos, or experienced a visit by some merchant, or welcomed the guardián himself when it came time for the fiesta of the patron saint. But the Indians of those villages did have to journey to their cabeceras de distrito, their cabeceras de doctrina, or even to Mérida itself to conduct their affairs.

The congregación of Tizimín, situated halfway between Valladolid and the peninsula's northeastern port of Río Lagartos, was an obligatory stopping point for everyone headed to the coast. Tizimín lay far from Mérida, and for that reason royal officials found supervision over the town's happenings difficult, if not impossible, and since its foundation in 1560, it had grown to become a significant population center, even weathering the blows of the demographic crisis (1564–1580).[104] Indeed, by 1583 its Indian population had reached a robust two thousand. Moreover, since 1565 the friars had turned the pueblo into a guardianía with twenty-one pueblos de visita. Henceforth, it was the largest Franciscan district in Yucatán, quite possibly the most populous, and its guardián wielded a huge influence over surrounding villages.

Spaniards did not fail to notice these advantages. In the century's final third, lured by an increasing demand for indigo, a blue dye made from plants, they began to convert Tizimín into a center of commerce.[105] By 1580 Alonso Díaz, encomendero of Dzonotchuil, together with his wife, sister, and brother-in-law Francisco Pinto made his home there. So, too, Gaspar Pinto (possibly Francisco's brother) had settled here with his own family. Diego López de Recalde, encomendero of Tiscacauchén, also came with his relatives, as did Diego Burgos Casino, the encomendero of Tizimín, who frequented the town.[106]

Spurred by European demand for dye, Spaniards founded *estancias*, relatively small and poorly capitalized properties, around the guardianía pueblos in order to cultivate indigo. They invested nothing whatsoever in land, but rather expropriated the monte around the pueblos.[107] They also took over houses of the caciques in order to turn them into *ingenios*, or mills (in this case for processing indigo), and took over the *norias* (water wheels) of the Indians.[108] In the course of this process Alonso Díaz and Francisco Pinto set up an estancia half a league from Tizimín. Diego de Burgos Casino had his own estancia named Tecantó, near his encomienda pueblo, Tecanxoc. Diego de Osorio created Tahbalal, close to Tesoco; Francisco de Cárdenas did the same near his encomienda village of Kikil.[109] These individuals worked in concert with the caciques of the villages of Tizimín guardianía to obtain the needed Indian workersto grow and sell indigo, making Tizimín a dynamic center for business ventures.[110]

But the extraction of this dye proved difficult work for the Indians, and in 1581 the Crown prohibited employing them for this purpose. This stricture, coupled with a decline in European indigo prices, made further estancias unattractive.[111] But, despite the indigo industry's decline, Tizimín retained its popularity among entrepreneurs. One of these was don Antonio Rodríguez. He had once been *alcalde* (that is, an official charged under the king's name with guarding a villa, city, fort, or castle) of the port of Sisal, and at some moment before 1580 he convinced Yucatecan governor don Guillén de las Casas (1577–1582) to appoint him guard of the port of Río Lagartos. There, among other activities, he was able to manage the encomiendas of Sucilá, Yaxcabá, and Mexquitán, all of which were Tizimín's pueblos de visita, and all payed tribute to his ward Rodrigo de Cisneros. As royal appointee, don Antonio bore the rod of justice, and as his brother-in-law friar Gaspar de Nájerahad been a *definidor* (a Franciscan appointed to provide counsel on matters of religion and administration) since 1581, his cordial relations with clergy and secular Spaniards alike favored his project.[112]

Antonio Rodríguez eventually took up residence in Tizimín, and on the pretext that the port of Río Lagartos needed guards, he asked for the caciques of Chuyubchuen, Panabá, Kikil, and Sucopó to bring Indian workers. On a weekly or monthly basis these caciques obligingly fetched a huge number of *macehuales* (a widely adapted Nahuatl term for indigneous commoners) "for their turn." Once they came to the port, he used them to extract salt, to fish, or to make ashes for soap.[113]

Rodríguez used his ties with the Franciscans, together with the power of his office, to bring "a huge quantity of Indians" to Río Lagartos, as the cacique of Calotmul put it. Any Spaniard who wanted to launch a new business had to come to don Antonio to rent Indian workers. Don Antonio was so powerful that he became one of Yucatán's most famous labor contractors. For example, Francisco de Cárdenas, encomendero of Kikil, worked with him to have Indians fell dyewood in the monte, carry it to the camino real, and from there transport it via mule team to Río Lagartos. Rodríguez's wife, meanwhile, took advantage of her husband's proximity to Tizimín's Franciscans; with the guardián's intercession, the gobernadores and principales of the congregación would send her two widows to spin, weave, and make bodices and threads for sale.[114]

Wine sellers also flocked to Tizimín. They made a point of arriving several days before major holidays such as the fiesta of the Three Kings, the celebration of the town's patron saints (January 6), and San Francisco (October 4), Christmas, and Easter. Lodging in the *mesón*, a community-maintained hotel for travelers, they solicited the convent guardián's permission to do business among the Indians. Once their petition was approved, the vendors commenced their sales traveling among the guardianía's various pueblos de visita. The caciques and principales of Tizimín guardianía also awaited the arrival of a Portuguese named Antonio Alfonso, a reputable wine seller, using community funds to buy from him the so-called *caldo para las limosnas*—that is, the wine delivered as alms to the convent's guardian—which they consumed during the banquets that they celebrated with other caciques and principales in nearby pueblos.[115] Spaniards also brought wine in order to retail it later in the congregación, in other villages, or to whatever cacique or principal came to their home to purchase it.[116]

This process of economic colonization also affected daily life among Tizimín's macehuales. Spanish presence soon made its way into domestic spaces, since Spaniards took up lodging in houses that had been designed for the *naguatatos* (a Nahuatl-derived word for interpreters) and *maestros de escuela* (school teachers), or in the homes of caciques. Gonzalo Chuil said of these uninvited guests: "some of them are so intrusive that they go to inhabit the cacique-gobernador's home against his will, and even if he makes clear that a mesón is available, they refuse to stay there."[117]

Spaniards similarly invaded indigenous family life as they began to form common-law relationships with the women of Tizimín. Illicit sex was an elemental mechanism of power when it involved relations between masters and slaves, or was a means of social ascent for one of the protagonists.[118] This mechanism of power helps in understanding the attitude of Alonso Díaz toward the women of Dzonotchuil, his encomienda village. He carried on illicit relations with Ana Cauich, Ana Noh, and Catalina Be, all married women. As a result of his encounters, the first two became pregnant, while Catalina died in childbirth, along with Díaz's infant son.[119]

Congregaciones held various pueblos together in the same place; they functioned as nodes of the colonial process, and for that reason also became potential flashpoints of conflict. Indeed, colonial governors frequently complained that the influx of Spaniards and *castas* (a generic term for people of mixed ancestry) harmed the Indians, that the territory was too immense for them to be able to impart justice, and that peddlers evaded paying the volume-based royal sales tax known as the *alcabala* along with the *almojarifazgos* (a tax on products entering or leaving a port). They also began to appoint magistrates called *corregidores*. By the mid-1560s Tizimín, Calkiní, Hunucmá, and Maní already had those royal officials stationed in them.[120] As López de Cogolludo put it, they were towns "sprung up in this land . . . [and] were like capitals of some fine territory."[121]

As the Franciscan order expanded in Yucatán from the 1560s onward, the friars continued moving innumerable caciques and their pueblos to other villages that were closer to the cabeceras that had already been established or were in the process of formation. This practice displaced huge numbers of people, so many that by 1582, thirty-one congregaciones contained what had once been eighty-one Yucatec Maya villages.[122]

In some cases these congregaciones were new creations. Those that the Franciscans formed out of the pueblos de visita when Tizimín became a cabecera de doctrina illustrate the point. Since this guardianía's territory was immense and its pueblos far-flung and distant from the cabecera, the Franciscans set about transferring caciques and their pueblos to places they deemed more appropriate. By 1582, in this district, there were seven reducciones that clustered eighteen of the original twenty-two settlements of the guardianía.[123]

Sometimes the opposite dynamic prevailed in that reducciones formed in the late 1550s and early 1560s were dismembered. Maní offers a useful illustration.[124] By 1547 or 1548 the Franciscans had established one of their first convents. Stirred to action by the notorious idolatry cases of 1561, the friars now moved twelve of the dependent pueblos in to the cabecera.[125] However, as soon as the friars had relocated two of Maní's dependent pueblos to the pre-Hispanic capital, the reducción began to disintegrate. In 1576 the Franciscans made Tekax into a cabecera de doctrina; while Pencuyut, which had been in Maní, was now relocated to another site, possibly its original location, and made one of Tekax's pueblos de visita. Some time later, the order returned Oxkutzcab to its original location. There they founded a second convent, to which they transferred Yaxá and Tikunché as pueblos de visita. Pustunich was relocated as a geograpically separate village, but also formed part of this new cabecera.

We know little about these population movements, but it is certain that in 1582 Panabchén, Sacalum, and Dzan were transferred, in all likelihood to Dzan's original site, and that the three villages became

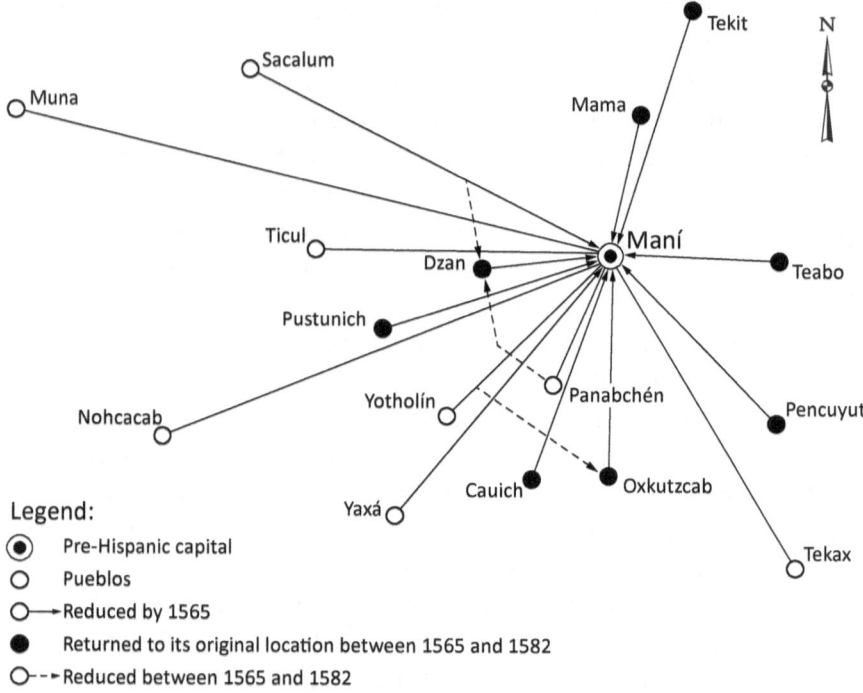

Legend:
- ◉ Pre-Hispanic capital
- ○ Pueblos
- ○→ Reduced by 1565
- ● Returned to its original location between 1565 and 1582
- ○--→ Reduced between 1565 and 1582

Map 4: Reducciones of Pueblos into a Single Location; The Cúuchcabal of Maní, 1565–1582. Drawn by Tom Jonas.

pueblos de visita for Maní. Mama, Tekit, and Teabo were relocated, possibly to the places where they had been prior to the Maní congregación; henceforth they appear in the documents as visitas. Ticul remained for a while in its pre-Hispanic capital of Maní, until at some undetermined moment it was moved—again, there is reason to believe that it returned to its original location. By the late 1580s, when friar Alonso Ponce visited Maní convent, he found only Tixul, a village that friars had relocated around 1550 from the site of Oxkutzcab.[126]

The early colonizing process thus cut in a number of directions. Both the awarding of encomiendas and the religious and political organization that the Spanish designed for the administration of indigenous society contributed to fragmenting the delicate web of personal ties that the overlords had built up with the lords at such pains during the century before Spanish invasion. Indeed the consequences were

Table 2.2
Reducciones into a Single Location, 1582

Pre-Hispanic Entity	Pre-Hispanic Status	New Location, & Attached Pueblos
Calkiní	cúuchcabalob	*CALKINÍ,*[1,+] together with: Halachó[1] Kinlacam[IND] Kukab* Mopilá[C] Nunkiní[C] Panbilchén[IND] Sacalum*[IND] Sihó
Chancenote	cúuchcabalob	*Tixholop,** together with: Tzemcay*
Dzidzantún	cúuchcabalob	*Izamal,*[2,+] together with: La Concepción Pomolché *Tecoh,*[2] together with: Cuxbilá* Tocbadz *Chalanté*, together with: Uitzil* *Sitilpech,*[2] together with: Chaltunpuhuy *Temax*, together with: Haltuniche* *Tixcochoh,** together with: Tixculum
Homún	cúuchcabalob	*Homún,*[3,+] together with: Cuzamá
Maní	cúuchcabalob	*MANÍ,*[+] together with: Tixul *Dzan*, together with: Panabchén Sacalum *Oxkutzcab,** together with: Tikunché Yaxá
Sací	cúuchcabalob	*Tizimín,*[S,+] together with: Dzonotchuil[S] Tekay[CH] Tiscacauché[S]
Sotuta	cúuchcabalob	*SOTUTA,*[+] together with: Yaxá *Tibolón*, together with: Tabi

Pre-Hispanic Entity	Pre-Hispanic Status	New Location, & Attached Pueblos
		Usil, together with: Cibak*
Tihosuco	cúuchcabalob	*Sacalaca*, together with: Canpocolché
Acanceh	independent pueblo	*Acanceh*,[3] together with: Chaltún Timucuy Tixiol*
Bécal	independent pueblo	*Bécal*,[1] together with: Nohcacab*
Calotmul	independent pueblo	*Calotmul*,[4] together with: Yocoboz*
Chichimilá	independent pueblo	*Chichimilá*, together with: Chibxul
Chuyubchuén	independent pueblo	*Chuyubchuén*, together with: Yalsihón
Dzonotaké	independent pueblo	*Dzonotaké*, together with: Sinsimato
Espita	independent pueblo	*Espita*, together with: Tzabcanul*
Hunucmá	independent pueblo	*Hunucmá*,[5] together with: Sihunchén Yabacú*
Kikil	independent pueblo	*Kikil*,[4] together with: Chocholá
Kinchil	independent pueblo	*Kinchil*, together with: Bolonboxché Tzemé
Panabá	independent pueblo	*Panabá*,[4] together with: Mexcitán Titzitz*
Sucilá	independent pueblo	*Sucilá*, together with: Yocchec
Tahmuy	independent pueblo	*Tahmuy*, together with: Yaxcabá*

Pre-Hispanic Entity	Pre-Hispanic Status	New Location, & Attached Pueblos
Tizonot	independent pueblo	*Tizonot,** together with: Muxupip*

Sources: "Residencia de . . . Quijada (1565), in AGI, Justicia, legajo 245, ff. 1001–526; "Carta de don Guillén . . . (25 de marzo de 1582)," in DHY, 2:55–65; López Cogolludo, *Historia de Yucatán*, 232–39; and Ciudad Real, *Tratado*, 2:367.

Note: Italicized names indicate new locations under reducción system; capital letters indicate pre-Hispanic capitals.
1 Located on the camino real from Mérida to Campeche
2 Located on the camino real from Mérida to Valladolid
3 Located on the camino real from Mérida to Maní
4 Located on the camino real from Valladolid to Río Lagartos
5 Located on the camino real from Mérida to Sisal
* Unidentified pueblo
+ Cabeza de guardianía
C Dependent pueblo of the Calkiní cúuchcabal
CH Dependent pueblo of the Chichén Itzá cúuchcabal
IND Independent pueblo
S Dependent pueblo of the Sací cúuchcabal

so powerful were that by the mid-1560s the halach uinicob had disappeared altogether along with their cúuchcabalob.

But other dynamics counterbalanced this fragmentation. The colonial policy of reducción constituted the first step in transforming batabil into pueblo, the fundamental unit of colonial Maya political organization. It was to the pueblo that vassals now adhered, but as naturales and vecinos, that is, as residents. The next step was to transform the inner workings of these early colonial villages via the indigenous cabildos, or *cuerpos de república*, with the aim of centralizing functions within them, functions that, to the colonial eye, the lords and principales had hitherto exercised in too diffuse and dispersed a fashion.

CHAPTER 3

Gobernadores and Indian Cabildos

From the moment Francisco de Montejo first set foot in Yucatán in 1526, until the middle of the sixteenth century, the Spanish did little to alter norms of authority among Maya peoples. But in 1552 the new lords of the land began to concentrate family chieftains in the cabeceras and build a territorially based power for the caciques. Above all, Spanish authorities labored to craft institutions that centralized politics and administration in order to transform the pre-Hispanic señorío. And they envisioned their greatest creation, the nascent villages, as new and innovative governing bodies that would serve those ends.

The conquistadors immediately equated certain indigenous ranks with offices of their own cabildos, or Spanish city councils. For example, the encomendero of Canpocolché noted, "They have as governors . . . a batab." Or, in the words of encomendero Juan Rodríguez, the lord of Sucopó was accompanied by "two or three men as *regidores*."[1] In the Spanish mind, then, all pueblos that had a cacique should also have a cabildo.

The cabildo, also known as the república, was to provide the inherently centralizing force that colonial authorities were looking for. Unlike the Spanish cabildos, their indigenous counterparts had a visible head in the gobernador (governor), the individual responsible for any of the various matters concerning the pueblo. At first the colonial authorities simply designated the lord or batab of a subject population as its gobernador. In this dual function, widely known throughout

Mesoamerica as the *cacique-gobernador*, indigenous lordship coexisted with powers conferred by the Spanish. The cabildo's imposition was a key part of Spanish colonialism, since the objective was to impose centralization on the dispersed pre-Hispanic señoríos, far too diffuse for Iberian tastes.[2] This was the context for the Crown's promotion of institutions like the *caja de comunidad* (community chest) fund (extensively discussed below) in the daily life of the pueblo.

When exactly did the cabildos come into being? It has been suggested that the process began with the visita of Tomás López Medel (1552–1554) and concluded with that of Diego García de Palacio (1583–1584).[3] In reality, the imposition and adoption of cabildos among Indian pueblos followed a slow and troubled path, and did not definitively displace the lordships until the century's end. Factors in both the Spanish and Indian worlds played a hand.

Regarding the Spanish, the colonial authorities perhaps erred on the side of ambition, for they tried to impose a cabildo in every place that had a cacique—that is, in almost two hundred pueblos. Needless to say, it was a simple matter to appoint the local cacique as gobernador; but creating functional institutions in every village presented a far steeper challenge, and even by the 1580s the project remained incomplete. Beyond the obvious complexities of the matter, Spanish initiatives in setting up the cabildos vacillated between 1550 and 1580, while colonial presence in the Maya world remained weak. For their part, the encomenderos proved more interested in having caciques deliver tribute in a timely fashion, and in quantities set by the tasaciones, than in setting up some bold new administrative system. The Franciscans, too, played a role in slowing the process. Often drawing upon the preexisting organization, they promoted certain individuals to help in evangelization. But they mainly concerned themselves with forming new villages, setting up *doctrina* schools for religious instruction, combating idolatry, and developing community funds. Finally, the Maya themselves helped to drag out the process of creating cabildos. As might be expected, the lords and principales opposed any change that trimmed their power. Attempts to model the early colonial pueblos on the basis of the repúblicas after 1550 brought imperial and indigenous powers into conflict, thereby complicating and prolonging the best-laid plans.

THE RISE OF THE GOBERNADOR AND OTHER OFFICIALS

As is well known, in many regions of Mesoamerica the transformation of indigenous political organization began with the gobernador, an office that almost invariably fell to those persons who played some decisive role in pre-Hispanic politics.[4] Yucatán presents no exception. During his visita, the astute don Tomás López did not fail to notice that the halach uinic and batab wielded the greatest influence among their people. Don Tomás referred to both indiscriminately as "caciques"; thinking in territorial terms, he saw the former as governor of his people or "province," while interpreting the latter as governor of the pueblo or village.[5]

Acting under this somewhat skewed assumption, don Tomás designated don Franciso Namon Iuit, halach uinic of Hocabá, as cacique and gobernador of his "province"; don Diego and don Lorenzo Iuit, respectively caciques of Tiscanbanchel and Huhí, as well as dependents of don Francisco, both now became gobernadores of their individual villages.[6] It is possible that the oidor also named don Francisco de Montejo Xiu, the halach uinic of Maní, governor of his "province;" at the same time he appointed a group of subordinate caciques as gobernadores of their villages, for they appear as such from 1557 onward. Henceforth, the title "cacique-gobernador" appears in the documentation as recognition of the role's duality.[7] In the same way, we find exotic combinations of Spanish, Taíno, and Maya terms. For example, Batab Uz, lord of the village of Tekax, was at times called "don Diego Batab Uz, cacique and governador."[8]

It appears that after López Medel departed, the designation of caciques as gobernadores advanced slowly. But in 1560 the *visitador* (royal inspector) Jofre de Loaysa reinvigorated the project, for he authorized the appointment of practically all the batab dependents of Nacahum Cochuah and Namox Chel, the respective overlords of the cúuchcabalob of Tihosuco and Dzidzantún. Don Diego de Quijada finished the process during the early years of his administration, for by 1562 nearly two hundred villages organized through the congregaciones already had their respective gobernadores.[9] The process had lasted a decade; the señoríos had suffered no real political transformation beyond the reductión of people into cabeceras, and the lords now sported the title of gobernador.

Another significant change during this period was the emergence of the alcalde. This figure's gradual rise as dispenser of justice, a function that he shared with the gobernador, was a bona fide innovation in Maya señoríos, for the alcalde's presence signaled the eventual suppression or displacement of the cacique's political and judicial functions. Alcaldes began to appear by 1560, when Jofre de Loaysa, during his visita to the peninsula, authorized this new official to hear and resolve Indian legal issues. In 1567 peninsular governor Luis de Céspedes Oviedo expanded the alcalde's purview to include the arrest of mestizos and mulattos whom he caught living in the villages; such offenders were to be sent to Mérida for punishment.[10]

The regidor marked another innovation in the world of the early village. This term, again borrowed from preexisting Spanish practice, referred to a cabildo officer charged with seeing to the welfare of the república. His duties included making certain that the physical headquarters of the cabildo were clean and "adorned," and that the village had a marketplace. In sum, he oversaw the norms for urbanization as expressed in reducción policy.[11]

The functions of the ah cuch cab now underwent redefinition. On one hand, he lost the responsibility for gathering the people for war, celebrations, and banquets; on the other, he continued to organize labor and collect tribute for the encomendero.[12] And when the colonial order began to organize the cajas de comunidad for the villages, the task fell to him. From that moment on, both Spaniards and Indians indiscriminately referred to the ah cuch cab as *mayordomo* or *a cux cabo* (a variant of the pre-Hispanic term).[13] In other words, the faculties of his office allowed him to adapt to the structure of the cabildo, and even to conserve his pre-Hispanic name.[14]

The arrival of Christianity also generated new offices. Evangelization implied interaction between Indians and Franciscans at the level of languages. Friars had to learn Yucatec Maya, and also had to devise ways to write it, so that it would be comprehensible using the Roman alphabet, in order to teach it to the next generation of priests who would Christianize the natives. Conversely, some Indians not only learned to speak Castilian but also to write their own words in the exotic script of the newcomers. The Yucatecans involved in these tasks were the first *escribanos* (literally, "scribes"). Little is known of when the doctrina schools came to exist, but they quickly yielded fruit, since by 1554 two of their students had become escribanos in Yaxkukul; three years later, Maní had an escribano as well, but, it appears, it was someone who retained a knowledge of Maya glyph-writing.[15]

Modifications of village authority did not stop there. Spaniards also imposed officials who, while not participating in the república's decisions, nevertheless facilitated centralization. Among these was an office of considerable variety, the so-called *alguaciles* (roughly, "sheriffs") who appeared in the 1550s. Again, the name borrowed from Spanish political terminology and practice for low-level policing. Owing to the Franciscans' evangelization campaigns, the first variety to appear was the *alguacil de doctrina*, also known as the *alguacil de escuela*.[16] His job was to gather the Indians for mass and for doctrina classes, and to prevent drunken sprees, pre-Christian rites, and public immorality.[17] In 1567 don Luis de Céspedes Oviedo added other responsibilities, such as arresting errant non-Indians, as he had also tasked the alcalde.[18] In the 1560s there were also *alguaciles de tributo* and *alguaciles de milpas*. The former were "to prompt the Indians in their tribute payments," while the latter saw to it that village Maya carried out their plantings.[19] At times the alguaciles bore the name of *tupiles*, not a pre-Hispanic Maya artifact but rather a Nahuatl term that the Spanish imported. At this same time villages saw the first appearance of the Indian jailers known as *carceleros*.[20]

These various officials of the repúblicas did not always result from top-down colonial imposition. Indeed, some caciques and principales used these new positions to legitimize their own authority and prestige, or else strove for new status and power under the terms the Spanish introduced. The new circumstances motivated ambitious Indians to seek appointments from colonial authorities. For example, in 1563 don Martín Couoh, gobernador of Champotón, asked don Diego de Quijada to authorize him to appoint two alcaldes and two alguaciles. Similarly, don Francisco Canul, gobernador of Tenabo, appeared before the alcalde mayor in Mérida in 1564 to promote the appointment of two alcaldes and four regidores.[21]

Even though the imposition of the república officers was only beginning in the 1560s, the intention was clear enough. For every one of the almost two hundred villages, the cabildo was to regulate the lives of Indians who were "naturales" (those born in a particular place), along with those who were "vecinos" or *avencindados* (those resident in a particular place, regardless of their community of birth). Cabildos, the idea ran, had to displace the power of the overlords in their capital villages, since the overlords' intervention would no longer be necessary. During this same time, numerous individuals managed their respective villages under the title of cacique-gobernador. To take only a few examples, don Francisco Cocom, son of Nachí Cocom, was halach uinic of Sotuta; don Juan Pech, a descendent of Naum Pech, was halach uinic of Motul; and don Francisco Xiu, descendent of Ah Kukil Xiu, served as halach uinic of Calotmul.[22] But by the mid-1560s the political ties that bound these descendants of overlords to the remains of their old señoríos had virtually disappeared, and the political entity known as cúuchcabal followed its overlord into virtual extinction.

The repúblicas also redefined the powers of the lords. Given that the Spanish initially named the caciques as gobernadores, they continued to govern and to impart justice, invoking their old precontact prestige. But their new offices authorized them to protect and defend the Indians; to see to it that Franciscans consoled and confessed sick Mayas; to look after the possessions of underage heirs; to prevent drunkenness; to extirpate the old rites and ceremonies; to watch for, correct, and punish public vices; to assure that Mayas carried out their plantings; to make certain that Indians attended doctrina classes and paid their tribute; to maintain order and harmony generally; and as if all this were not enough, to serve in a catchall capacity as the "fathers of the repúblicas." Moreover, gobernadores had to maintain a census that tabulated married, single, and baptized subjects—information that both encomenderos and priests required for calculating tribute. Finally, the governors were to construct and repair roads and to administer surplus grain needed to offset years of shortage.[23]

Above all, however, the Spanish thought in terms of territoriality. As a result of this fact, the lords could only carry out their functions within the confines of their own villages, and not over their original far-flung subject population that, despite all of the restrictions colonial power had placed on their movement, had managed to pull up stakes and settle in other villages.[24] And just as precontact legitimacy had issued from below—from the family chieftains, to the batabob, and then to the halach uinic—the power of the gobernador now emanated from political decisions outside the Maya world.[25] In sixteenth- and seventeenth-century Yucatán, the gobernador did not hold an office by reason of popular will, but rather had received a colonial appointment, and during his time in office, he very much depended on the decisions of higher-ups.[26] This redefinition of office also modified the gobernador's right to benefit from common labor. Indeed, the terms of governorship presupposed that this new functionary received a fixed sum as salary. From the start, respecting the indigenous tradition of control over human energy by the elite, the title of the gobernadores only specified the labors that the Indians were to carry out on the cacique-gobernador's behalf. For example, don Juan Iuit, cacique of Hoctún, stated that when don Diego de Quijada had made him gobernador, he had also imparted to him another right, namely, to make use of the "work and help from the Indians [of] the [pueblo] by reason of his office."[27] But over time this arrangement changed. In 1583 Diego García de Palacio, visitador of the Audiencia of Mexico, ruled that the gobernador could no longer make use of Indian labor, since he was entitled to nothing more than a salary.[28]

INDIAN CABILDOS, REDUCCIONES, AND POLITICAL ADJUSTMENTS

As the final third of the sixteenth century began, the cabildo of the early villages remained very much a work in progress. However, that did not stop the colonial authorities from promoting centralization in pueblos that had been congregated into a single place. Thus began a series of political reaccommodations. In particular, two innovations of the república greatly simplified the old hierarchy of the cúuchcabal. The first was the governorship, and the second was the alcaldía (both offices filled by Indians of the pre-Hispanic capital); but each pueblo maintained its own gobernador and regidores. The Spanish authorities encouraged these tendencies. They also tried to impose a single república in these congregaciones that had been organized from a dependent cúuchcabal.

The case of Chancenote exemplifies unification through governorship. At the conclusion of the Spanish conquest, Chancenote was a pre-Hispanic capital with the lordships of Tizno, Tecaz, Holcol, Tezamay, Temaza, Tibatún, Tixmucul, Tixholop, Tixcancal, and Quehac.[29] During the reducciones, all but the last of two were moved to the location of Chancenote. However, Indian resistance to congregación, and the violent means Franciscans used to carry it out, so severely impacted the caciques that the first four of these villages practically ceased to exist. In 1579 encomendero Juan de Urrutia said, "the cause of their total destruction has been moving them, reducing many villages into one, and this with excessive and brutal force."[30]

The disappearance of these lordships brought on a period of instability. Given his deteriorating personal ties with other lords, the halach uinic of the Tzeh lineage lost control of the capital; and by the late 1550s don Juan Uluac rose to become cacique of Chancenote as well as the four lost lordships of Tizno, Tecoz, Holcol, and Tezamay. In 1560 Jofre de Loaysa confirmed these changes when he named Uluac as the sole gobernador of the villages during the former's visita.[31]

In similar fashion, the disappearance of Temaza's cacique illustrates how Spanish authorities fostered centralization in Chancenote. Nahau Chan, lord of Temaza, died sometime in the first half of the 1500s, and was succeeded by his son, don Juan Chan. The evidence suggests that when the village was relocated to Chancenote, don Juan was displaced, if not as cacique, then at least as gobernador. Indeed, between 1556 and 1558 don Alonso Ortiz Delgueta, the alcalde mayor of Yucatán, appointed don Pedro Canul to the job. And when both don Juan and don Pedro died between 1565 and 1571, don Luis de Céspedes Oviedo named don Juan Chan as gobernador of both pueblos.[32] Upon his death, don Francisco Solís, then governor of the peninsula (1582–1586), appointed don Juan Chan Pat, son of don Juan Chan, as Chancenote's gobernador.[33] By this time, Temaza had already lost its identity as a pueblo.

The pre-Hispanic capital of Popolá presents a similar case. Its encomendero, Diego Sarmiento de Figueroa, fumed when the Franciscans had burned his thirteen tributary villages with the aim of congregating their people in Popolá, which was home of the sole cabildo.[34] Although lacking in the scope of the previous cases, something similar happened in the pueblo of Ekmul. It was folded into its capital of Sotuta. By the 1580s Ekmul's cacique had been subordinated to the governorship of don Francisco Cocom, son of Nachí Cocom.[35]

Still another example comes from Calkiní and its gobernador, don Francisco Che. In this instance we see how reducing various pueblos to a single location fed the indigenous elite's passion for political unification and centralization. During the congregaciones the Franciscans had combined nine pueblos in the site of Calkiní, making it one of the largest population nuclei in the peninsula, and what friar Alonso Ponce called, "the second largest in the province of Yucatán."[36] On one occasion the gobernador and principales appeared before don Diego de Quijada and argued that since Calkiní was the reducción's most important pueblo, "he should grant them permission for two alcaldes to have jurisdiction over all the . . . pueblos. . . . Which he did."[37]

The petition may have affected other cases as well. Perhaps with the Calkiní request in mind, don Diego de Quijada carried out similar changes during a visita to Tecoh, the location of Tocbadz and Chaltunpuhuy, dependents of the pre-Hispanic capital at Dzidzantun; Tunkás as an independent pueblo; and Sahcabá, an unidentified pueblo. He appointed Juan Macún, cacique of Tunkás, as gobernador of all the congregación's pueblos, and Andrés Uc and Luis May, as the alcaldes. In the interests of representation, he named a regidor for each of the unincorporated pueblos, thus forming a single cabildo.[38]

Two circumstances converged to trouble the development and consolidation of these unified cabildos.[39] First, from the 1560s onward, as the Franciscan order expanded and Yucatecan territory was rearranged accordingly, some of the reducciones of the 1550s and 1560s ended up being dismembered.[40] Moreover, the late sixteenth- and early seventeenth-century congregaciones brought a new phase of relocations. Reducciones that had endured up to the 1580s consequently disintegrated as new ones appeared.[41]

This reordering of territory and the second congregación program at century's end truncated centralization in reducciones where the process had already begun. Again, the case of Calkiní is instructive. The dismemberment that it sustained not only limited the jurisdiction of its alcaldes, but also led the involved pueblos to organize their own independent repúblicas. Tepakán did so first, appearing half a league from Calkiní in the mid-1580s.[42] Afterwards came Nunkiní and Mopilá.[43] The first of these was possibly restricted to its original location, while the second was joined to Tepakán, where both appear in the mid-1600s with their respective gobernadores, alcaldes, regidores, and escribanos.[44]

The cases of Tixmucul and Tixholop confirm the pattern. Originally dependent villages of Chancenote, they were moved after 1565, possibly to their previous locations. In the early 1580s the first of these lay three leagues from the pre-Hispanic capital; Tixholop was two leagues away, and, when combined with Tzemcay, made up a new congregación.[45] In these and similar cases, rearrangement helped pueblo caciques avoid ceding power to gobernadores of their capitals.

In Maní, too, reorganization halted centralization. As Franciscans began to work among the señoríos of Maní's cúuchcabal, the twelve dependent pueblos were gradually relocated away, until by the late 1580s only Tixul remained in the pre-Hispanic capital.[46] Whether Maní's cabildo was unable to force its jurisdiction upon Tixul, or whether the cacique and people of Tixul simply opposed the brunt of unification, is a point that remains unknown. What is clear is that by the late 1580s the dependent pueblos had their own repúblicas, and as friar Alonso Ponce said, "in the pueblo [of Maní] are two parcialidades, one is called Maní and the other is Tezul [Tixul]. Each has its governor, its alcaldes, cabildo, and jurisdiction."[47] The same could not be said of Dzan, a village restored to its original location; or of Panabchén, which began to appear as a new reducción under the exclusive governorship of don Jorge Xiu.[48]

Caciques, too, opposed centralization, for under this arrangement they stood to lose power to the gobernadores. Not surprisingly, some caciques made arrangements, whether tacit or explicit, to cling to their autonomy. Such may have been the case when the caciques of Tekay, Tiscacauchén, and Dzonotchuil integrated into Tizimín. As previously mentioned, this last pueblo had been selected as cabecera de doctrina and as the seat of the corregidor. This privileged position allowed Tizimín to consolidate its position. However, as of 1580, all four pueblos still defended their autonomy.[49] Even though in 1583 the oidor Diego García de Palacio ordered that Tizimín only have one gobernador, by the early 1600s each pueblo of the congregación had its own gobernador and cabildo.[50] Clearly, then, some caciques found a way to maintain their position in the new order.

CAJAS DE COMUNIDAD AND CENTRALIZED ADMINISTRATION

Another institution that helped centralize village administration was the caja de comunidad, briefly mentioned above. The cajas started as a Franciscan initiative to provide villages with the wherewithal necessary to operate their doctrina schools. In order to give pueblo children a Christian education, the friars lodged them in accommodations near the monasteries, "in houses that every village provided for them, all were together in the same place."[51] As the Franciscans extended their operations throughout Yucatán, new doctrina schools continued to appear, and as the years passed these schools became gathering places for "children and young sacristans, who read and write, and *cantores* who sing and lead masses in song in unison with organ, flutes, *chirimías* [a wooden wind instrument], sackbuts, cornets, and musicians with trumpets, horns, and organs that they are accustomed to playing."[52] To help maintain these schools, the students' parents raised funds by selling cotton blankets and collecting contributions; these funds, in turn, came to be known as the "cajas de comunidad" (community chests), so called because they were kept in chests, or *cajas*.

Examples of this practice abound. By 1556 the school of Maní had already raked in an impressive one thousand pesos in gold. The cacique administered and also helped to raise these resources, here labeled "bienes propios" ("personal funds").[53] In May 1557 don Francisco de Montejo Xiu, cacique of Maní, and don Francisco Che of Ticul, represented "the Indians . . . in the school of Maní monastery" when they signed a contract for six years with Joaquín de Leguizamo, Mérida's richest merchant.[54] The caciques agreed to provide Leguizamo with one thousand pesos in gold to invest in his business activities in New Spain. After six years the profits or losses would be shared equally. The contract concluded by stating "that [if] in the space of six years, the schools . . . have more funds, they can entrust them to don Joaquín de Leguizamo under the same conditions." Within less than a month, on June 23, 1557, they invested 364 additional pesos. When the arrangement finally concluded in 1563, the Maní school received 2,101 pesos for their caja de comunidad.[55]

As in Maní, the caciques and principales of other villages also began to round up caja funds for their schools, all under the Franciscans' watchful eyes. Indians so embraced the practice of collecting money that by 1565 innumerable pueblos had their own cajas, enjoyed appreciable monies, and operated with a system whereby administrators regulated income and expenditures. Take, for example, the case of Homún. In 1563 don Gaspar Tun, cacique and gobernador, along with the principales Andrés Qui and Juan Hao, kept detailed records of funds that reached to 829 tostones (a silver coin worth four reales): 279 in cash; 180 owed by Damián de Góngora of Mérida; 120 owed by the encomendero Juan Vela; from Gómez de Castillo, one hundred tostones for a chain and cross of gold; and 150 tostones that various Indians had borrowed "to ameliorate their hunger and their needs, as demonstrated by the documents they have presented."[56]

Caja monies came from diverse sources. Some derived from the sale of corn, cotton, chile, and beans from community-cultivated milpas. The exact quantity depended on the area planted and the price of the product. For example, in the early 1580s the indígenas of Dzonotchuil planted three hundred mecates; Tiscacauchén had two hundred and Tizimín one hundred. Between 1573 and 1583 Espita's caja made 205 pesos on the sale of eight hundred cargas of corn, two hundred of cotton, and ten of chile—an appreciable sum indeed.[57]

Indigenous leaders also organized special collections to celebrate the village's patron saint, on the feast days of Easter and Christmas, to purchase ornaments for the church or maintain the friars. The sum of these collections naturally varied. In every village the fiestas of the patron saint took precedent; one part of the collection went to the cacique and another part to the Franciscans. Every March 19th, for the fiesta of Espita's patron saint, San José, the Indians gave three mantas of cotton to the friar "who comes to oversee the fiesta," and three mantas to the gobernador and principales, plus "ten roosters for the principales and gobernador, and five chickens . . . and two pounds of wax and four pairs of sandals for the friar."[58]

Another substantial source for the caja was the return on the system of *repartimiento de indios*, in which the Indians received cash payment in exchange for such compulsory labor as building houses or providing agricultural work for Spaniards.[59] The sale of venison reliably turned a few pesos. To obtain this coveted meat, Mayas usually organized hunting parties. In 1583 Gonzalo Chuil, Calotmul's escribano, reported that the pueblo had "the custom of hunting deer . . . and of ever deer they slay, they removed a leg, the maw, and the skin, and gave them to whoever had killed that deer. They sold the rest, and kept the returns in the caja de comunidad."[60] Finally, the cajas received tribute surplus, that is, the difference between what was owed to the encomendero, and what had really been collected.[61]

In terms of their physical construction, the cajas were made of wood and had three keys, each guarded by a different functionary. By 1560 almost all Yucatecan villages had a place where they jealously guarded the money for their schools. For example, the Maní caja had a double lock and was in turn kept within another locked chest.[62] During those years no hard and fast rules determined who should hold the keys, but one of those keys usually remained in the hands of the gobernador, and the others with two principales. One of these latter bore the title of mayordomo, and it was expected that he and the escribano would give *cuenta y razón* (that is, keep records of) the funds. These four functionaries had to answer to Spanish authorities for managing the village money.[63]

The villages also had another form of patrimony that did not physically enter into the cajas: the so-called *bienes de comunidad*, or community property. This practice was still irregular in the second half of the 1500s, but it became more important as the years passed. In 1563, for example, Homún possessed "an iron bar and other tools" that were used for building the convent.[64] For the most part, however, the bienes fell into one of two categories. The first was livestock, especially horses, that the villages used to turn water wheels and transport travelers. The other was constructions, especially the community or government houses, many of which were of masonry by 1580. Friar Alonso Ponce described Maní thus: "there are very large casas reales, of brick and mortar . . . and so is the jail."[65]

Also included in this second category were the inns (*mesones*) and stables. Generally speaking, the *pueblos pasajeros*, that is, pueblos located along the caminos reales, had an inn to put up travelers.[66] These buildings consisted of two rooms: one for Spaniards, another for Indians. An Indian husband and wife were charged with attending to the travelers, whether on a weekly, monthly, or annual basis. Villages without mesones or community houses lodged wayfarers in the homes of caciques. Some villages constructed a stable *ex profeso* (specifically for travelers' horses), but those that did not kept animals on the patio of the community house.[67]

ROYAL POLICY AND OPPOSITION TO THE CABILDOS

At least initially, the new order seemed to hold out hopes for continuity. Indeed, since the visita of don Tomás López in 1552 until the end of the first year of the administration of don Diego de Quijada (c. 1562), numerous lords and principales had successfully weathered the conquest. Many took a lively interest in crafting the repúblicas (after all, some nobles solicited appointment to the new offices). But even if not actively involved, they at least continued to observe the unfolding events. As long as the governorship passed to the cacique and the new positions to the principales, the república's imposition did not necessarily disrupt the señoríos' power structure. This gave the impression that everything would remain as it was, and that Spanish rule guaranteed social continuity for the Indians. Indeed, royal authorities proceeded cautiously in those years, and tended to respect the political hierarchy in most matters.

In 1562, however, the situation changed dramatically. The discovery of idolatrous practices convinced authorities that the huge number of Indians involved in these rites evidenced the power and prestige that the lords still wielded among their people. (See chapter 4 for a detailed discussion of these events.) For this reason, don Diego de Quijada launched an aggressive campaign against indigenous authority. His offensive had two thrusts. The first was to reduce the power of the caciques by removing them from governorships. This happened with the lords of Tahcab, Ekpedz, Sacalaca, Uitzil, and Ticul, where caciques had received gubernatorial appointments.[68]

The second thrust was to accelerate the creation of república offices in order to make cabildos the norm throughout Yucatán, by extension allowing colonial authorities stricter control over the population. In 1565 Francisco de Montejo the Nephew wrote that don Diego de Quijada had "placed in the Indian pueblos . . . indigenous alcaldes and regidores, which he created for the governance of those pueblos." Along the same lines, encomendero Francisco de Bracamonte reported Quijano "had placed . . . in many pueblos . . . alguaciles, alcaldes, and governors, and other officers."[69]

This diminution of power naturally raised hackles among the caciques. During the *juicio de residencia,* a judicial review conducted at the end of each colonial administrator's term of office, the lords took the opportunity to denounce the approach as authoritarian, and declared that in 1563 titles of gobernador and other officers had been given without considering petitions.[70] Don Gaspar Tun, cacique and gobernador of Homún, was even more explicit: "Some three months ago [late 1564], the alcalde mayor came to my village and against my will . . . appointed alcaldes and regidores and procurador, offices that had never existed in the [village]."[71]

However, the caciques-gobernadores nursed a different attitude concerning the proliferation of the alguaciles. Since the caciques-gobernadores had neither judicial nor political nor administrative responsibilities, they did not constitute a threat. Rather, alguaciles simply carried out orders. In 1579 Juan Farfán, encomendero of Yalcón, described them as assistants to the gobernador.[72] Indians themselves perceived that, even though it was the gobernador's responsibility to guarantee all Indians planted their fields, he sent alguaciles to conduct the actual oversight. Diego Yuc, *alguacil mayor* (the head of all other alguaciles of a village), said that the gobernadores of Tizimín, Tekay, Tiscacauchén, and Dzonotchuil always "attended to the matters of their repúblicas, and regarding the Indians who make their milpas, although they do not visit them punctually, they nonetheless send the alguaciles to visit and inspect."[73]

Cacique opposition was not misguided, for don Diego de Quijada's plan did indeed pose a threat. The caciques clearly perceived offices such as alcalde and regidor, and even the cabildo itself, as potential rivals. The alcalde mayor's authoritarian tactics thus threatened to halt, however temporarily, the consolidation of these governing bodies. Even in the late 1570s cacique resistance remained a potent force in the villages. But Spaniards relentlessly promoted the new system. Francisco Palomino, *defensor de los naturales* (a Spanish official charged with protecting the Indians and with representing them in their numerous petitions, quarrels, and lawsuits), wrote that in Yucatán the Indians did not have "government or a way to live"; therefore it was best that "there be alcaldes and regidores and other officers of the cabildo of the same Indians," as was the case in New Spain, Guatemala, and other parts of colonial America.[74]

Except for the governorship, the cabildos and officers that appeared between 1550 and 1580 did so in an isolated fashion and as a result of the labors of Tomás López Medel, Jofre de Loaysa, and Diego de Quijada. From 1554 to 1560, the alcaldes mayores did not seem worried overmuch about transforming village politics. They failed to craft a system that would somehow establish Crown presence in Yucatán, and were similarly unable to rein in interests of encomenderos and friars. In fact, royal officials wrote to Philip II in April 1558 accusing the alcaldes mayores of vacillating in carrying out controversial policies for fear of being removed from office.[75]

Such was the context for the Crown's decision to strip the Audiencia of New Spain of its right to name alcaldes mayores. The idea was to place the matter in the hands of Spain itself. was Don Diego de Quijada received the first such royal appointment when he came to Yucatán on July 1, 1561.[76] Convinced that his royal appointment conferred absolute power, he began to implement a variety of orders, hitherto ignored, with the aim of normalizing relations between Indians and

Spaniards. On July 18, less than three weeks after his arrival, don Diego issued his first decree revoking the *mandamiento,* or authorization, to use Indians through repartimiento. In his somewhat mistaken understanding of the matter, Jofre de Loaysa had issued such mandamiento as a personal service component of tribute. The mandamiento in reality amounted to licenses or permits granted by Spanish authorities, ordering caciques and principales to provide a specified number of Indians each week to a particular Spaniard—encomendero or otherwise—in exchange for a salary.[77] Encomenderos were the first to be affected by Quijano's reforms. Tensions mounted, especially since one of the first measures, citing royal edict, called for bachelor encomenderos to marry and establish households.[78]

Oddly enough, and in spite of the foregoing measure, don Diego enjoyed the support of certain encomenderos from the very start. He even convinced the cabildo of Mérida to write to the Crown requesting that he be named governor and given Montejo's now-defunct title of *capitán-general* for ten years. Simultaneously, Quijano asked that he be given a raise in salary, along with the power to give out vacant encomiendas and to dispense charity from the tributes that had formerly belonged to the Adelantado.[79]

Interested in advancing Crown prerogatives in Yucatán, in March 1562 don Diego de Quijada decided to carry out a *juicio de residencia* (official investigation) of the Campeche *ayuntamiento* (town council), and to name a teniente de alcalde to assume charge of the port and its affairs. Upon realizing that the cabildo was in the hands of a nucleus of encomenderos, he removed the alcaldes elected for 1562. This decision ultimately blew up in Quijada's face. He antagonized the encomenderos, who appealed to the Audiencia of Mexico. This body decided to restore Campeche's dismissed alcalde; Quijada was barely able to impose his teniente and establish his presence in the villa.[80]

It was in May 1562, in the middle of these tussles, that friars discovered evidence of idolatrous rites in Maní. As the highest civil authority, Quijada participated in an astonishingly harsh inquisition, and firmly supported the event's overseer, friar Diego de Landa, at that moment the Yucatecan Franciscans' *provincial* (that is, the supervisor over the convents of a provincia, or ecclesiastical administrative unit). Criticism of the alcalde mayor intensified, and many encomenderos and Spanish settlers threw most of the blame on him, alleging that Landa would not have fallen into such excesses were it not for the alcalde's approval. As soon as the opportunity presented itself, encomenderos accused Quijada of causing most of the deaths and injuries suffered during the investigations. At the same time Quijada, acting in concert with royal policy, had prohibited *tamemes* (human porters), thus incurring the wrath not only of the vecinos and encomenderos, but of the bishop as well.[81]

Pressured by Spanish interests and against those of indigenous lords, don Diego tried to force cabildos on all the pueblos. To that end, he began an offensive of dismissing caciques from the governorships of their pueblos. What his campaign lacked in persuasion, it more than made up for in force. Quijada's aggressive approach not only roused the Indians involved, but awoke a more generalized opposition among the indigenous elite.

After Quijada departed, the next man to tackle this issue was don Luis de Céspedes Oviedo, governor from 1565 to 1571. Rather than focusing on the imposition of cabildos, he concentrated on strengthening the police power of alcaldes and alguaciles.[82] Although successive authorities took an interim appointment of Spanish alcaldes mayores and corregidores as a way of expanding the Crown's power in the Maya sphere, these designees tended to dedicate themselves to working the Indians through the *repartimiento de mercancía*, a forced sale of Spanish products to the Indians, or else by raiding the cajas de comunidad.[83]

For example, Juan de Contreras, teniente de alcalde de Valladolid under Quijada, distinguished himself by forcing the sale of cacao in his pueblos.[84] During his 1565 juicio de residencia, caciques denounced the injuries Contreras's repartimientos had caused, but he held on until 1571. And in those years he used his repartimientos to become a leading cotton vendor, obtaining Indian-produced fiber and selling it to villages that had none, or whose production was insufficient for creating mantas, especially in villages close to Mérida.[85]

Repartimiento de mercancía invariably enraged caciques, the necessary enforcers of this unpopular practice. Encomenderos, too, detested the practice, for they saw it as benefiting rival claimants to Maya surplus.[86] Nevertheless, the practice endured. With the exception of

López Medel and Loaysa, Crown representatives before and after Quijada dedicated themselves to their own interests, and did little in the way of building new political organizations in the pueblos.

During the three decades between the visitas of don Tomás López Medel and don Diego García de Palacio, encomenderos themselves showed no interest in radical transformations, either. Nor did they remove or appoint caciques arbitrarily, since they depended on these same caciques for tribute collection both before and after the tasaciones. Ultimately, they needed the caciques to recruit labor for their nascent enterprises, for the construction of homes, and as domestic servants.[87]

Nor did Franciscans have much interest in the matter, even though they were the principal architects of the reducción program. They did prioritize the creation of alguaciles de doctrina to bring Indians together for evangelization projects. The establishment of the cajas de comunidad helped make the mayordomo, under the title of ah cuch cab, a common figure in the pueblos. But evangelization competed more directly with the indigenous hierarchy, and for that reason the Franciscans, from the very beginning, kept more of a police-like watch over caciques and principales. One such act of guardianship turned up in Maní, 1561, when don Francisco de Montejo Xiu and other caciques and principales were tried on charges of drunkenness.[88] Still, the most palpable display of all was the inquisition against indigenous nobility of the cúuchcabalob of Maní, Sotuta, and Hocabá (discussed at length in chapter 4).

GOVERNMENT OF EARLY COLONIAL VILLAGES

Little is known of the internal workings of the early colonial villages from the López Medel to the García de Palacio years. Their organization revealed the presence of gobernadores, alcaldes, regidores, mayordomos, *fiscales* (Indians responsible for teaching Christian doctrine), and other officers. But even as villages assembled their new repúblicas, the batab still served as gobernador and the principales (chuntanob) as officers, and together they continued to guide the destiny of their old señoríos. In practical terms, Spanish authorities recognized this fact, for when referring to indigenous leaders they invoked such terms as "cacique and principales," or "cacique-gobernador and principales." Only in the early 1600s did other terms make their timid appearance in the indigenous documents: "gobernador, alcaldesob y regidoresob," and in Spanish writings, "gobernador, alcaldes y regidores."[89]

The larger picture, then, is one of continuity. The caciques, whether as batabob or gobernadores, were those individuals to whom all decisions gravitated. They still governed their old lordships; and if the principales took part in those decisions, they did so in an altogether secondary capacity. Now in their capacity as gobernadores, the batabob continued to manage "the affairs of their repúblicas." For example, judicial papers provide abundant evidence that the gobernadores intervened in cases of adultery, a violation of both pre-Hispanic and Christian matrimony.[90]

Adultery was a crime in the pre-Hispanic period, and it fell to the lords and principales to punish it. Landa reports that an adulterer would be tied to a pole and handed over to the woman's husband. If the latter individual chose to pardon, then the offender would be set free; if not, then the culprit would be killed by an enormous stone that was dropped on his head. Women deemed guilty suffered infamy or discredit, and their husbands usually abandoned them.[91] Still another punishment was to riddle the adulterer with arrows.[92] Both the right of spousal pardon, and the death penalty for offenders disappeared under colonial rules; in their place, the cacique applied the whip. Thus, when Juan Chab and Inés Pech were caught in the act, Juan Ku, gobernador of Pencuyut, condemned them to twenty lashes each.[93] The same happened to Inés Tun, who contrived to make off with don Francisco Dzul every time her husband went to his milpa; and to Inés Ku, who took advantage of her husband's trips to collect honey in the monte.[94] In these cases, the damaged reputation lingered, and unlike the pre-Hispanic period, it was the injured husband, unrestrained by the cacique or principales, who applied the punishment. When Alonso Puch discovered that his wife was unfaithful, he whipped her and cut off her hair. Such a punishment constituted a profound humiliation for a woman, since the absence of long hair announced her misdeed.[95]

Caciques also castigated pimps. This crime originated in European concepts of propriety, and was considered as offensive as adultery. Ana Na, who arranged for Alonso Díaz and Francisco Pinto to have affairs with married women, was condemned as "promoter of sin" and subjected to harsh and humiliating sanctions.[96] Don Juan Chuil, cacique-gobernador of Dzonotchuil, thus punished her by forcing her to wear a *sanbenito*, the Inquisitional tunic that publicly announced her crime; for good measure, he also gave her her fifty lashes.[97]

Like gobernadores, caciques could also punish Indians for laziness. When don Juan Chuil, cacique-gobernador of Dzonotchuil, learned that certain Indians had not yet begun their plantings, he ordered them to be whipped "as idlers and for not having made their milpas and not clearing and caring for their milpas as they should."[98] In the same way, caciques saw to it that Indians attended doctrina classes. Turning again to don Juan Ku, Pencuyut's gobernador, we find him diligent in that regard, for as he said to Andrés Huh, he had to "be careful of doctrina."[99]

But not all matters were so clear cut. Defending the Indians against Spanish injuries raised ticklish questions, since caciques had no jurisdiction over the colonizers. Thus in 1580, when the caciques of Dzonotchuil, Tiscacauchén, Tizimín, and Tecay ordered Martín Rodríguez to fence in his pigs and horses because they were rampaging through Indian milpas, Rodríguez ignored the order until Francisco Hernández de la Cueva, *juez de residencia* (conductor of an administrator's term of office) of don Guillén de las Casas, forced him to obey.[100] Yucatecan colonial justice and administration thus proved less effective when confronted with double standards for Maya and Spaniard.

There is no doubt that caciques also played a key role in tribute, since as gobernadores they saw to its production and punctual delivery. The 1549 tasaciones set by the Audiencia of Guatemala mandated that Yucatecan pueblos divide tribute into three payments a year; based on that decision, the caciques separated the houses of their señoríos into three groups, regardless of the number of residents, and made each part deliver its third of the tribute payment each year.[101] Or, as Gonzalo Chuil, escribano of Calotmul, put it, "the cacique makes three groups out of his pueblo. First, one third pays its tribute, then the second, and so forth."[102]

However, with the demographic collapse in the final third of the sixteenth century, the caciques confronted the problem of a population that could no longer produce the amount stipulated in the tasaciones. In March 1563 Pedro Gómez, treasurer of the royal hacienda, complained to the Crown that it had now become custom for the caciques to delay two or three months in submitting their quotas. As a result, pueblos were becoming "indebted" to their encomenderos, that is, chronically falling behind on payments.[103] As the population continued to decline, it became impossible to meet tribute demands; drought, famine, and disease in the years 1571–1572 worsened the pueblos' plight, and the caciques suspended their trips to the district cabeceras (Mérida, Campeche, Valladolid, and Bacalar) to hand over payments.[104] Spaniards now began to solicit orders to force caciques to render full tribute on time. For example, in 1572 royal officials of the villa of Campeche, charged with overseeing Crown encomiendas, jailed the cacique of Champotón merely for lacking a single *pierna de manta* (a bolt of cloth the length of a human leg) for August of that year.[105]

Faced with adversity, the caciques and principales forced women to gather in their houses to produce mantas that the former could hand over at the specified time.[106] Collective work was a pre-Hispanic tradition among Indian women, as previously described in our examination of the rueda. But these original gatherings were a space in which the women could "tell their jokes of ridicule and invent new ones, talking all the time."[107] With the demographic crisis, this casual atmosphere turned sour. The cacique now forced them to gather and supervised them the entire time, keeping the labor as intense as possible so that he could meet tribute deadlines. In 1573 the defensor de los naturales reported that the women "spin and weave the tribute mantas; they are forced to go together to the cacique's house and there they labor in the open air."[108] Within a decade this type of artisan's workshop came to be a place apart from the home of the cacique and principales. For, by the early 1580s, there was no Yucatecan pueblo without its *camulna*—that is, a community house where Indian women had to weave cloth from morning until night.[109]

Caciques were also responsible for providing colonizers with manual laborers. Spaniards and the gobernador settled on the number of Indians, how long they would work, and what pay they would receive; the gobernador, with the chuntanob or principales, selected men and women from among the two-thirds of the homes not currently preparing tribute orders to fill the agreed labor quotas.[110]

But the cacique's duties did not stop there. Almost any cost in this society eventually found its way to the backs of the Indians, a fact that compelled Maya authorities time and again to serve as collectors for new and often ad hoc levies. The Crown had made the encomendero cover costs of evangelization, the rationale being that his responsibility for their worldly and spiritual welfare was precisely what justified his tributary rights. However, Spaniards seldom complied with this order, as evidenced by its repeated reiteration.[111] For this reason Indians ended up paying for the priest's vestments, for clothes and frontpieces of linen or silk that adorned the altar, for the chalice, the bell, the cloth of the cross, and for the missal in order to adorn the divine cult.[112] Franciscans asked the gobernadores and principales to cover these costs by assigning quotas among their people, either in money or kind, to purchase ornaments to celebrate religious rites.

One example of this sort of cost-shifting comes from Tizimín, 1580. With the fiesta of the Three Kings approaching, the gobernador and principales of the twenty-two pueblos that made up town's guardianía came to the cabecera to hear mass. Afterwards there was a meeting, and the guardián, friar Pedro de Vergara, took the opportunity to ask the Indian elite to buy a *manga de la cruz*, a popular type of mantle or cloth adornment, for the church. They accepted, and agreed on a pierna de manta (a leg-length bolt of cloth) of tribute to cover the costs. Although we do not know how much cloth the guardián received, Juan Tamay, the fiscal and alguacil of Dzonotchuil, remembered that his pueblo and those of Tizimín, Tekay, and Tiscacauchén had rendered four hundred mantas to buy the manga de la cruz.[113]

In one way or another, the caciques and principales who governed and dispensed justice in their old señoríos were spokesmen for the Spanish demands in the villages, and for the demands their own vassals made on the outside world. This was no easy position, since to fail to meet those demands—whether of encomenderos, priests, functionaries, or settlers—carried sanctions such as verbal abuse, lashes, and imprisonment. And from within their old señoríos, they faced opposing demands and the complaints of their vassals.

Such was the case of don Luis Pech, coadjutor (assistant) of the gobernador of Kiní village. In early February 1573 Salvador García came to his pueblo with a permit to bring an Indian woman as servant to Mérida. Disposed to comply, don Luis asked García to depart, since his presence in the village had caused the Indians to hide. The latter agreed, and don Luis and his principales decided to send Ix Pot, a widow, since the other widows "were so old that they could not serve." But Ix Pot's relative questioned don Luis's authority and went to friar Melchor de Tarazona, guardián of Motul, to complain. Tarazona ordered don Luis to come to the doctrina cabecera; once there, "he publicly whipped him, causing a tremendous uproar and scandal among the Indians" for sending Ix Pot who, even though a widow, was a young woman.[114]

These sorts of injuries constantly jeopardized the recognition of caciques in their own villages, where personal ties mattered. The situation worked against their "rule or dominion." The predicament added to the gradual separation of caciques from the governorship, a process accelerated by the demographic collapse. The loss of economic prerogatives allowed don Diego García de Palacio, oidor of the Audiencia of New Spain, during his visita of 1583–1584, not only to regulate the functions of the cabildos, but also to extend these institutions throughout Yucatán.[115] With this visita's actions, the period of political transition within the Maya lordship effectively came to an end.

CHAPTER 4

DECLINE OF THE CACIQUES

This study has continually emphasized the importance of the batab, cacique, or lord in the construction of the colonial system. We now explore his destiny in the early years of the Spanish order in greater detail. Batabob during these years had survived the wars of invasion as well as the turbulence that defined nascent colonial society. For long years they had been educated under its cultural norms, and without doubt they represented the niceties of the historical traditions and rituals of their ancestors. For that reason the Batab stood as the visible and conspicuous figure around whom the lordship, the fundamental units of the pre-Hispanic political order, revolved.

At the moment Montejo set foot in Yucatán, the batabob were a select group. Aside from the fact that they made up part of the almehenob, or nobility, and were recognized as such, they also divided into groups sharing a common ancestor.[1] Each of these groups had its unique traditions, the differences among which often traced back to the causes that had motivated their ancestors to destroy Mayapán. And as related groups, they monopolized and exercised power among themselves, and restricted access to that power.

By the mid-sixteenth century some governing lineages, such as the Xiu and the Cocom, had roots in Yucatán dating as far back as the tenth century A.D. Others, such as the Chel, Tzeh, Canul, and Pech possibly appeared in the 1300s and 1400s, since available sources provided no documentation of their existence prior to that period. The histories of the Iuit and Cochuah remain obscure, but this is not to say that they lacked traditions of their own.

Whether or not Spaniards understood it, at mid-sixteenth century the combination of the caciques' historical traditions and multiple powers was beyond doubt material expressions of lordly "rule or dominion," that is, the exercise of their jurisdiction. To limit or restrain the powers that directly conflicted with colonial authority bore consequences for the cacique. This limitation began a slow process of sundering the network of personal ties that sustained the power they had accumulated since the mid-1300s, and which brought and held together the lives of hundreds of family chieftains who recognized these caciques as their lords.

Similarly, the ancestral rights that caciques held over the labor force were circumscribed, owing to the fact that Spanish policy tended to distinguish between what was considered the nobility's rightful income and what was deemed mere accessory. Unlike other Mesoamerican lords, the Yucatecan caciques possessed no territorial or patrimonial properties. For this reason, when Crown policy began to limit their economic prerogatives, their means of surviving difficult times dwindled accordingly.

Removing caciques from the governorships had a similar corrosive effect, permanently diminishing their authority in the new colonial world. By the early 1580s caciques were in open crisis, and their expulsion from positions of leadership in their pueblos was nearly complete. This amounted to a tragedy for indigenous society, a defining moment in the passage into a new colonial order.

PRIVILEGES OF THE CACIQUES

As in other areas of Mesoamerica, Spanish policy began by conferring a set of formal privileges to Yucatecan caciques, privileges that allowed them to establish their authority and prestige in the early colonial years. In the second half of the sixteenth century, the honorific title of "don" began to preface the names of these newly baptized Christians.[2] They also received the right to own and ride horses. This equestrian honor placed them—both symbolically and physically—above the common Indian, who invariably traveled on foot. Don Francisco Canul and his namesake, respectively caciques of Tenabo and Tepekán, could not resist the tempting image of themselves on horseback, and went to don Diego de Quijada to request that their dreams be made reality.[3] At this same time, caciques started to build masonry homes, and to wear boots, stockings, felt hats, cloth capes, and the baggy, ankle-length pants known as *zaragüelles*. In the early 1580s Martín de Palomar described their clothing thus: "They go about dressed as Spaniards. No one wore *calzas atadas* [a full-length legging popular among Spaniards], but rather zaragüelles, stockings or boots, and mounted on horseback."[4] For years this form of dress was more or less the norm among the indigenous elite.[5] Their interaction with the colonizers' world turned them into ladinos, that is, speakers of Spanish and practitioners of Spanish culture.[6]

Various other privileges defined cacique life. Until the 1560s, at least, they continued to enjoy rights to Indian labor and tribute. During the later 1500s Spaniards also turned to them for isolated military functions. Don Juan Canul, cacique of Hunucmá, presents one such case. In 1571, when he informed don Diego de Santillán, governor of Yucatán, that French pirates had come ashore at the port of Sisal, he was named captain-general of the Indians in and near his village.[7] Although we lack conclusive evidence, it is possible that the appointment of caciques as captains owed to the Spanish need to have, in coastal pueblos, persons capable of organizing and dividing an armed force of Indians to guard—and if need be, to defend—the peninsula's vast coastline during the sixteenth and seventeenth centuries, when pirate attacks were continual. Although we know little about the matter, such appointments doubtless involved ritual elements that affirmed the cacique's authority above and beyond its original limits.[8]

Despite such honors and distinctions, caciques confronted unprecedented changes. They had survived the upheavals of conquest and colonization, and the demographic and agricultural crises that followed. But then came new Spanish limitations on their powers, and the weakening of personal ties to their old vassals or cuchteelob. The now-definitive presence of the *pax hispánica* meant more than a simple restriction in old patterns of intra-Indian wars. The caciques' ancient power of levying soldiers was now cancelled altogether.[9] In the future, when a cacique, in his capacity as captain, organized a small military force, he would do so under Spanish supervision.[10]

So too, the cacique's right to own slaves came under assault in the early colonial years, when Spanish power in the peninsula was still tenuous. The first friars led this offensive. Protected by the 1542 New Laws, and driven by the idea that slavery contradicted man's natural and divine rights, the Franciscans assigned themselves the task of liberating the slaves of the batabob and halach uinicob. The method was simple: make the master's baptism contingent upon the slave's manumission.[11] Their methods seemed to have borne fruit in the villages around Campeche and Mérida. But not so in Maní, where caciques opposed the friars' ultimatums. The opposition was so intense that the caciques, apparently behind the back of their halach uinic, Ah Kukum Xiu (later called don Francisco de Montejo Xiu), resolved to assassinate the intrusive Franciscans. Only a convergence of circumstances saved the intended victims. The instigators were captured and condemned to death, but the intervention of friar Luis de Villalpando halted the executions.[12]

The second half of the sixteenth century was characterized by a Spanish campaign to limit the caciques' power and prerogatives. Don Tomás López Medel began the offensive. And, just as he started to rein in the encomenderos, he also showed a genuine concern that the indigenous society live in peace, and that it receive temporal and spiritual oversight on the part of Spaniards. The group of *ordenanzas* (statutes) that Medel dictated were aimed at the most intimate details of villages, and his concept of Christianity led him to regulate even the daily life of Indian families. In this micromanagerial spirit, for example, he ordered that the Indians be obligated to go to church twice a day, to pray the Ave María and Our Father, to commend themselves to God, to bless the table before eating, and to cross themselves before getting up.[13]

His long residence and the visita he carried out in the Yucatecan pueblos allowed Don Tomás to understand the lords' dominion among their people; he also came to realize those same lords' centrality in the political structure of the señoríos.[14] The caciques worried him greatly, and many of his measures, aside from questioning their powers generally, were aimed at those ritual functions that directly clashed with Christianity. López Medel thus ordered the lords not to preach or to pass on their rites and religion.[15] But he remained cautious regarding their political power; he attacked them indirectly by encouraging the Indians to complain about whatever excess their caciques committed.[16] During the years of his visita, Spaniards still could not afford to do without the lords in governing Maya society.

Regarding the caciques' right to hold slaves, don Tomás continued the offensive begun by the Franciscans several years earlier. Observing that Jesus Christ had liberated mankind, he prohibited Indians from owning slaves, and ordered anyone so held to be liberated immediately.[17] Those bondsmen belonging to caciques or principales were quickly liberated. In fact, the very practice disappeared quickly from Indian society, owing to Crown opposition to the practice, as manifested in the 1542 New Laws.[18] Even the Maya whom Spaniards had captured during the 1546–1547 rebellion regained their freedom.[19]

Still, López Medel had grander restructurings in mind. His larger intention was to undermine the lordship by socially degrading the institution, for he thought that a "throng" of principales was a source of confusion and discord. López Medel thus decided that while all villages would have a cacique, those with less than fifty inhabitants would have only one principal, the oldest and most virtuous man among them; those with fifty to one hundred inhabitants, two principales; those with 150 to two hundred inhabitants, three principales; four hundred inhabitants, four or five principales; and finally, those with more than five hundred inhabitants, a maximum of six principales. The remaining principales, in don Tomás's radical order, "were to be removed, and to remain macehuales."[20]

López Medel's dispositions, many of which smacked of utopianism, clearly aimed at demoting the caciques. But after his visita, authorities seem to have made little effort to carry out his plans, for as previously mentioned, the alcaldes who governed until 1560 were unable to effect a wholesale political restructuring that made the villages more responsive to Crown wishes. At the same time, between 1554 and 1560 the Franciscans had little interest in the ordenanzas; rather, with the oidor's support, they dedicated themselves to the business of reducción. Even so, don Tomás's decrees still foreshadowed hard times for the caciques.

Don Diego de Quijada's presence in the early 1560s greatly restricted cacique powers. And while he acted with blatant regalism against encomendero interests, he also treated Maya elites in much the same fashion. From the start he allowed the Franciscans (a group every bit as intransigent and repressive as Quijada himself) to combat the lords' rituals and ceremonies. Within a few days of Quijada's arrival, the guardián of Maní denounced don Francisco de Montejo Xiu, the halach uinic of the village's cúuchcabal, and don Juan Xiu, cacique of Hunactí, of organizing drinking parties with their principales. Gatherings in which the lords ate and drank were a cultural tradition and deeply ceremonial in nature. But the guardián saw these festivities as mere bacchanalias and at odds with Christianity. Prompted by the friar's accusations, don Diego de Quijada tried and sentenced those involved.[21]

Punishment fell particularly hard on don Francisco de Montejo Xiu. Don Diego confiscated his property and condemned him: "here in the casa real and cabildo [of Mérida], I sentence him to receive fifty lashes and be suspended as cacique of Maní for six months, during which time he is to be banished from the same; and is not to return for that period, unless it is to hear mass and divine services on Sundays and feast days. . . . I also sentence him to pay twenty pesos in gold."

The halach uinic's accomplice, Juan Xiu, also had his property confiscated, and was suspended as cacique for six months; and all the principales who took part in the gathering were whipped and banished.[22]

These draconian punishments marked a precedent for the caciques. The temporary destitution of an overlord and the accompanying corporal punishments not only struck at the "rule or dominion" of the nobility, but also at their prestige. And just as López Medel had desired in his 1552 ordenanzas, they encouraged discord among the Indians. Indeed, Ana Hao and María Dzul took advantage of the occasion to accuse don Francisco of forcing sexual relations upon them when they brought him *pozole* (a beverage of crudely ground corn). Similarly, Francisco Chi, principal of Maní, denounced Montejo Xiu for having made the principales sell two *xiquipiles* (16,000 beans) of chocolate among the naturales.[23]

Don Diego's and the Franciscans' reputation for high-handedness won eternal notoriety for an event that was to become a milestone in colonial history. Thus far, all appeared to have gone well. The Franciscans had founded monasteries, learned Maya in order to preach the word of God, baptized the Indians, and formed the early colonial villages. The Maya had attended mass and listed attentively to the sermons "as if they had been Christians for five hundred years. So too, the friars had taught the children to read and write and sing, and to play [instruments] and to be Christians."[24] And yet in villages throughout the peninsula, the lords still maintained their knowledge and power of traditional Maya ritual. So it was that at the beginning of May 1562, some Indian youths informed friar Pedro de Ciudad Rodrigo, guardián of Maní convent, that they had found some idols and skulls in a cave. It immediately became apparent that pre-Hispanic religious beliefs had persisted, despite a decade of evangelization. In a pique of frustration, the friar immediately launched an investigation, and ordered all the Indians living close to the discovery to be brought before him.[25]

The accused immediately confessed, and began to implicate others. The investigative snowball thus began to grow, and with it, the Franciscans' bewilderment. By the end of May hundreds of imprisoned Indians from Maní and its dependent villages filled the jail, the hospital, the houses, and the stores of Maní. Under interrogation, they revealed that they possessed idols to whom they had made sacrifices in order to obtain better crops or more successful hunts. Learning of the situation, friar Diego de Landa, the Franciscan provincial, went to Maní, took control of the increasingly grave situation, and requested the support of don Diego de Quijada.[26]

Convinced that Maní's caciques and principales were complicit in the idolatries, Landa ordered their arrests, while the other friars continued to investigate in the surrounding villages.[27] The interrogations began peacefully enough, but with the massive detentions, the friars' methods took a radical turn: they now began to extract information through torture. Indeed, Landa believed that the power of the caciques was so enormous that there was no "Indian, man or woman, who will denounce the lord, or the principales, even if burned alive."[28]

Thus persuaded—for many of the Indians refused to confess—the friars proceeded with tortures. Gaspar Col, gobernador of Tzucacab, testified as follows:

> they tied [the Indians'] wrists with strong cords, and they hoisted them in the air by their feet, naked from the waist up, and lashed them with whips and applied drops of burning wax in their exposed flesh; and they twisted their thumbs and the big toes of their feet; and having bound their hands and feet, they twisted them with a stick until the bonds tightened and caused great pain; and this was to make them confess and tell that they had idols and did indeed commit idolatry; and once this was concluded, then they placed their feet in stocks, and when there were no more holes in the stocks, then they tied the prisoners' hands behind their backs and held them in collars, and in this way the prisoners slept and remained.[29]

Under this atmosphere of repression, the detained caciques and principales constituted a serious concern. Fearing that they might inspire unrest and resistance, on July 4, 1562 Landa asked don Diego de Quijada to move them to Mérida. The provincial had heard rumors that from jail, don Francisco de Montejo Xiu had ordered his followers to set a fire that would enable him to escape, for as lord of the entire Maní cúuchcabal, he stood in imminent danger.[30] Unnerved by the trials in Maní, caciques in towns subject to Hocabá and Sotuta began to take preventative measures. Don Francisco Namon Iuit, halach uinic of Hocabá, and the lords of Sotuta demanded action more radical than that proposed by Montejo Xiu. Shortly after Maní's auto-da-fé (inquisitional public punishment) of July 12, 1562, don Francisco de Montejo Xiu summoned the caciques of Yaxcabá and Sotuta, and argued for the necessity of killing the encomenderos, the friars, and all the Spaniards of the village.[31]

The unrest spread rapidly. Indeed, the Sotuta lords' intention of fomenting a general uprising had already spread to Sacalaca, a dependent village of Tihosuco. Evidence on this point comes from a certain Padre Lorenzo de Monterroso, who had served as a priest in the pre-Hispanic capital of Sotuta in the late 1540s and early 1550s, and who, in disciplining some Indian idolaters, had picked up key information on Maya intentions. He claimed that Pedro Ix of Sotuta had come with his principales for a summit, and that they carried a *coyol*, or banner, indicating that the Indians sought war.³² Although the conspirators' arrest frustrated the plan, don Francisco de Montejo Xiu, even before his arrest and removal to Mérida, had instructed his principales to pressure the macehuales not to divulge the lords' idolatries.³³

These judicial proceedings carried devastating consequences for the authority and prestige of the Maya nobility. On July 11 Landa announced his sentences. He stripped the caciques of their cacicazgos, then had them whipped, sheared, and then jailed in Mérida. In addition to corporal punishments, many principales were degraded socially. For example, Juan Ucán and Hernando Ceh, respective principales of Teabo and Tahdziú, lost their titles forever.³⁴ Landa considered macehuales minor offenders, and gave them nothing more than two- or three-real fines and a few lashes.³⁵

The following day, the most important auto-da-fé in the history of Yucatán was held in Maní. It began with a solemn procession through the village, headed by Landa himself. Behind him marched the Maya penitents, "with *corozas* [dunce caps] on their heads and naked from the waist up, with idols in their hands and with sanbenitos, most of these latter made of mantas of yellow cotton with red crosses."³⁶ Once the procession was over, the penitents were arraigned before a tribunal made up of Franciscans and the alcalde mayor himself, don Diego de Quijada. Quijada took a missal in hand, knelt before a cross, swore to uphold the faith of Jesus Christ, and then executed the sentences. Not even dead Maya escaped punishment; those who in life had been idolaters were disinterred and dressed in sanbenitos. Their bones were thrown into fires and burned to ashes. The auto-da-fé ended with a solemn mass of penitence. Gaspar Antonio, interpreter-general of the Indians, translated the details of the punishment as it took place for the benefit of the Maya penitents and spectators.

Franciscan repression of the indigenous elite and their vassals sparked a deep division among Spaniards. Opposition quickly emerged among encomenderos of subject villages around Maní, Sotuta, and Hocabá; and in the cabildo of Mérida itself. These individuals had extensive experience in the peninsula, and understood that intransigent attitudes on the part of extirpating friars could provoke an Indian uprising. They therefore began to manifest their disapproval of Landa's methods; and they sent Francisco de Bracamonte and Joaquín de Leguizamo, regidores of Mérida, to ask Landa that the order "not conduct said affair with such rigor, and rather they begged that . . . little by little they try to learn why the Indians had engaged in these evil practices." To this request Landa tartly replied that "[for] those who rise up or rebel . . . or give themselves to the devil, there was no reason to abandon the rigor with which they began, because it was appropriate, for they had committed many sacrifices and idolatries."[37]

Confronted with this reply, and fearing catastrophe, the Spanish opposition group began to conspire against Landa and his ally, don Diego de Quijada, with the aim of presenting information about events in Yucatán before the Audiencia of New Spain.[38]

Indian discontent and Spanish infighting set the stage for the arrival of Bishop and friar Francisco de Toral, on August 14, 1562. As the highest ecclesiastical authority and quite against the wishes of Landa, he assumed control of the situation. His attitude toward the Indians, together with his ideas of evangelization, differed radically from the provincial's own thinking. Consonant with his essentially renaissance mentality, Toral believed that Indians, as neophytes in matters of religion, should be evangelized by means of persuasion; Landa, to the contrary, hewed to the medieval approach of violent coercion.[39] Armed with these conflicting world views, the bishop and the provincial found themselves locked in unending tussles throughout the second half of 1562. But Toral's authority gradually prevailed, and on January 2, 1563, after making his own inquiry regarding the idolatries, he decided to reduce the nobles' penalties, and subsequently liberated them.[40] After eight months of confrontations between these two factions (the order's provincial, the Franciscan brothers, and the alcalde mayor on one side, and the indigenous elite, the encomenderos, and the bishop on the other), one of the most controversial episodes in the history of Yucatán's religious persecution came to a close.

THE CRISIS OF LORDSHIP

While these religious and administrative struggles raged, Yucatecan caciques also suffered from changes in control of material riches. Unlike central Mexico, where indigenous lords possessed abundant resources that included tribute, services, lands, *terrazgueros* (sharecroppers), and so forth, Yucatán's lords and principales owned scant material wealth.[41] Their situation was hardly buoyant. An inventory of don Francisco de Montejo Xiu's goods, made in the early 1560s, when Spanish authorities had yet to mount a serious campaign against the lords' economic privileges, provides a perfect illustration of this fact. The inventory makes no mention of territorial possessions, of lineage properties, or even of landholdings somehow inherent in his rank as halach uinic. Nor did he claim terrazgueros. His riches, if the term applies, consisted of a bed and mattress, two cedar boxes with locks, nine chairs, a table, and a masonry home that, per pre-Hispanic rights he had used Indian labor to build.[42] Few substantial differences distinguished his possessions from those of the macehuales. The description of the house of Juan Chan, principal of Maní, corroborated this portrait: it was of poles and straw.[43]

Without the land that might have allowed them to weather times of economic crisis, Yucatecan lords found themselves vulnerable when the Crown began to limit their rights to commoner labor. But until the early 1560s, save for the end–of–war levies and the manumission of slaves, the caciques had suffered few economic restrictions at the hands of Spaniards.

This state of affairs changed when don Diego de Quijada, as part of overall Spanish policy, began to trim the caciques' economic plans. Following the January 31, 1552 cédula, he issued orders clarifying the nature of those rights. Then in 1563 he limited don Juan May, cacique of Yaxkukul, parcialidad of Cuzamá, to the following Indian services: they were to cultivate a half fanega (roughly, 3,200 square meters) of milpa for him, build his home, and as needed provide it with repairs; he was also to receive a married couple as servants. By 1565 the alcalde mayor extended his new rules to all the lords.[44] It would seem that beyond these bare-bones services, the alcalde mayor gave no thought to having the Indians provide their caciques with some sort of tribute; rather, the entire practice was simply eliminated.

Quijada also took the critical step of restricting cacique control of labor repartimiento. From his administration onward, the lords could only use the Indians of their villages for Crown-authorized projects.

A cacique would thus require an order from a Spanish authority stating the number of Indians requisitioned, the term of their employment, and the salary they were to receive.[45] If his needs exceeded the time and number of Indians authorized, the cacique could only make up the difference through measures established by the colonial regime; or else he would have to work through less formal means, namely, by use of his old influence upon the macehuales.

But Quijada's successors failed to enforce the ban on tribute in any consistent fashion; nor did they always scrutinize all that carefully how caciques used commoner labor. The actual application of these laws remained a touchy process. On one hand, caciques still enjoyed village authority; on the other, Spaniards needed their influence, and caciques were thus able to parlay their responsibilities into opportunities for power. In matters of both labor and tribute, they claimed anything left over after satisfying Spanish demands, or simply continued to collect, claiming that quotas were still unmet. Although, in 1567 don Luis de Céspedes Oviedo, governor of Yucatán, ordered caciques to sell the remainder of tributary goods and to place the returns in their cajas de comunidad. He also threatened to destitute, or to fine with double-payment, any cacique who over-collected. Still, this latter abuse persisted for years.[46]

Much the same happened with money of the cajas de comunidad. At convenient moments these funds became playthings for the lords or caciques. The friars asked them to organize huge contributions of cotton mantas and other products among the commoners in order to raise money to purchase silver for the church, or to pay for masses, processions, silk capes, bells, and so forth. In exchange, the Franciscans turned a blind eye before the caciques and principales "squandering" money on fiestas for the villages' patron saints. Between 1573 and 1583 alone, the native elite of Tizimín, Dzonotchuil, Tekay, and Tiscacauchén spent 165 pesos and six *tomines* (a *tomín* representing one-eighth of a Spanish gold coin) to celebrate the feast of the Three Kings. These monies came from four collections in the four pueblos during those years.[47]

The visita of oidor Diego García de Palacio in late 1583 had a huge impact in all these matters. He brought with him a series of fiscal and political initiatives already in place in central Mexico, and extended them throughout the peninsula. In terms of fiscal matters, García de Palacio simplified and homogenized the old tributary system bequeathed by the Audiencia of Guatemala in 1549.[48] He established fixed, limited payment for all Indian tributaries. Specifically, for every Indian he ordered two cotton piernas de manta, a fanega of corn, and two fowl: one a Castilian chicken, and the other a turkey native to the region.[49] This measure meant that caciques no longer determined who paid and who did not. In sum, the indigenous nobility lost a significant part of its traditional control over matters of economy.[50]

At the same time, don Diego García de Palacio instituted other measures aimed at making caciques something less than they had once been. He decreed that any gift from lords had to be at their own cost, and not that of the commoners, at the risk of paying four times in his own money what he had illegally taken, along with the loss of his office. Finally, García prohibited the lords from accepting gratuities from the commoners in exchange for authorizing marriages. And again, he insisted that caciques not demand tribute from macehuales, or extract service from them without express order from the governor or a Spanish magistrate.[51]

Regarding politics, García de Palacio's presence meant the institutionalization of the indigenous cabildo. Indeed, this body gained strength and presence in the villages. Spanish authorities ordered them to prevent caciques from flaunting personal services. Bureaucratic formula now prevailed: caciques had to ask the defensor de naturales to take their request for labor to the colonial authorities, who would in turn advance the request to the village's cabildo. These latter would read and analyze the request and, if approved, send it back to the república.[52]

FROM LORDSHIP TO GOVERNORSHIP

As previously stated, when Spanish authorities began organizing the Indian repúblicas, necessity compelled them to take advantage of the indigenous hierarchy by appointing caciques—that is, batabob—as gobernadores.[53] These gobernadores monopolized power and access through their knowledge of Suyuá, that cryptic tongue passed from father to son that allowed successors to claim the title of batab or halach uinic.[54] If this ancient tradition conflicted with the elective character that Spanish policy imposed on indigenous governance in other Mesoamerican regions, it mattered little, because in Yucatán, royal authorities showed little interest in native ritual when designating gobernadores.

For this reason, every time a new Spanish representative came to Yucatán, his first step was to confirm or remove the gobernador in each of the pueblos. The procedure was simple enough. Calling together the caciques, the Spanish representative would void the appointments of his predecessor; once the Maya in question paid a fee, he would extend new appointments, informing the recipients that they could only hold the office as long as no other royal authority decreed otherwise.[55]

This practice naturally subjected the governorships to the caprices of the royal representative; the cacique would have to follow colonial norms to keep his office.[56] In this way, Suyuá was gradually displaced by a mechanism that allowed governing lineages to monopolize the "rule or dominion" of the villages, and for that reason, to represent the señorío before the outside world.

Before the early 1560s, when knowledge of Suyuá still controlled access to power, the alcaldes mayores who administered Yucatán seldom changed out the lords' successors with any great frequency. But the wars of conquest, together with the Franciscans' violent methods of congregación, weakened the nobility's control of succession. The Maya priests and principales of the señorío and lineages, forces that guaranteed retention of power, no longer excluded "interlopers" by interrogating them in the ancient language of court. There could be no more threat of hanging them, cutting out their tongues, or gouging out their eyes, as had been the practice before the Montejos arrived.

The Cochuah lineage presents a case in point. When the conquest began, this lineage governed Tihosuco and the lordships of Ekpedz and Ichmul. But during the campaigns of conquest, the lords and their people suffered abuse and repression almost to the point of disappearing altogether. Nacahun Cochuah, the halach uinic, perished, as did his successor (or successors), priests, and principales. Don Melchor and don Agustín Cochuah, respective lords of Ekpedz and Ichmul, survivors of those terrible years, failed to fill the power vacuum, and could not stop a certain interloper, Xol, later baptized Francisco, from taking command of the señorío from its capital.[57] During his visita of 1560, Jofre de Loaysa granted Xol the title of gobernador of Tihosuco.[58] Something similar played out among the Tzeh lineage.[59] Dislocations stemming from the reducciones caused them to lose control of Chancenote, their pre-Hispanic capital, and helped someone from Uluac to ascend to the cacicazgo.[60] As with Xol, Loaysa made the usurper from Uluac the new gobernador.[61]

Don Diego de Quijada inaugurated a second phase of cacique decline when he and his successors, just like their counterparts in central Mexico, launched a premeditated campaign of divesting traditional caciques of their governorships.[62] We know little about the circumstances that prompted don Diego de Quijada to ignore those caciques' existence and to appoint other, non-elite Indians as gobernadores. But this is exactly what happened in Ekpedz, Sacalaca, Temax, Uitzil, Tahcab, Tocbadz, Calotmul, and Pustunich. These changes stirred controversy in the pueblos; principales of Tahcab, referring to the events of the time, reported that the presence of the gobernador alongside the continued existence of the cacique had resulted in the fact "that among the principales there has been and remains much confusion."[63] Under these circumstances, many family chieftains decided to maintain personal ties with their caciques, thus accepting their "rule or dominion," while other chieftains adhered to the orders of the new and rival functionary. The appearance of intrusive gobernadores thus underscored the fact that the lords' days were numbered, and that the network of personal ties was disintegrating.

In some villages the effect of this partial transition was even more radical: residents began to doubt the power of *both* authorities. The principales of Sacalaca señorío put the matter thus: "neither of them [the cacique nor the gobernador] command, nor are they obeyed, and there is much confusion and disorder . . . for lack of a leader."[64] The unfolding of these events is unclear, but it is possible that increasing factionalism, along with struggles for control of the village, eroded the personal ties that bound indigenous society to its lords.

When the late sixteenth-century demographic crisis hit Yucatán, don Diego de Quijada exploited the situation as a chance to purge caciques from their governorships. In this way, the death of Lorenzo

Uluac, cacique and gobernador of Ticul, was the ideal opportunity to impose Francisco Che as gobernador, independent of the existence of don Juan, Uluac's son, who was only confirmed in the cacicazgo and nothing else.[65] It is possible that in this case, as in others, the lord's successors did not tolerate the pressure and accepted that a new individual take charge of the governorship; this newcomer, in turn, displaced them from the village's dealings with the colonial world. If one thing characterized Quijada, it was his campaign to remove systematically the caciques that had survived the early colonial turbulence; for by 1565, the final year of his administration, some thirteen new individuals (in addition to those already mentioned) assumed governorships in the villages.[66]

Don Diego de Quijada acted even more directly against the halach uinicob. He whipped, exiled, and suspended from his cacicazgo don Francisco de Montejo Xiu in the aforementioned case of drunkenness and inappropriate sexual conduct. So, too, don Francisco Namon Iuit and don Lorenzo Cocom were removed from office and jailed because of idolatries. But in 1563, when friar Francisco de Toral, bishop of Yucatán, reduced their sentences, Quijada's posture changed to one of neutrality, and he ceased to prioritize the caciques' elimination from the governorships.

Significantly, don Diego respected the successors of those halach uinicob who died during his administration. Don Francisco Cocom, son of don Juan Cocom (immortalized by his pre-Hispanic name of Nachí Cocom), began to rule Sotuta as cacique and gobernador in 1563, and continued until at least 1580. Nor did the alcalde mayor harass Melchor Pech, gobernador of Motul. Don Melchor descended from Naum Pech, also known as don Francisco de Montejo Pech, halach uinic of Motul.[67] Still, even though these individuals managed to hold a joint appointment of cacique and gobernador, they nevertheless ruled a people territorially limited to the pueblos that were pre-Hispanic capitals, and wielded economic prerogatives no different from those of other caciques. In addition to these cases, there were other instances when it was death, and not Quijada, who separated the overlords from their office. The rulers of Calkiní, Tihosuco, and Chancenote died during the invasion or shortly afterward. The overlords of Hocabá and Maní dropped out of the political landscape during the governments of don Luis de Céspedes Oviedo and don Diego de Santillán, respectively.

The Spanish authorities' determination to separate caciques from their gobernadores played out in an atmosphere hardly favorable for indigenous society. Indeed, during the last third of the 1500s crop plagues, droughts, famines, and epidemics struck with such severity that the population dropped significantly. First came a prolonged dry spell in 1564; then from 1569 to 1570, plague; from 1575 to 1576, drought and famine; in 1580 typhus and measles; from 1587 to 1588, locusts; in 1590, locusts, famine, measles, and typhus; and in 1592 and 1593, more locusts. In sum, demographic and agrarian crises intermittently scourged the villages the Franciscans had formed.[68]

In this dire situation, flight was virtually the only answer. Those lords and vassals who had survived the Montejos now reacted to each plague or famine by taking refuge in the dense woods of the peninsula's base. When a lord relocated with a number of family chieftains, he had to begin the slow process of reconstituting his señoríos. But if they were the vassals of other caciques, they often chose to adhere to the preexisting señoríos of the region of Dzuluinicob or Cehache, or at least set up households alongside their relatives there, to found a new residential cluster. These changes had the cumulative effect of weakening or ending their ties to an older society or political order.

Meanwhile, those caciques and family chieftains who chose to remain in the northeast faced considerably altered circumstances. They no longer had the option of searching for a more powerful cacique or halach uinic, whether of their own lineage or of another, who could shelter them in trying times. The new colonial rulers had limited elite power to their own territory, and restricted it from alliances that transcended the newly founded villages. Thus limited to the boundaries of their villages, the caciques watched as the demographic crisis in one way or another cut into their networks of personal ties. The lords thus passed from the scene and were replaced by new leaders: gobernadores acting with Spanish colonial support.

The history of the Xiu illustrates this process. As previously established, the Xiu caciques belonged to a lineage endowed with a long historical tradition. Although their ancestors' origins remain controversial, the Xiu had nonetheless been a presence in the Maya world since the late tenth century. Their lords formed part of the Mayapán ruling confederation. When that city fell, two capitals replaced it: the more famous one in Maní, and a lesser-known counterpart in Calotmul. The lineage controlled a group of señoríos that recognized one or the other of these capitals, with the exception of Cuncunul, which maintained its independence until the mid-1500s.

When the Spanish came to Yucatán, they found a ruler in Maní named Ah Kukum Xiu, and in Calotmul a certain Ah Kukil Xiu, possibly the former's uncle.[69] The first was baptized don Francisco de Montejo Xiu and the second don Juan Montejo Xiu. In the early colonial years these two men, out of respect for indigenous hierarchy, were made gobernadores of their pueblos and, per Spanish notions of territory, of their "provinces." Until the early 1560s such caciques suffered little demotion in power, except in matters conflicting with Christian doctrine.

As previously indicated, the tenure of don Diego de Quijada inaugurated a campaign against the cacique's authority and prestige. In Maní, for example, lordship passed from the indigenous landscape with the death of Ah Kukum Xiu, better known as don Francisco de Montejo Xiu. In 1561 when don Francisco was suspended from his cacicazgo and banished from his village, then later jailed for idolatry, a principal named Juan Ku became governor of Maní. However, don Francisco's speedy liberation allowed him to reassume reins of the village. At some point in the late 1560s or early 1570s he died without descendants, and no evidence suggests that priests, principales, or other surviving lords named a successor.

Gaspar Antonio Xiu descended from the Xiu lineage on his mother's side, and even though he evidently lacked the requisite education in Suyuá, was named gobernador by don Diego de Santillán, Spanish provisional governor from 1571 to 1573. But the defensor de los naturales challenged the designation, and in 1573 accused Santillán of promoting Xiu despite opposition from Indians, priests, and lay Spaniards. He also denounced the salary of 150 pesos in gold that Xiu received at the cost of the Indians. It is unknown whether Santillán suspended him or whether Gaspar Antonio simply resigned, but by 1575 Francisco Be was Maní's gobernador.[70]

Little is known of Ah Kukil Xiu (don Juan Montejo Xiu), the halach uinic of Calotmul. He may have died in the mid-1550s, for by 1557 a certain don Hernando Xiu appeared as his successor. The picture of don Hernando Xiu, and of don Alonso Xiu, cacique of Pustunich, is considerably clearer, since they happened to live during the turbulent administration of don Diego de Quijada. Neither don Hernando nor don Alonso cherished fond memories of the alcalde mayor, since without any particular reason, he made Andrés May and Juan Cuyoc governors of their respective villages.

The prestige, authority, and strength of the personal ties of don Hernando and don Alonso played an important role in helping them to dodge the pressures that beset them. Indeed, in spite of the demographic collapse, don Hernando, along with his successor don Francisco, managed to hang on to Calotmul's governorships.[71] Similarly, don Alonso, for whom the presence of Juan Cuyoc was anathema, survived the plagues and famines, and despite his rival's presence, managed to uphold his own authority as cacique and gobernador of the village at least until 1580.

Few documents record the lives of don Juan Xiu, or a second individual of that same name, or a don Pedro Xiu, respective caciques of Tzucacab, Hunactí, and Yaxa. But unlike many caciques, they found themselves caught in the demographic crisis, and were suddenly challenged by indigenous gobernadores whom the Spanish appointed. The first to disappear was don Juan Xiu of Tzucacab. While evidence remains inconclusive, indications are that Quijada opportunistically named Gaspar Col to rule the village. The other don Juan Xiu (of Hunactí), and don Pedro Xiu of Yaxá, died soon afterward. Their deaths provided the chance for authorities to name new individuals to their roles. Thus, by 1572 Pablo Can was Hunactí's gobernador, and three years later Francisco Dzan assumed the same role for Yaxá.[72]

If the demographic crisis struck the lineages indiscriminately, it was a mathematical certainty that those governing fewer than five señoríos were virtually eliminated as leaders of their pueblos. The case of the Iuit lords demonstrates how, with populations declining, Spaniards took advantage of the severed descent lines by imposing their own preferred gobernadores. The Iuit were lords of Hocabá, a pre-Hispanic capital, and of the señoríos of Huhí, Hoctún, and Tiscanbanchel; and don Tomás López named them gobernadores of their respective villages. At the time of the conquest, Nadzul Iuit was the halach uinic of the cúuchcabal of Hocabá; shortly after 1550 he died, and per indigenous practice, his son don Francisco Namon Iuit succeeded him. But don Francisco died, possibly as a result of the plague of 1569–1570; neither his son (if indeed he had one) nor one of his brothers succeeded him as gobernador. Rather, by 1572 that role had passed to a new individual, one Lorenzo Cen.

Shortly afterward came the consecutive deaths of Francisco Iuit's brothers don Lorenzo, don Diego, and don Juan, respectively caciques of Huhí, Tiscanbanchel, and Hoctún. Spaniards then appointed Indians from other lineages as the new gobernadores. By the end of the sixteenth century, we find Martín Puc, Francisco Ku, and Lorenzo Uc in these roles. The Iuit retained only the governorships of Xocchel. In pre-Hispanic times this village was a dependency of Hocabá, and when the Spanish arrived, don Juan Blanco Iuit, Francisco Namon Iuit's fifth brother, was recognized as cacique; he also resided in the señorío and possibly was head of that lineage. Nevertheless, in reality the batab was a member of the Che clan. In recognition of that unnamed Che's lordship, the Spanish designated him gobernador at some moment in the 1550s. Around 1565 both he and don Juan Blanco died, and Blanco's brothers continued to govern their lordships; that is, the lineages still showed only limited evidence of erosion from the demographic collapse; they managed to impose Juan Francisco Iuit, don Juan Blanco's son and their own nephew, as gobernador. It is difficult to determine whether or not the Indians recognized him as their lord, for the documentation only refers to him as gobernador. He must have died a few years later, for documents state that in 1569 his own son Juan occupied the governorship, and as late as 1597 another Iuit, a certain don Diego, appears in that position.[73]

If a headcount of lords was what mattered, the Pech, Canul, and Cupul lineages had (within limits) the greatest chance of resisting and surviving the demographic collapse and the blows of colonialism, at least until the early 1580s.[74] We cannot know with certainty what artifices the caciques of these lineages used to escape displacement in their villages. However, the case of don Pedro Pech, batab of Kiní, illustrates one possible approach. He survived the conquest, and being cacique, he was named the village's gobernador. Apparently Pech lacked a direct successor, and in 1571 he was now too old for the job; his brother don Luis, in agreement with the elderly don Pedro, went to don Diego de Santillán, who had gained appointment as Yucatán's governor, and asked the latter for the title of coadjutor, that is, as assistant to his brother in fulfilling the latter's obligations as gobernador.[75] The eventual death of don Pedro made don Luis gobernador in his own right, and per laws of Indian succession he ascended as lord of Kiní and secured the governorship to control the village.

Now more than ever Maya lords needed such artificial strategies. Perhaps this explains how the Pech lineage caciques of Ixil, Chicxulub, Kuncheil, Cacalchén, Chuburná, Nolo, and Motul, successfully kept parvenus from taking away the governorships of their villages when faced with royal offensives. The descendants of caciques of the first three of those villages held their own until the early 1570s. The caciques of Cacalchén remained in power until 1576, while the descendants of caciques in the latter three towns did so for a decade beyond that.[76]

Perhaps the Spanish initially failed to notice the practice. But as the demographic crisis worsened, the lineages were taxed to their limits. The Pech caciques of Mocochá and Tixkokob illustrate the point. When the lords of these villages died, their sons inherited the cacicazgos. However, the Spanish soon stripped them of their titles as gobernadores, either because the caciques' offspring did not adapt well to the new regulations, or else because the Spanish simply found them unsuitable for one reason or another. The encomendero of the villages justified the change by charging them with simple incompetence; regarding Mocochá, he claimed that the reason was that "he to whom the cacicazgo came . . . was unequal to it." With reference to Tixkokob, he indicated that "although this village has a native cacique, he did not receive the governorship, as he was unsuitable." Behind these justifications lay the fact that Spaniards had selected other individuals for the task: in Mocochá, an Indian of that village named Juan Ciau, and in Tixkokob, Lorenzo Pech, a resident of San Cristóbal, a village made up of *naborios* (that is, Indians unattached to a pueblo).[77]

One way or another, by the early 1580s the process of purging the caciques from governorships of their old señoríos had reached a critical point. Such was the political and social context when in late 1583 don Diego García de Palacio, oidor of the Audiencia of New Spain, conducted a visita in Yucatán. His fiscal reforms, aimed mainly at limiting the lords' economic privileges, have already been discussed. In matters of politics, the visitador dedicated himself to organizing the repúblicas, and he issued a series of rules, both specific and general, to breathe life into these institutions. Among other things, he determined that the cabildos were to consist of a gobernador, alcaldes, regidores, a mayordomo, and the alguaciles.[78] Although his instructions say nothing of the gobernador, the other officers were to be elected annually on the first of January.[79]

Diego García de Palacio likewise established responsibilities. The governor, alcaldes, and regidores were to see to it that the naturales worked one set of milpas in order to sustain themselves, and another to supply their caja de comunidad. They were to keep village accounts in order: they had to record the tasación of tribute and the subsequent payments made to encomenderos.[80] García also determined that the gobernador was to allocate yields from the cornfield allocated for the caja and was to assign the alcaldes and regidores a salary in corn so obtained, but only after paying the maestros de escuela, the cantores, the sacristan, and those who prepared food for special events.[81] Among don Diego's most important decisions regarding cabildo integration was to allow macehual participation. Principales were to hold half the offices, and commoners the other half; both were to be "indios of full understanding, good Christians and careful with the fruits of their milpa, and with their women and children."[82]

García de Palacio's guidelines worked their inexorable way into the administrative and political life of the señoríos. Indeed, from his visit onward the repúblicas gradually became the norm in Yucatecan villages. If this happened, it was because during don Diego's years in Yucatán, the powers of the caciques had fallen into open crisis because of the Spanish onslaught. With few exceptions, their heirs had also been displaced from the governorships, and for that reason those heirs lacked the prestige and power necessary for weaving personal ties with the descendants of their forefathers' vassals. This fact, in turn, isolated them from the "rule or dominion" that would have allowed them to present the same resistance their fathers had shown in confronting the new cabildos.

The sixteenth century's final two decades spelled hard times indeed for old Maya elites. The slow spread of the repúblicas, the limitations of cacique power, the trimming of economic privilege through bureaucratic oversight, the near-total displacement of the caciques' personal ties and their replacement by concepts of territory, and their exclusion from the governorships all ended by plunging the historical lords or caciques of the old lineages into a crisis without precedent. Two linguistic conventions reflect this change. One was that any Indian appointed to the governorship now enjoyed the right to be called "don." In other words, the cabildo became a social ladder, and from the early seventeenth century onward, any individual who accepted an office in the república now came to be seen as a principal.[83]

The second and perhaps more significant modification of vocabulary was that any individual appointed as gobernador also began to call himself cacique, and eventually batab. Before the blows of Spanish policy, the honorific title of "don" lost its original impact. Colonial authorities could recognize any Indian as batab, whether or not they came from a ruling lineage. In some cases, even an occasional mestizo or mulatto, uneducated in the mysteries of Suyuá, could avail themselves, however nominally, of the rank of batab. Without doubt, by 1600 the Yucatec Maya villages, heirs of the batabilob or señoríos, had moved squarely into the colonial world.[84]

Conclusion

Throughout the pages of this book I have traced the history of the batab. This figure distinguished himself by weaving an intricate and durable web of personal ties with his cuchteeloob in order to animate his batabil or lordship and convert it into the basic unit of Maya political organization. From his appearance in the mid-fourteenth century, the lord and his lordship participated in, and adapted himself to, the great political restructuring and reaccommodations carried out by the overlords. Despite the fact that individual batabs fell victim to armed conflict or demographic and agrarian crises, the institution of batabil nonetheless abided.

During the first phases of colonial rule, the cacique's fortress of personal ties resisted the Spanish onslaught. But that same fortress crumbled once the new order consolidated itself. The circumscription of power within a limited and well-defined territory, the suppression of ancient privileges, and the cacique's expulsion from pueblo governance (an expulsion hastened by demographic collapse) all helped to displace the lords and their personal ties from indigenous life. From that moment on, lordship began a slow and uneven transition to the colonial village, and was remade into the new corporate entity to which the Indian was attached as natural and vecino.

Assigning the population to the early pueblos and embedding them in that system turned out to be a longer and more involved process than the Spanish had imagined. With the lords of the ancient lineages now gone, innumerable family groups who were descendants of the old cuchteeloob little by little began to flee to the monte, for areas far from the indiscreet gaze of encomenderos and friars. They found new homes near water sources, and there re-created their personal ties through blood kinship and through matrimony. This phenomenon revealed two sides of the same coin: on one side, the dissolution of the personal ties the lords had forged with their former vassals; and on the other, the new Indian gobernadores' inability to consolidate a territorial power with their respective cabildos.

The pueblos' migration into the monte surged during moments of epidemic, drought, plague, and famine. When these disasters abated, many family chiefs, along with their offspring, returned to the villages to which they were "naturales y vecinos." Or, better said, Spaniards organized what can only be called raids with the aim of "reducing" them to those villages. Despite all these efforts, groups of family chiefs, much in the style of their ancestors, elected to settle in residential clusters that they had come upon during their flight, or else founded new hamlets in the dense wilderness that abounded throughout the length and breadth of the peninsula. These practices continued until the early 1800s. But wherever and however they chose to live, the peninsula's indigenous people could no longer ignore the changes that the Spanish conquest and reorganization had introduced. By the end of the seventeenth century, political power based on the principle of territorial association had become a fundamental reality in the daily life of Yucatec Maya society.

APPENDIX A

The Cúuchcabalob of the Mid-Sixteenth Century

This appendix lists the cúuchcabalob, their dependent lordships, and the independent batabilob at the moment of Spanish contact. It is organized in alphabetical order, and consists of four columns. The first indicates the place-names of the batabilob integrated therein. The second column states the ruling lineage. The third column provides the names of the encomendero to whom each batabil was assigned, while the fourth indicates the source from which the information was taken (see Sources for Appendices A and B). The symbol (*) indicates that the place-name does not appear in existing maps, while italicized letters designate señoríos where the Franciscans founded cabeceras de doctrina. A brief review of the cúuchcabal's history prefaces each table.

CALKINÍ

Calkiní was founded by Ah Tzab Canul in the second half of the fifteenth century. According to Maya tradition, this individual descended from Mexican mercenaries who had come to Mayapán at the invitation of the city's Cocom lord. The Canul lineage fragmented after the fall of the multepal. One group went to the Petén, while eight batabob under the command of Na May Canché migrated to the western part of the peninsula, where they subsequently established themselves. Struggles arose between the Canul and Na May Canché, a fact that led the Canul lineage to disperse. It was under these conditions that Ah Tzab Canul founded Calkiní. His successor died shortly after the Spanish invasion. Thereupon one Nah Pot Canché rose to power, and was confirmed in that power by the Spanish. In 1561 Calkiní was chosen as a cabecera de doctrina. See Okoshi Harada, *Códice de Calkiní*; this source identifies Calkiní as a cúuchcabal.

Table A.1
The Cúuchcabal of Calkiní (Campeche)

Batabilob	Lineage	Encomendero in 1565	Source
CALKINÍ	Canul	Francisco Pérez	8
Matú	unknown	unknown	8
Mopilá	Euán	Pedro Martín	8
Nunkiní	Canul	Francisco Quiroz	8
Tepakán	Canul	Gregorio Cetina	8
Tzemez Akal	unknown	unknown	8
Xicinchah*	Tayú	unknown	8

CALOTMUL

The founder of the Calotmul cúuchcabal remains unknown, but when the Spanish arrived, one Ah Kukul Xiu was its halach uinic. A few details concerning its expansion do survive. The batab of Tahdziú was apparently the first to fall under Calotmul's dominion. However, Calotmul was unable to subjugate Tahdziú definitively, since intestine wars convulsed the area up to the moment the Spanish arrived. The batab of Sal was subjugated at a relatively late date. However, Sal itself seems to have been free from internal conflicts for most of its history. Its first batab was Napuc Camal, who gathered the inhabitants and founded Tixbalatún. Holpop Hau succeeded him, and moved his residence to Tahbuleb. Upon his death, authority passed to his stepson, Napuc Chablé, and then to a certain Na Hau Te. Quite possibly the halach uinic of Calotmul took advantage of a break in succession to impose an individual belonging to his own lineage. The exact date remains unknown, but it seems that this occurred just prior to the Spanish invasion. Following Na Hau Te's death, the Sal lordship passed to an Indian later baptized under the name of Juan Xiu. Around the time of European contact, Ah Kukum Xiu, the halach uinic of Maní married doña María Xiu, possibly the daughter of Ah Kukil Xiu. At some point Peto, one of Calotmul's señoríos, achieved the status of Franciscan *vicaría*, a position that it held in 1582. See "Relación de Tahdziú," in *RHGY* 1:389–91; "Relación de Titzal," in *RHGY* 1:236–37; and Roys, *Political Geography*, 77. Calotmul appears as a cúuchcabal in "Residencia de Diego de Quijada," in AGI Justicia, legajo 245, ff. 1112v–43v.

Table A.2
The Cúuchcabal of Calotmul (Mérida)

Batabilob	Lineage	Encomendero in 1565	Source
CALOTMUL	Xiu	Rodrigo Alvarez	1
Hunactí	Xiu	Juan Gómez	1
Peto	Pot	Juan de Aguilar	1
Sal	Te	"El menor de Alonos Julian"	1
Tahdziú	Ceh	"El menor de Francisco Vásquez"	1
Tzucacab	Xiu	Pedro Alvarez	1

CAN PECH

There are no clues as to the identity of the founder of Can Pech or his lords, but it was clearly the place of residence of a halach uinic. During the final phase of the invasion, the Spanish selected this pre-Hispanic capital as the site for the villa of San Francisco de Campeche. Later on, in the early 1560s, Campeche became the seat of the teniente de alcalde mayor. In the previous decade the first friars to reach Yucatán chose this place when establishing their first convent, and for that reason it acquired the status of cabecera de doctrina. See Chamberlain, *The Conquest*, 202–203. Fernández de Ovieda, *Historia general*, vol. 1, chap. 126, states that a halach uinic made his residence here. In 1565 Can Pech was given in encomienda to the Spanish Crown, and not to a private encomendero (see sources 63 and 64), and Chamberlain, *The Conquest*, 202–203.

CHANCENOTE

After the fall of Mayapán, Kahual Op Tzeh founded Chancenote as his cúuchcabal. The dominion of his successors remained unquestionable, at least until shortly before the Spanish invasion. Some references survive regarding Nahau Chan, lord of Temaza. This lord lived in Tiscocom, and subordinated eight batabilob, which he appears to have ruled for sixty years. Prior to his death, and close to the time of the invasion, Nahau Chan and his followers moved to Temaza for reasons unknown. This place flourished and went on to become a batabil of some importance. According to its encomendero, "the best and most people" lived in Chancenote's dependent pueblos. In 1576 the Franciscans turned this pre-Hispanic capital into a cabecera de doctrina. For the two most important sources concerning the Chancenote cúuchcabal, see "Probanza del capitán don Juan Chan cacique y señor natural de los pueblos de Chancenote y sus sujetos (1622)," in AGI, Audiencia de México, legajo 140, ramo 2; and "Relación de Chahuac-há," in *RHGY* 2:243–50.

Table A.3
The Cúuchcabal of Chancenote (Valladolid)

Batabilob	Lineage	Encomendero in 1565	Source
CHANCENOTE	Tzeh	Juan de Urrutia	58
Cehac*	Tuyub	"El menor de Diego Burgos"	7
Holcol*	unknown	unknown	58
Tecaz*	unknown	unknown	58
Temaza*	Chan	Juan de Urrutia	1, 58
Tezamay*	unknown	unknown	58
Tibatún*	Tzeh	Alonso Villanueva	7
Tixcancal	Tzeh	Juan López de Mena	1
Tixholop*	Puc	Francisco de Cieza, Alonzo Villanueva	52
Tixmucul	Tzeh	Alonso Villanueva	52
Tizno*	unknown	unknown	58

CHAUAC-HÁ

Its history is unknown. Spaniards called it the "province" of Chikinchel ("the western woods"). In early 1543 Francisco de Montejo the

Nephew first founded the city of Valladolid on the site of this pre-Hispanic capital, but the area's unhealthy surroundings forced the Spaniards to relocate Valladolid to another such capital, that of Sací. See "Relación de la villa de Valladolid," in *RHGY* 2:28; and "Relación de Chauac-há," in *RHGY* 2: 244, 249. The latter reference establishes Chauac-há's status as pre-Hispanic capital. Encomienda rights over the batab of Chauac-Há were originally awarded to Juan de Urrutia (see source 58), while the batab of Sinsimato went to an unidentified conquistador (see source 52).

CHETUMAL

Information concerning this cúuchcabal comes from Juan Farfán. He reports having participated in the conquest of the Uaymiles, "who also go under the name of the province of Chetumal." See "Relación de Kanpocolché," in *RHGY* 2:320. However, the identity of the owner of the encomienda rights to Chetumal remains unknown (see source 67).

CHICHÉN ITZÁ

The history of Chichén Itzá traces back several centuries prior to the Spanish presence, when this city served as the political center of northern Yucatán. Its decline from the mid-1100s onward severely restricted its domain. Nevertheless, it managed to maintain the status of capital until the middle of the sixteenth century. Naobom Cupul was its halach uinic at the time of the invasion, and he commanded the loyalties of several batabilob in the Tizimín area. See "Relación de Sodzil," in *RHGY* 2:125–26; "Relación de Ichmul," in *RHGY* 2:298. The "Crónica de Yaxkukul," 21, 26, provides a source establishing Chichén Itzá as a cúuchcabal.

Table A.4
The Cúuchcabal of Chichén Itzá (Valladolid)

Batabiloob	Lineage	Encomendero in 1565	Source
CHICHÉN ITZÁ	Cupul	unknown	49, 65
Sodzil	Batún	Martín Ruiz de Arce	49
Tikuch	Cupul	Blas González	49, 59
Tekay	Miz	Alvaro Osorio	49

COZUMEL

While failing to establish the name of its capital, numerous sources indicate that the island of Cozumel was ruled by a halach uinic; see Fernández de Oviedo, *Historia general*, vol. 7, chap. 9; and López de Gómara, *Historia de la conquista*, chaps. 10 and 14. However, the identity of the island's encomendero remains unknown (see sources 63 and 64).

DZIDZANTÚN

Ah Chel founded this cúuchcabal. He was the son-in-law of a Mayapán priest, from whom he learned his arts. According to an indigenous tradition collected by Landa, the priest warned Ah Chel of the imminent collapse of the multepal, whereupon Ah Chel relocated to the north of the peninsula, and established his capital in Tecoh. At some unknown date he or his successors moved the cúuchcabal to Dzidzantún, where the Spanish found a certain Namox Chel ruling as halach uinic. In the second half of the 1500s the Franciscans established four cabeceras de doctrina in the area. The first was in the señorío of Izamal (1549), the second was in the pre-Hispanic capital (1567), the third in the batabil of Tekantó (1576), and the fourth in Temax. See Landa, *Relación*, chap. 9. Vol. 1 of *RHGY* contains numerous references to Dzidzantún as a political center.

Table A.5
The Cúuchcabal of Dzidzantún (Mérida)

Batabilob	Lineage	Encomendero in 1565	Source
DZIDZANTÚN	Chel	Martín Sánchez	3, 65
Buctzotz	Ucán	Francisco de Montejo	3
Cansahcab	Chel	unknown	3
Chalanté	Cupul	Sebastián Vásquez Alonso Rojas	7
Chaltunpuhuy*	Motul	Beltrán Cetina	7
Ciciltum	Can	Pedro Hernández	7
Dzilam	Chel	Francisco de Montejo	3, 68
Izamal	Che	"La hija de García Hernández"	3

Batabilob	Lineage	Encomendero in 1565	Source
Kantunil	Dzul	Francisco López	7
Kimbilá	Pech	Rodrigo Alonso Flores	3, 7
Pixilá	Uitz	Rodrigo Alonso Flores	3
Pomolché	Ucán	Spanish Crown	7
Sinanché	Euán	Ambrosio Villafrades	3, 68
Sitilpech	Chin	Lucas de Paredes	7
Sudzal	Motul	Sebastián Vásquez	3
Tecal	Canché	Diego Briceño	7
Tecoh	unknown	unknown	3
Tekantó	Pot	Cristóbal Sánchez	3
Temax	Ek	"Juan de Sosa el menor"	3
Tepakán	Couoh	Cristóbal Sánchez	3
Teya	Tun	Alonso de Castro	3
Tixcochoh	Tun	"El hijo de Juan del Rey"	3
Tixculum	Dzib	"Juan Bote el menor"	7
Tixtual*	Batún	Alonso Julián	3
Tocbadz	Uicab	Blas Hernández	7
Uitzil*	Pech	Francisco Palomo	7
Xanabá	Huchín	Francisco de Arceo	7
Yobaín	Chel	San Martín y Galiano	3, 68

EKBALAM

Ekbalam was founded by Coch Cal Balam, an individual of unknown antecedents. The secular history of its rulers can be divided into two stages. One stretches from Ekbalam's foundation to the death of Heblaychac. The other covers the period of domination by the Cupul lineage, which possibly rose to power in the late fifteenth or early sixteenth century. During the Spanish invasion Namon Cupul ruled the cúuchcabal, which included at least seven batabilob; of these, we only know with certainty the names of the last two places on the list, and by association, the location of the first. See "Relación de Ekbalam," *RHGY* 2:137–39; and "Relación de Nabalam," in *RHGY* 2:186. The first of these two sources document's Ekbalam's status as capital and its rule as a central power. Encomienda rights over the batabob of Ekbalam and Hunabkú, both of the Cupul lineage went Juan Gutiérrez

Picón, while rights over the batabob of Nabalam and Tahcab (Cupul and Tun, respectively) went to Juan de Contreras (see sources 1 and 48).

HOCABÁ

The name of its founder is unknown. At the time of the Spanish invasion, its halach uinic was Nadzul Iuit. According to Roys, the halach uinic may have had a Mexican origin, since "iuit" means "feather" in Nahuatl. The Franciscans founded two cabeceras de doctrina here, the first in the señorío of Homún in 1561, and the second in the capital in 1576. See "Relación de Hocabá," in *RHGY* 1:133; and Roys, *Political Geography*, 55. In *RHGY* vol. 1 and *DDQAMY* vol. 1 we find innumerable references to the fact that Hocabá was a political center and the residence of a halach uinic.

Table A.6
The Cúuchcabal of Hocabá (Mérida)

Batabilob	Lineage	Encomendero in 1565	Source
HOCABÁ	Iuit	Melchor y Francisco Pacheco	62
Cuzumá	unknown	unknown	7
Hoctún	Iuit	Melchor y Francisco Pacheco, Gaspar Juárez de Avila	62
Homún	Tun	Gómez de Castillo; Juan Vela	62
Huhí	Iuit	Melchor y Francisco Pacheco	1
Sahcabá	Pot	Melchor y Francisco Pacheco	62
Sanahcat	Tzab	Melchor y Francisco Pacheco	1
Tahmek	unknown	unknown	62
Tiscanbanchel	Iuit	Melchor y Francisco Pacheco	1, 62
Xocchel	Che	Melchor y Francisco Pacheco; Gaspar Juárez de Avila	62

MANÍ

While Mani's founder remains unidentified, there is no doubt that it was a political capital constructed by an individual belonging to the Xiu lineage. In the late 1500s its halach uinic was Ah Kukum Xiu, better known as don Francisco de Montejo Xiu. This cúuchcabal was given in encomienda a don Francisco Montejo the Adelantado. At some time around 1550, when the Crown stripped Montejo of his enormous encomienda holdings, the component señoríos were divided among various conquistadors. The Franciscans created three cabeceras de doctrina here during the century's second half: the first in Maní (1549), the second in the señorío of Tekax (1567), and the third in Oxkutzcab (1581). See Roys, *Political Geography*, 61. As with the preceding cúuchcabal, the first volumes of *RHGY* and *DDQAMY* contain abundant references to the fact that Maní was a political center. Moreover, in Ciudad Real, *Calepino maya*, 123, we find the phrase, "u cuchcabal Maní."

Table A.7
The Cúuchcabal of Maní (Mérida)

Batabilob	Lineage	Encomendero in 1565	Source
MANÍ	Xiu	Spanish Crown	66
Cauich	Xiu	Pedro Hernández	55
Dzan	Xiu	Alonso Rosado	1, 26, 55
Mama	Che	Juan de Aguilar	55
Muna	Pacab	Alonso Rosado	1, 26, 55
Nohcacab	unknown	Paceb Hernando Muñoz Zapata	7
Panabchén	Xiu	Alonso Rosado	55
Pencuyut	Ku	Ana Campos	55
Pustunich	Xiu	Juan Gómez	55
Sacalum	Che	Francisco Pacheco	55
Teabo	Nauat	"Juan Bote el menor"	55
Tekax	Uz	Francisco de Bracamonte	55
Tekit	unknown	Hernando Bracamonte	55
Ticul	Uluac	Spanish Crown	55
Tikunché*	Xiu	Beltrán de Cetina	55
Yaxá	Xiu	Francisco Tamayo	55
Yicmán*	Xiu	unknown	55
Yotholín	Xiu	Diego López	55

MOTUL

According to Indian traditions recorded by the encomenderos, this capital was founded by Sac Mutul, from whom the name derives. Apparently it was abandoned for many years until being occupied by Nohcabal Pech after the fall of Mayapán. During the second half of the sixteenth century the friars established three cabeceras de doctrina here: the first in the batabil of Conkal (1549), the second in the pre-Hispanic capital (1567), and the third in the señorío of Tixkokob (1581). See "Relación de Motul," in *RHGY* 2:269.

Table A.8
The Cúuchcabal of Motul (Mérida)

Batabilob	Lineage	Encomendero in 1565	Source
MOTUL	Pech	Francisco Bracamonte	4, 66
Aké	Pech	unknown	4
Baca	Pech	Melchor Pacheco	4, 68
Bokabá	Oxté	unknown	4
Cacalchén	Pech	Francisco Tamayo	4
Chicxulub	Pech	unknown	4
Cholul	Pech	unknown	4
Chuburnú	Pech	Francisco de Montejo	7
Conkal	Pech	Francisco de Montejo	4, 68
Dzemul	Pech	Spanish Crown	4
Euán	Pech	Juan Gómez	4
Itzimná	Itzimná	unknown	7
Ixil	Pech	Julián Doncel	4, 68
Kibá	Pech	unknown	4
Kiní	Pech	Spanish Crown	4
Kumún*	Pech	unknown	4
Kuncheil	Pech	Gonzalo Méndez	4
Kuxché*	Che	unknown	4
Mocochá	Pech	Francisco de Montejo	4, 68
Muxupip	Pech	? Castilla	4
Nolo	Pech	Francisco de Montejo	7, 68
Sitpach	Pech	unknown	4
Suma	Ek	Antón Bojórquez	4
Telchac	Pech	Spanish Crown	4, 68
Ticulul*	Pech	unknown	4
Tichauinic*	Canché	unknown	7
Tixkokob	Pech	Francisco de Montejo	4, 68
Ucí	Pech	Juan Bautista Cárdenas	4
Yaxkukul	Pech	Spanish Crown	4, 68

POPOLÁ

Of unknown founder, Popolá possibly rose as a cúuchcabal during the second half of the fifteenth century. We have relatively solid information regarding its rulers, all members of the Cupul lineage, until the 1550s. Its first documented halach uinic was Namay Cupul, who was succeeded by Achichuen Cupul. At the time of the invasion,

APPENDIX A

one Nadzul Cupul governed its cúuchcabal, and still held the titles of cacique and gobernador in 1565. As a cúuchcabal, Popolá contained thirteen batabilob, but their names remain a mystery. This cúuchcabal was awarded to encomendero Francisco de Cieza. See "Relación de Popolá," in *RHGY* 2:215–16; this source indicates that its batabilob lived under a centralized form of rule.

SACÍ

Documentary sources suggest that two halach uinicob linked by kinship ties lived in this capital. Each independently governed his own batabilob. Here they are classified as Sací 1 and Sací 2. Ah Tzuc Cupul ruled the former. We know little of which or how many dependent batabilob he governed, but evidence indicates that his dominion extended to the señorío of Tizimín and possibly even to a pair of neighboring batabilob located some ten leagues to the north. Perhaps these northern batabilob were Dzonotchuil and Tiscacauché. The halach uinic of Sací 2 was Nadzul Cupul, and he included Pixoy and Dzitnup among his señoríos. Both halach uinicob had disappeared by 1550. In 1544 the Spanish founded the villa of Valladolid on the site. In the 1550s Sací became the seat of a teniente de alcalde mayor. Around 1550 the Franciscans turned it into a cabecera de doctrina. See "Relación de la villa de Valladolid," in *RHGY* 2:37; "Relación de Pixoy," in *RHGY* 2: 51, 60; and "Relación de Dzicab," in *RHGY* 2:205. In the "Crónica de Yaxkukul," 21, 26, the place-name of Sací is asociated with the term cúuuchcabal.

Table A.9
The Cúuchcabal of Sací 1 (Valladolid)

Batabilob	Lineage	Encomendero in 1565	Source
SACÍ	Cupul	unknown	65
Dzonotchuil	Chuil	Diego de Ayala	60
Tizimín	Xol	"El menor de Diego Burgos"	53
Tiscacauché	Cupul	Juan López Ricalde	44
The Cúuchcabal of Sací 2 (Valladolid)			
SACÍ	Cupul	unknown	33, 65
Dzitnup	Uc	Andrés González	33
Pixoy	Cupul	"el menor de Gaspar González"	61

SOTUTA

According to traditional narratives collected by Landa, the first capital of this cúuchcabal was founded in the mid-1400s in Tibolón by the sole survivor of the Cocom lord of Mayapán. Although the circumstances remain unknown, the capital was later moved to Sotuta, where the Spanish found Nachí Cocom, or don Juan Cocom, serving as its halach uinic. Around 1576 the Franciscans turned this pre-Hispanic capital into a cabecera de doctrina. See Landa, *Relación*, chap. 9; and "Relación de Sotuta," in *RHGY* 1:146. In the *RHGY* vol. 1 and in *DDQAMY* vol. 1, we find numerous references to Sotuta as a political center.

Table A.10
The Cúuchcabal of Sotuta (Mérida)

Batabilob	Lineage	Encomendero in 1565	Source
SOTUTA	Cocom	Juan de Magaña y ? Méndez	1
Ekmul*	Cocom	Bartolomé Rojo	1
Mopilá	Canul	Pedro Campos	13
Sahcabá	Cocom	Gaspar Ruiz, & "El menor de Antonio Yélvez"	13
Suyuá	unknown	unknown	1
Tabi	unknown	unknown	7
Tibolón	Ix	Juan de Magaña	13
Tixcacaltuyú	Tuyú	Francisco Manrique	13
Tixcanchunup	Ix	Pedro García	1, 13
Usil	Tun	Bartolomé Rojo	1, 13
Yaxá	Naual	Gonzalo Cea	1
Yaxcabá	Pech	Joaquín de Leguizamo	13

TIHOSUCO

Nothing is known of its founder, but at the moment of conquest, Nacahum Cochuah was its halach uinic. He died during or shortly after the wars of invasion. Sometime around 1576 the Franciscans set up a cabecera de doctrina in the señorío of Ichmul. Antonio Méndez, encomendero of Tihosuco, reported that this province was ruled by the aforementioned halach uinic, and that his "seat and location" was at Tihosuco. See "Relación de Tihotzuc," in *RHGY* 2:198.

Table A.11
The Cúuchcabal of Tihosuco (Valladolid)

Batabilob	Lineage	Encomendero in 1565	Source
TIHOSUCO	Cochuah	Antonio Méndez	32
Canpocolché	Cauich	Juan Farfán	67
Chikindzonot	Pot	Antonio Méndez	32
Chunhuhub	unknown	unknown	70
Ekpedz	Cochuah	Juan de Loría	1
Ichmul	Cochuah	Blas González	59
Sabán	Ceh	Martín Ruiz	7
Sacalaca	Uicab	Juan Flamenco; Esteban Ginovés; Pedro Valencia	1
Samyol*	unknown	Diego Sarmiento de Figueroa	52
Tabi	unknown	unknown	53
Uaymax	unknown	Juan López de Mena	7

INDEPENDENT BATABILOB

This category consists of the lordships that no longer recognized the authority of a halach uinic after the fall of the multepal. It was composed of the batabilob of "the province of Chakán," those of the "province of Chikinchel," some of the batabilob of the "province of the Cupul and the Canul," and others of those whom no evidence establishes them as subordinate señoríos of some cúuchcabal. In the table below, the letters M, C, and V indicate the individual batabil's district: Mérida, Campeche, or Valladolid, respectively.

Table A.12
Independent Batabilob

Batabilob	Lineage	Encomendero in 1565	Source
Acanceh	unknown	unknown	1
Aculemax* (V)	Cuy	"El menor de Cisneros"	1
Bacabchén	Canul	unknown	7, 8
Bécal (C)	Canul	Alonso García	1
Bolonpoxché (M)	Canul	Lucas de Paredes	1
Cachi (V)	unknown	Baltasar de Montenegro	1
Calotmul (V)	Canul	Marcos de Anaya	1
Caucel (M)	Euán	Luis de Santa Cruz	1
Chaltún (M)	Cocom	Francisco de Arceo	1
Champotón (C)	Couoh	Spanish Crown	1
Chemax (V)	Dzul	Juan López de Mena	1
Chibxul (V)	Caamal	Alonso Villanueva	1
Chichimilá (V)	Ek	Juan de Urrutia	1
Chocholá (V)	Yam	Juan Farfán	1
Chuinchuén (V)	May	Juan López de Ricalde	1
Chulilhá	Canul	unknown	7, 8
Conil (V)	Polá	"El menor de Gaspar González"	1
Cuncunul (V)	Xiu	Juan de Cárdenas	1
Dzibilkal (M)	Canul	unknown	1
Dzitás (V)	Canul	Pedro Molina	1
Dzitbalché (C)	Canul	Alonso Tenorio	1
Dzonotaké (V)	Na	Juan López de Ricalde	1
Ebtún (V)	Cupul	Esteban Ginovés, Juan de la Cruz	1
Ecab (V)	unknown	Juan de Cárdenas	1
Espita (V)	Dzib	Luis de Baeza	1
Halachó (C)	Canul	"El menor de Juan de Porras"	1
Haltuniché*	Caamal	Gonzalo Cea	1
Hecelchakán (C)	Canul	Pedro Martín Bonilla	1
Hunucmá (M)	Canul	Francisco de Montejo	1
Huhbilchén (	Cupul	unknown	5, 1
Kantunilkín (V)	Chan	Juan Vellido	1
Kanxoc (V)	Pot	Martín Ruiz	1
Kaua (V)	unknown	Esteban Ginovés	1
Kikil (V)	Noh	Miguel de Tablada	1, 68
Kinchil (M)	Canul	Gaspar Ruiz	1
Kinlacam (C)	Canul	Gregorio de Cetina	1
Kukab (C)	Ci	Gregorio de Cetina	1
Loché (V)	Dzib	Diego de Anaya	1
Maxcanú (C)	Canul	Alonso Pérez	1
Mexcitán (V)	Cupul	"El menor de Cisneros"	1
Oxcum 1 (M)	Caamal	Alonso Julian	1

Batabilob	Lineage	Encomendero in 1565	Source
Oxcum 2 (M)	Cantún	Alonso de Rojas	1
Panbilchén (C)	Canul	"El menor de Juan de Porras"	1
Pocboc (C)	Canul	Martín de Ciderio	1
Polbalam (C)	unknown	Francisco de Cieza	1
Pomuch (C)	Canul	Bartolomé González	1
Sahcabá* (M)	Pot	Hernando Bracamonte	1
Salacum* (C)	Canul	Juan Insuasti	1
Samahil (M)	Mo	Rodrigo Alvarez	1
Sihó (C)	Canul	Esteban Martín	1
Sihunchén (M)	Canul	Francisco Tamayo	1
Sisal (V)	Caamal	Baltazar de Montenegro	1
Sucopó (V)	Chuc	Juan Rodríguez	1
Tahmuy (V)	Na	"El menor de Cisneros"	1
Tecoh (M)	Cocom	Juan de Montejano	1
Tekom (V)	unknown	Juan de Cárdenas	1
Temozón (V)	Cen	Andrés González	1
Temul* (V)	unknown	Juan Rodríguez	1
Tenabo (C)	Canul	Juan García de Llanos	1, 68
Tepip (V)	Pech	Juan Loría	1
Tesoco (V)	Cupul	? Osorio	1
Tesul* (V)	Miz	Pedro Molina y Pedro Valencia	1
Tihó (Mérida)	unknown	unknown	7
Tikunché (C)	Canul	Juan Insuasti	1
Timucuy (M)	Pech	Gaspar Juárez de Avila	1
Tinum (V)	Cupul	Juan Cano	1
Tixbecyá (M)	Cocom	"El menor de Antonio Yélvez"	1
Tixcacalcupul	Kauil	Juan de Cárdenas	1
Tixhualahtún (V)	unknown	Bernardo Sánchez	1
Tixiol (M)	Pech	Francisco Palomo	1
Tixol (V)	Miz	Alonso Medina	1
Tunkás (M)	Macún	Francisco Palomo	1
Tzeme (M)	Tun	Rodrigo de Escalona	1
Uayma	Caamal	Juan Vellido	1
Ucú (M)	Pech	Juan Vela	1
Umán (M)	Pot	Juan de Montejo	1
Xocén (V)	Xoc	Alonso González	1
Yabacú (V)	Canul	Giraldo Díaz	1
Yalcobá (V)	Cupul	Alonso Medina	1
Yalcón (V)	Xoc	Lucas Pimental	1
Yalsihón (V)	Cupul	Juan Cárdenas	1
Yaxcabá* (V)	Puc	Luis Díaz	1
Yocchec (V)	Pax	Antonio Méndez	1
Zamá (V)	Cauich	Diego Martín	1

APPENDIX B

Lineages, Caciques, and Gobernadores

In the early 1560s the halach uinic and batab—both now referred to as caciques—were imposed as governors, the former over his village and province, and the latter over his village alone. Yucatán's oldest colonial documentation, much like that of other Mesoamerican regions, gives some indication of the functional duality contained in the cacique-gobernador arrangement. The critical moment came when the Spanish began to impose in the governorship individuals who were not heirs to the cacicazgo. This appendix reconstructs how that process unfolded during the second half of the sixteenth century, in which time the caciques began to disappear as governors of their villages.

The names of the caciques appear under the patronymic of their lineage. It is important to note that the lineages have been reconstructed exclusively on the basis of the similarity of surnames, and using the sources closest in time to the era of the Spanish invasion. The appendix is clustered by lineages, in alphabetical order. Within each lineage is a subgrouping of associated villages in alphabetical order, showing the pre-Hispanic and Spanish name of each, together with that village's precontact cúuchcabal in parentheses.

For each village, the appendix provides three columns of information. The first column shows the names of all known caciques of the period. The second presents the year in which a cacique appears as gobernador. The third column provides the source or sources of the information given.

In addition to the above information, the appendix includes keys to other points of importance. Names in capital letters indicate pre-Hispanic capitals. Italicized names indicate a break in the ruling lineage. The parenthetical (P) indicates that the individual in question was a principal. The cross (†)indicates the caciques who had already died by 1569. Finally, the asterisk (*) designates place names that cannot be located on existing maps.

THE BATÚN LINEAGE

Sodzil, or San Juan Bautista (Cúuchcabaloob: Chichén Itzá)

Name	Period	Source
Francisco Batún	1565	1

Tixtual* (Dzidzantún)

Hernando Batún	1565	1
Hernando Batún	1567	3
Hernando Batún[a]	1569	6
Juan Dzul	1580	24

THE CAAMAL LINEAGE

Chibxul (unattached)

Diego Caamal†	1565	1

Haltuniché* (unattached)

Pedro Caamal	1565	1

Oxcum (1)[b] (unattached)

Juan Caamal	1565	1

---

[a] Hernando Batún died in 1576 and was succeeded by his illegitimate son, name unknown. This son apparently died in the late 1570s.

[b] During the period of reducciones this batabil was divided. This part was moved to Umán and there governed by a certain Juan Caamal. The other part remained in its original location. It remains unclear which of these parts was governed around 1580 by Hernando Canul.

APPENDIX B

Sisal, or San Bernardino (unattached)

Name	Period	Source
Batab Caamal[a]	invasion	50
Juan Caamal[b]	1579	50

Uayma (unattached)

Pedro Caamal	1565	1
Juan Caamal	1569	6

THE CANCHÉ LINEAGE

Itzimná (Motul)

Pablo Canché	1572	7

Tecal (Dzidzantún)

Pedro Canché†	1565	1
Pedro Canché[c]	1580	22

Tichauinic* (Motul)

Pedro Canché	1567	4

THE CANUL LINEAGE

Bacabchen (unattached)

Copá Cab Canul	pre-Hispanic	8

Bécal, or La Natividad de Nuestra Señora (unattached)

Antonio Canul	1565	1

Bolonpoxché, or La Pura Concepción (unattached)

Juan Canul	1565	1

CALKINÍ, or San Luis Obispo (Calkiní)

Ah Tzab Canul	pre-Hispanic	8

[a] Baptized under the name Juan Caamal.
[b] Son of Batab Caamal.
[c] Son of Pedro Canché.

Name	Period	Source
Napot Canché	invasion	8
Gonzalo Che	1565	1
Gonzalo Che	1567	2
Alonso Canché	1581	36

Calotmul, or San Esteban[a] *(unattached)*

Pedro Canul	1565	1

Chulihá (unattached)

Napuc Canul	invasion	8

Dzibikal, or San Francisco (unattached)

Nah Couoh Canul	invasion	8
Francisco Uicab	1568	7

Dzitbalché, or La Asunción de Nuestra Señora (unattached)

Juan Canul	1565	1

Halachó, or Santiago (unattached)

Pedro Canul	1565	1
Pedro Canul	1576	2

Hecelchakán, or San Francisco (unattached)

Pedro Canul	1565	1
Lucas Canul	1576	9

Hunucmá, or San Francisco (unattached)

Juan Canul	1565	1
Juan Canul	1580	19

Kinchil, or San Mateo (unattached)

Juan Canul	1565	1

Kinlacam, or San Luis Obispo (unattached)

Diego Canul	1565	1
Diego Canul	1567	2

Maxcanú, or San Miguel (unattached)

Na Hau Canul	invasion	8
Hernando Canul	1567	1

[a] A batabil located to the south of Tizimín; not to be confused with the cúuchcabal of Calotmul.

APPENDIX B

Mopilá, San Mateo Apóstol[a] *(Sotuta)*

Name	Period	Source
Juan Canul	1561	13
Juan Canul	1562	13
Juan Canul	1565	1

Nunkiní, San Diego Alcalá (Calkiní)

Juan Canul	1565	1
Juan Canul	1567	2
Jorge Canul[b]	1580	8
Jorge Canul	1595	8

Panbilchén* (unattached)

Diego Canul	1565	1
Francisco Canul	1567	2

Pocboc, or Los Santos Reyes (unattached)

Pedro Canul	1565	1

Pomuch, La Circuncisión (unattached)

Miguel Canul	1565	1

Sacalum* (unattached)

Lorenzo Canul	1565	1
Lorenzo Canul	1567	7

Sihó, or San Luis Obispo (unattached)

Ah Chacah Canul	pre-Hispanic	8
Francisco Uicab	1565	1
Francisco Uicab	1567	2
Juan Canul	1580	16

Sihunchén, San Francisco (unattached)

Juan Canul	1565	1

Tenabo, or La Asunción de Nuestra Señora (unattached)

Naun Canul	invasion	8
Francisco Canul	1565	2

[a] Not to be confused with the other Mopilá, a batabil dependent on the cúuchcabal of Calkiní.

[b] Son of Juan Canul.

Tepakán, or San Bartolomé[a] *(Calkiní)*

Name	Period	Source
Francisco Canul	1565	1
Francisco Chin	1567	2

Tikunché[b] *(unattached)*

Francisco Canul	1565	1

Yabacú, or San Francisco* (unattached)

Franisco Canul	1565	1
Diego Chan	1580	16

THE CAUICH LINEAGE

Canpocolché (Tihosuco)

Francisco Cauich	1565	1
Juan Cauich	1569	6

Zamá (unattached)

Francisco Cauich	1565	1

THE CEH LINEAGE

Sabán (Tihosuco)

Diego Ceh	1565	1

Tahdziú, or San Bernardino (Calotmul)

Diego Ceh	1565	1
Diego Ceh	1580	18

THE CHAN LINEAGE

Kantunilkín (unattached)

Juan Chan	1565	1

[a] Not to be confused with the other Tepakán, a batabil dependent on the cúuchcabal of Dzidzantún.

[b] A batabil located to the south of Calkiní; not to be confused with the other Tikunché, a batabil dependent on the cúuchcabal of Maní.

APPENDIX B

Temaza* (Chancenote)

Name	Period	Source
Nahua Chan	pre-Hispanic	37
Juan Chan[a]	invasion	37
Pedro Canul	1565	1
Juan Chan	1569	37
Juan Chan Pat[b]	1580	37

Tikunché*[c] (Maní)

Diego Chan	1562	12
Diego Chan	1565	1
Juan Uluac	1575	9

THE CHE LINEAGE

Izamal, or San Antonio de Padua (Dzidzantún)

Pedro Che	1565	1
Pedro Che†	1567	3

Kuxché* (Motul)

Pablo Che	1567	4

Mama, or La Asunción de Nuestra Señora (Maní)

Juan Che	1562	12
Francisco Uluac	1565	1
Francisco Uluac	1575	9

Sacalum, or San Antonio de Padua (Maní)

Gaspar Che	1565	1

Xocchel, San Juan Bautista (Hocabá)

Batab Che[d]	invasion	10

---

[a] Son of Nahua Chan; his pre-Hispanic name is unknown.

[b] Son of Juan Chan and grandson of Nahua Chan; for those interested in the history of the Chan lineage, see Quezada, "Don Juan Chan."

[c] Not to be confused with the other Tikunché, a batabil located to the south of Calkiní.

[d] Baptized under the name of Francisco Che.

Name	Period	Source
Francisco Che[a]	1562	10
Juan Francisco Iuit	1565	1
Juan Iuit[b]	1569	6
Diego Iuit	1597	40

THE CHEL LINEAGE

Canshacab, San Francisco (Dzidzantún)

Francisco Chel	1562	10
Andrés Chel	1567	3

DZIDZUNTÁN, or Santa Clara (Dzidzantún)

Francisco Chel	1565	1
Francisco Chel	1567	3
Francisco Chel	1569	6

Dzilam, or San Francisco (Dzidzantún)

Uamux Chel	invasion	46
Juan Chan	1567	3
Francisco Pech	1567	9

Yobaín, or San Lorenzo (Dzidzantún)

(?) Chel[c]	invasion	46
Francisco Chel	1567	3
Juan Chan	1579	38
Juan Pech	1607	39

THE COCHUAH LINEAGE

Ekpedz, or San Laurencio (Tihosuco)

Melchor Cochuah/ Alonso Cupul[d]	1565	1

[a] In this year Juan Blanco Iuit was also recognized as cacique. His brothers were don Lorenzo, don Juan, and don Diego Iuit, respective lords of Huhí, Hoctún, and Tiscanbanchel.

[b] Son of Juan Francisco Iuit.

[c] Landa indicates that at the time of the Spanish invasion, Yobaín was ruled by a young member of the Chel lineage.

[d] In 1563 don Diego de Quijada issued the title of gobernador to Alonso Cupul.

Ichmul, or San Bernardino de Siena (Tihosuco)

Name	Period	Source
Agustín Cochuah	1565	1
Agustín Cochuah	1569	

TIHOSUCO, or San Agustín (Tihosuco)

Nacahun Cochuah	invasion	32
Francisco Xol	1565	1
Francisco Xol	1569	6

THE COCOM LINEAGE

Chaltún, or La Natividad de Nuestra Señora (unattached)

Lorenzo Cocom	1565	1

Ekmul, or La Asunción de Nuestra Señora* (Sotuta)

Lorenzo Cocom	1565	1

Sahcabá[a] *(Sotuta)*

Baltazar Cocom	1559	31
Baltazar Cocom[b]	1561	13
Baltazar Cocom	1562	13
Baltazar Cocom	1565	1

SOTUTA, or San Pedro y San Pablo (Sotuta)

Nachí Cocom[c]	invasion	31
Lorenzo Cocom[d]	1561	13
Francisco Cocom[e]	1562	13
Francisco Cocom	1565	1
Francisco Cocom	1580	31

Tecoh, or La Asunción de Nuestra Señora[f] *(unattached)*

Juan Cocom	1565	1

---

[a] Not to be confused with the other Sahcabá, a dependent batabil of the Hocabá cúuchcabal, and of another batabil as of yet unidentified.

[b] In that year Hernando Cocom appears as señor and cacique.

[c] Baptized under the name of Juan Cocom.

[d] Brother of Nachí Cocom.

[e] Son of Nachí Cocom.

[f] An independent batabil located to the south of Acanceh; not to be confused with the other Tecoh, the first location of Ah Chel.

Tixbecyá, or San Juan Bautista (unattached)

Name	Period	Source
Diego Cocom	1565	1
Diego Cocom	1569	1

THE COUOH LINEAGE

Champotón (unattached)

Martín Couoh	1565	1

Tepakán, or San Juan Evangelista[a] (Dzidzantún)

Francisco Couoh[b]	invasion	23
Pedro Cauich	1565	1
Pedro Cauich	1567	3
Tomás Chin	1569	2
Juan Mo (P)	1580	23

THE CUPUL LINEAGE

Chalanté, San Miguel (Dzidzantún)

Francisco Cupul	1565	1
Francisco Tepal	1569	6

CHICHÉN ITZÁ, San Juan Bautista (Chichén Itzá)

Naobon Cupul	invasion	49

Dzitás, Santa Inés (unattached)

Juan Cupul	1565	1
Juan Cupul	1569	6

Ebtún, or San Bartolomé Apóstol (unattached)

Juan Cupul	1565	1
Juan Cupul[c]	1569	6, 47

[a] Not to be confused with the other Tepakán, a dependent batabil of the Calkiní cúuchcabal.

[b] This individual's pre-Hispanic patronymic remains unknown; rather, all we have is his baptismal name of Francisco Couoh. His son Hernando Couoh succeeded him.

[c] By the end of the sixteenth century the Cupul lineage had disappeared from the village's political landscape.

APPENDIX B

EKBALAM (Ekbalam)

Name	Period	Source
Na Mon Cupul	invasion	48
Juan Cupul	1579	56

Huhbilchén* (unattached)

(?) Cupul	invasion	51

Hunabkú, or San Juan Bautista (Ekbalam)

Pedro Cupul	1565	1
Juan Cupul	1569	6

Mexcitán, San Pedro (unattached)

Juan Cupul	1565	1
Juan Cupul	1569	6

Nabalam, or San Agustín (Ekbalam)

Pedro Cupul	1565	1
Pedro Cupul	1569	6
Juan Cupul	1571	57

Pixoy, or Santa Ana (Sací 2)

Melchor Cupul†	1565	1

POPOLÁ, or San Francisco (Popolá)

Na May Cupul	pre-Hispanic	52
Achichuen Cupul	pre-Hispanic	52
Na Dzul Cupul[a]	invasion	52
Juan Cupul	1565	1

SACÍ (1) (Sací)

Ah Tzuc Cupul	invasion	53

SACÍ (2) (Sací)

Na Dzul Cupul	invasion	33

Tesoco, or San Lorenzo (unattached)

Pedro Cupul	1565	6
Pedro Cupul	1569	6

[a] He was baptized under the name of Juan Cupul.

Tikuch, or La Visitación de Nuestra Señora (Chichén Itzá)

Name	Period	Source
Marcos Cupul	1565	1
Marcos Cupul	1569	6

Tinum, or La Pura Concepción (unattached)

Juan Cupul	1565	1
Francisco Cantum	1569	6

Tixcacauché, or Los Santos Reyes (Sací 1)

Francisco Cupul	1565	1
Francisco Cupul	1569	6
Juan Canché	1580	44

Yalcobá, or San Andrés Apóstol (unattached)

Pedro Cupul	1565	1
Pedro Cupul	1569	6

Yalsihón (unattached)

Francisco Cupul	1565	1

THE DZIB LINEAGE

Espita, or San José (unattached)

Francisco Dzib	1565	1
Francisco Dzib	1569	6
Francisco Cupul	1580	45

Loché, or San Agustín (unattached)

Jorge Dzib	1565	1

Tixculum, San Pedro (Dzidzantún)

Francisco Dzib	1565	1

THE DZUL LINEAGE

Chemax, or San Antonio de Padua (unattached)

Juan Dzul	1565	1

Kantunil, or San Francisco (Dzidzantún)

Name	Period	Source
Pedro Dzul	1565	1
Pedro Dzul	1569	6
Andrés Tu	1580	16
Diego Chin (P)	1581	21

THE EK LINEAGE

Chichimilá, or San Francisco (unattached)

Lorenzo Ek	1565	1
Lorenzo Ek	1569	6

Suma, or San Bartolomé (Motul)

Juan Ek	1565	1
Juan Ek	1567	4
Juan Ek	1569	6

Temax, or San Miguel (Dzidzantún)

Pedro Ek	1565	1
Juan Chan[a]		
Pedro Ek	1567	3
Pedro Ek	1569	6

THE EUÁN LINEAGE

Caucel, or San Miguel (unattached)

Pedro Euán	1565	1
Juan Euán	1580	36

Mopilá, or San Bartolomé[b] (Calkiní)

Ah Tzab Euán	invasion	8
Miguel Canul	1565	1

[a] In 1565 Juan Chan appeared as gobernador, possibly appointed by don Diego de Quijada.
[b] Not to be confused with the other Mopilá, a dependent batabil of Sotuta's cúuchcabal.

Name	Period	Source
Miguel Canul	1567	2
Juan Noh	1580	36

Sinanché, or San Buenaventura (Dzidzantún)

Juan Euán	1567	3

THE IUIT LINEAGE

HOCABÁ, or San Francisco (Hocabá)

Nadzul Iuit	invasion	25
Francisco Namon Iuit	1562	11
Lorenzo Cen	1572	7

Hoctún, or San Miguel Arcángel (Hocabá)

Juan Iuit[a]	1552	10
Juan Iuit†	1565	6
Lorenzo Uc	1597	40

Huhí, or San Pedro Apóstol (Hocabá)

Lorenzo Iuit	1552	1
Lorenzo Iuit	1565	1
Martín Puch	1597	40

Tiscanbanchel (Hocabá)

Diego Iuit	1552	10
Diego Iuit	1565	1
Diego Iuit	1569	1
Francisco Ku	1597	40

THE IX LINEAGE

Tibolón, or San Juan Bautista (Sotuta)

Juan Ix	1561	13
Juan Ix	1562	13
Juan Chuil (P)	1572	1

[a] In 1562 Francisco Cocom also appeared as cacique.

Tixcanchunup (Sotuta)

Name	Period	Source
Juan Ix	1565	1
Pedro Ix	1572	7

THE MIZ LINEAGE

Tekay, or Los Santos Reyes (Chichén Itzá)

Pablo Miz	1580	44

Tesul* (unattached)

Pedro Miz	1565	1

Tixol* (unattached)

Juan Miz	1565	1

THE MOTUL LINEAGE

Chaltunpuhuy* (Dzidzantún)

Juan Motul	1565	1
Juan Motul	1569	6

Sudzal, or La Asunción de Nuestra Señora (Dzidzantún)

Francisco Motul	1565	1
Francisco Motul	1567	3
Francisco Motul	1569	6

THE NA LINEAGE

Dzonotaké, or Santo Domingo (unattached)

Luis Na	1565	1

Tahmuy, or San Esteban (unattached)

Diego Na	1565	1
Francisco Na	1569	6

THE PECH LINEAGE

Aké (Motul)

Name	Period	Source
Juan Pech	1567	4

Baca, or La Pura Concepción (Motul)

Name	Period	Source
Op Pech[a]	invasion	7
Pedro Pech	1567	4
Pedro Che	1572	7

Cacalchén, or San Pedro y San Pablo (Motul)

Name	Period	Source
Na Chan Pech	invasion	30
Luis Pech	1565	1
Luis Pech	1567	4
Luis Pech	1569	6
Francisco Pech	1576	9

Chicxulub, or Santiago (Motul)

Name	Period	Source
Ak Nakuk Pech[b]	invasion	7
Pedro Pech[c]	1552	7
Juan Pech	1567	4
Andrés Pech	1572	7

Cholul, or San Pedro Apóstol (Motul)

Name	Period	Source
Luis Pech	1567	4

Chuburná, or La Pura Concepción (Motul)

Name	Period	Source
Ah Itzam Pech[d]	invasion	19
Melchor Pech	1565	7
Juan Pech[e]	1580	16, 19

Conkal, or San Francisco (Motul)

Name	Period	Source
Ixkil Itzam Pech	invasion	7

[a] He was baptized under the name of Ambrosio Pech.
[b] He was baptized under the name of Pablo Pech.
[c] Son of Pablo Pech.
[d] When Ah Itzam Pech died he was succeeded by his son Antonio Pech.
[e] In 1581 the encomendero of Chuburná wrote, "the gobernador of the village is called don Antonio Pech, cacique natural of said place, son of Antonio Pec, grandson of Ah Itzam Pech, cacique and señor natural of that same village."

Name	Period	Source
Luis Pech[a]	1567	4
Alonso Pech	1576	9

Dzemul, or Santa Ana (Motul)

Luis Pech	1565	1
Luis Pech	1567	4
Ambrosio Pech	1572	7

Euán, or San Luis Obispo (Motul)

Diego Pech	1559	10
Diego Pech	1565	1
Diego Pech	1567	4
Diego Pech	1569	6

Ixil, or San Bernabé (Motul)

Ah Dzulub Pech	invasion	7
Pedro Pech	1567	4
Luis Pech	1572	7

Kibá (Motul)

Tomás Pech	1567	4

Kimbilá, or Santa Clara (Dzidzantún)

Francisco Pech	1565	1
Francisco Pech	1567	4
Francisco Pech	1571	43

Kiní, or San Mateo (Motul)

Pedro Pech	1565	1
Pedro Pech	1567	4
Luis Pech[b]	1571	43

Kumún* (Motul)

Martín Pech	1567	4

Kuncheil, or San Miguel Arcángel (Motul)

Ah Kom Pech[c]	invasion	7
Martín Pech	1565	1

[a] Possibly the son of Ixkil Itzam Pech.
[b] Brother and coadjuntor de gobernador of Pedro Pech.
[c] He was baptized as don Martín Pech.

Name	Period	Source
Martín Pech	1567	4
Martín Pech	1569	6
Francisco Pech	1572	7

Mocochá, or La Asunción de Nuestra Señora (Motul)

Miguel Pech	1567	4
Juan Ciau	1572	7
Juan Ciau	1580	19

MOTUL, *or San Juan Bautista (Motul)*

Noh Cabal Pech	pre-Hispanic	29
Naum Pech[a]	invasion	29
Francisco de Montejo Pech	1552	7
Melchor Pech	1565	1
Melchor Pech	1567	4
Juan Pech	1572	7
Juan Pech	1576	9
Juan Pech	1580	29

Muxupip, or Santiago (Motul)

Luis Pech	1558	10
Luis Pech	1567	4

Nolo, or San Bartolomé (Motul)

Ah Namon Pech	invasion	54
Francisco Pech	1562	10
Jorge Pech	1581	19

Sitpach, or San Juan Bautista (Motul)

Pedro Pech	1565	6
Francisco Pech	1567	4

Telchac, or San Francisco (Motul)

Juan Pech	1567	4
Pedro Pech	1567	9

[a] He was baptized under the name of don Francisco de Montejo Pech.

APPENDIX B

Tepip* (unattached)

Name	Period	Source
Juan Pech	1565	1

Ticulul* (Motul)

Andrés Pech	1567	4

Timucuy, or Los Santos Reyes (unattached)

Francisco Pech	1565	1

Tixiol, or La Natividad de Nuestra Señora* (unattached)

Pablo Pech	1565	1
Pablo Pech	1567	6
Francisco Pech	1569	6

Tixkokob, or San Bernardino de Siena (Motul)

Hernando Pech	1562	10
Lorenzo Pech	1580 (?)	19

Ucí, or San Antonio de Padua (unattached)

Francisco Pech	1565	1
Francisco Pech	1567	4

Ucú, or San Luis Obispo

Martín Pech	1565	1

Uitzil, or La Natividad de la Virgen*[a] (Dzidzantún)

Pedro Pech	1563	1
Francisco Chan		
Pedro Pech	1565	1
Francisco Chan		

Yaxcabá, or San Francisco (Sotuta)

Diego Pech/Juan Ku[b]	1555	13
Diego Pech/Juan Ku	1562	13
Juan Hau (P)	1565	1

[a] In 1563 don Diego de Quijada conferred the title of gobernador on Francisco Chan, despite the fact that Pedro Pech was apparently cacique.

[b] Both men appeared as gobernadores between 1555 and 1562. Possibly one was cacique and the other was gobernador.

Yaxkukul, or La Pura Concepción (Motul)

Name	Period	Source
Ah Macan Pech[a]	invasion	7
Pedro Pech	1567	4

THE POT LINEAGE

Chikindzonot, or La Asunción de Nuestra Señora (Tihosuco)

Francisco Pot	1565	1
Francisco Pot	1569	6

Peto, or La Asunción de Nuestra Señora (Calotmul)

Gaspar Pat	1565	2
Juan Col	1580	17

Sahcabá, or San Juan Evangelista[b] (Hocabá)

Juan Pot	1562	10
Juan Pot	1565	1
Juan Pot	1569	7
Juan Iuit	1597	40

Sahcabá (unattached)

Agustín Pot	1565	1
Juan Dzul	1569	6

Tekantó, or San Agustín (unattached)

Nacom Pot	invasion	23
Juan Aké	1565	1
Juan Aké	1567	3
Juan Pot[c]	1580	23

Umán, or San Francisco (unattached)

Francisco Pot	1565	1
Andrés Pot	1576	9

[a] He was baptized as Pedro Pech.

[b] Not to be confused with the dependent batabil of the Sotuta cúuchcabal, or with another as-of-yet unidentified batabil.

[c] Son of Nacom Pot. By 1580 a nephew of Juan Pot, an individual of name unknown, was gobernador.

THE PUC LINEAGE

Tixholop, or San Pedro* (Chancenote)

Name	Period	Source
Juan Puc	1565	1
Gabriel Chic	1569	6

Yaxcabá (unattached)

Francisco Puc	1565	1

THE TUN LINEAGE

Homún, or San Buenaventura (Hocabá)

Gaspar Tun	1562	12
Gaspar Tun	1565	1
Gaspar Tun	1567	41
Gaspar Tun[a]	1569	6

Tahcab, or San Bartolomé (Ekbalam)

Juan Tun/Juan Pantí[b]	1565	1
Juan Tun/Juan Pantí†	1569	6
Juan Tep	1571	56

Teya, or San Bernabé Apóstol (Dzidzantún)

Jorge Tun	1565	1
Juan Pol (P)	1567	3
Juan Pol	1569	6

Tixcocho, or San Juan Bautista (Dzidzantún)

Juan Tun	1565	1
Juan Tun	1567	3
Juan Tun	1569	6

Tzeme, or San Miguel (unattached)

Francisco Tun	1565	1

[a] He was removed from office in this year as a result of having been banished from his village.

[b] In 1563 don Diego de Quijada issued titles of gobernador for both Juan Tun and Juan Pantí. Apparently the former was cacique.

Usil, or Santiago (Sotuta)

Name	Period	Source
Tomás Tun	1558	13
Tomás Tun	1561	13
Pedro Yah	1562	13
Juan Cauich	1565	1
Juan Pech	1572	7

THE TZEH LINEAGE

CHANCENOTE, or San Francisco (Chancenote)

Kaual Op Tzeh	pre-Hispanic	37
Juan Uluac	1565	1
Juan Chan	1569	37
Juan Chan Pat[a]	1580	37

Tibatún* (Chancenote)

Luis Tzeh	1565	1

Tixcancal, or San Martín Obispo (Chancenote)

Alonso Tzeh	1565	1
Alonso Tzeh	1569	6

Tixmucul (Chancenote)

Luis Tzeh[†]	1565	1
Juan Uc	1601	7

THE UCÁN LINEAGE

Buctzotz, or La Pura Concepción (Dzidzantún)

Juan Ucán	1565	1
Juan Balam	1567	3
Martín Uitz	1580	19

---

[a] Son of Juan Chan and nephew of Nahau Chan; see notes 11 and 12 above.

Pomolché, or San Idefonso (Dzidzantún)

Name	Period	Source
Francisco Ucán	1565	1
Francisco Ucán	1569	6
Martín Balam	1576	9

THE UICAB LINEAGE

Sacalaca, or La Asunción de Nuestra Señora (Tihosuco)

Pedro Uicab[a]	1565	1

Tocbadz, or La Natividad de la Virgen (Dzidzantún)

Luis Uicab	1565	1
Francisco Uicab	1569	6

THE XIU LINEAGE

CALOTMUL, or San Pedro Apóstol (Calotmul)

Ah Kukil Xiu[b]	invasion	7
Juan Montejo Xiu	1557	7
Hernando Xiu/Andrés May[c]	1565	1
Francisco Xiu	1572	7

Cauich (Maní)

Juan Xiu	1565	1

Cancunul, or San Juan Bautista (unattached)

Juan Xiu	1565	1
Francisco Xiu	1569	6

Dzan, or Santiago Apóstol (Maní)

Napot Xiu	invasion	26

---

[a] In 1563 don Diego de Quijada issued titles of gobernador to both Pedro Uicab and Juan Xicum.

[b] Ah Kukul Xiu was baptized under the name of don Juan Montejo Xiu.

[c] In 1565 Andrés May appeared as gobernador, having been imposed by don Diego de Quijada.

Name	Period	Source
Miguel Cuyoc	1572	7
Jorge Xiu[a]	1580	26

Hunactí (Calotmul)

Juan Xiu[b]	1557	7
Hernando Xiu/Andres May	1565	2
Pablo Can	1572	7

MANÍ, or San Miguel Arcángel (Maní)

Ah Kukum Xiu[c]	invasion	7
Francisco de Montejo Xiu	1562	11
Juan Ku	1562	69
Francisco de Montejo Xiu	1565	1
Francisco de Montejo Xiu	1567	5
Gaspar Antonio Chi Xiu	1571	9
Francisco Be	1575	9

Panabchén (Maní)

Nabatún Xiu	invasion	26
Jorge Xiu[d]	1565	1
Jorge Xiu	1567	4
Jorge Xiu	1575	9
Jorge Xiu	1580	9

Pustunich, or La Asunción de Nuestra Señora (Maní)

Alonso Xiu/Juan Cuyoc[e]	1565	1
Alonso Xiu	1572	7
Alonso Xiu	1580	7

Tekit, or San Antonio de Padua (Maní)

Alonso Xiu	1562	12
Alonso Xiu	1565	1

[a] He was the son of Nabatún Xiu, and was also gobernador of Panabchén.
[b] He governed until 1561.
[c] He was baptized under the name of Franciso de Montejo Xiu.
[d] Son of Nabatún Xiu.
[e] Don Alonso Xiu was cacique, and in 1563 don Diego de Quijada named Juan Cuyoc gobernador.

Name	Period	Source
Alonso Xiu	1575	9
Diego Xiu	1580	28

Tzucacab, or Santa María Magdalena (Calotmul)

Juan Xiu	1557	55
Gaspar Col	1565	1
Gaspar Col	1572	7

Yaxá, or San Juan Bautista[a] *(Maní)*

Pedro Xiu	1562	12
Pedro Xiu	1565	1
Francisco Dzan	1575	9

Yicman* (Maní)

Ah Ziyah Xiu[b]	invasion	7
Diego Toz	1565	1

Yotholín, or San Felipe y Santiago (Maní)

(?) Xiu	invasion	7

THE XOC LINEAGE

Xoccén, or La Natividad de la Virgen (unattached)

Diego Xoc	1565	1
Diego Xoc	1569	6
Francisco Xoc	1580	34

Yalcón, or San Lucas (unattached)

Lorenzo Xoc	1565	1
Lorenzo Xoc	1565	6
Lorenzo Xoc	1580	35

---

[a] Not to be confused with the other Yaxá, a dependent batabil of the Sotuta cúuchcabal.
[b] Father of Ah Kukum Xiu, halach uinic of Maní.

OTHER LINEAGES

Aculemax (unattached)

Name	Period	Source
Andrés Cuy	1565	1

Bokobá, or La Asunción de Nuestra Señora (Motul)

Gaspar Oxté	1567	4

Cehac, or Santa Ana* (Chancenote)

Luis Tuyub	1565	1

Chocholá, or San Francisco (unattached)

Juan Yam	1565	1
Juan Yam/Agustín Noh[a]	1569	6

Chuinchén* (unattached)

Marcos May	1565	1

Citilcum, or San Pedro (Dzidzantún)

Ah Kul Can[b]	invasion	20
Gaspar Cahum	1565	1
Gaspar Cahum†	1567	3
Pedro Cahum[c]	1580	20

Conil (unattached)

Juan Polá	1565	1

Dzitnup (Sací 2)

Andrés Uc	1565	1

Dzonotchuil, or Los Santos Reyes (Sací 1)

Juan Chuil	1565	1
Juan Chuil	1569	6
Juan Chuil	1580	44

[a] In 1565 Juan Yam appears as gobernador, and by 1569 both he and Agustín Noh were listed as caciques.

[b] After his death he was succeeded by his son Francisco Can.

[c] Son of Gaspar Cahum.

APPENDIX B   167

Kanxoc, or San Cosme y San Damién (unattached)

Name	Period	Source
Juan Pol	1565	1

Kikil, or San Francisco (unattached)

Francisco Noh	1565	1

Kukab, or San Luis Obispo* (unattached)

Francisco Ci	1565	1
Francisco Ci	1567	2

Muna (Maní)

Alonso Pacab	invasion	26
Juan Pacab	1565	1
Juan Pacab	1575	9
Juan Pacab	1580	26

Oxcum 2ª (unattached)

Francisco Cantún	1565	1

Pencuyut, or San Bernabé (Maní)

Juan Ku	1562	12
Juan Ku	1565	1
Juan Ku	1583	42

Pixilá, or San Buenaventura (Dzidzantún)

Andrés Uitz	1565	1
Andrés Uitz	1567	3
Andrés Uitz	1569	6

Sal (Calotmul)

Nahua Te[b]	invasion	24
Gaspar Pol[c]	1580	24

Samahil, or San Pedro (unattached)

Francisco Mo	1565	1

[a] The batabil was divided during the reducción process. This part remained in its original location and was ruled by a certain Juan Cantún; see note 2 above.
[b] When Nahau Te died he was succeeded by Juan Xiu. The length of Juan Xiu's term of office remains unknown.
[c] He assumed office with the death of Juan Xiu at some unknown date.

Name	Period	Source
Juan Mo	1576	9
Juan Mo	1580	16

Sanahcat, or La Asunción de Nuestra Señora (Hocabá)

Diego Tzab	1562	10
Diego Tzab[a]	1565	1
Diego Tzab[b]	1569	6
Francisco Mo	1597	40

Sitilpech, or San Jerónimo (Dzidzantún)

Juan Chi	1565	1

Sucopó, or San Martín Obispo (unattached)

Miguel Chuc[†]	1565	1

Teabo, or San Pedro Apóstol (Maní)

Juan Nahuat[c]	invasion	27
Luis Euán	1565	1
Juan Chulín	1575	9
Juan Chulín	1580	27

Tekax, or San Juan Bautista (Maní)

Batab Uz[d]	invasion	13
Diego Uz	1562	14
Miguel Ek	1565	1

Temozón, or La Asunción de Nuestra Señora (unattached)

Francisco Cen[†]	1565	1

Ticul, or San Antonio de Padua (Maní)

Lorenzo Uluac[e]	invasion	1
Juan Uluac	1560	1

[a] Teniente de gobernador of Francisco Namon Iuit.
[b] In this year he appeared as gobernador of his village.
[c] His pre-Hispanic patronymic remains unknown, but he was recognized as the lord who had sworn obedience to the Spaniards.
[d] He was baptized under the name of Diego Uz.
[e] The year of his death remains unknown, but don Diego de Quijada recognized don Juan Uluac, his son, as the legitimate heir to his cacicazgo. In 1562 the alcalde mayor named Francisco Che as gobernador.

APPENDIX B

Name	Period	Source
Francisco Che	1562	15
Francisco Che	1565	1
Melchor Cobá	1575	9

Tixcacalcupul, or Santiago Apóstol (unattached)

Juan Kauil	1565	1
Juan Kauil	1569	6

Tixcacaltuyú, or San Juan Bautista (Sotuta)

Gonzalo Tuyú	1565	1

Tizimín, or Los Santos Reyes (Sací 1)

Melchor Xol	1565	1
Juan Huchín	1569	6

Tunkás, or Santo Tomás (unattached)

Juan Macún	1565	1
Juan Macún	1569	6

Xanabá, or San Nicolás (Dzidzantún)

Pablo Huchín	1565	1
Pedro Ku	1569	6

Xicinchah* (Calkiní)

Namay Tayu	invasion	8

Yaxá, or San Andrés Apóstol[a] (Sotuta)

Juan Naual	1565	1

Yocchec, or Santiago (unattached)

Pedro Pax	1565	1
Pedro Pax	1569	6

[a] Not to be confused with the other Yaxá, a dependent batabil of the Maní cúuchcabal.

Sources for Appendices A and B

1. "Residencia de Diego de Quijada (1565)," in AGI, Justicia, legajo 245, ff. 1000–560. This document provides the most complete listing of caciques and their respective villages and encomenderos for the year 1565.

2. "Carta de diez caciques de Nueva España a S. M., el rey don Felipe II, pidiendo religiosos de la orden de San Francisco (1567)," in *Cartas de Indias*, 2:368. This document includes the names of the ten caciques of the peninsula's western coast.

3. "Carta en donde los caciques piden a S. M., religiosos de la orden de San Francisco (1567)," in AGI, Audiencia de México, legajo 367. This document offers the most complete listing of the caciques associated with Dzidzantún.

4. "Carta en donde los caciques piden a S. M., que envíe religiosos franciscano (1567)," in AGI, Audiencia de México, legajo 367. This document contains the most complete listing of caciques associated with Motul.

5. "Carta de los indios gobernadores de varias provincias de Yucatán al rey don Felipe II, quejándose de los tormentos, muertes y robos que con ellos habían cometido los religiosos de la orden de San Francisco (1567)," in *Cartas de Indias*, 2:410. This document contains the names of three caciques associated with Maní.

6. "Residencia que don Diego de Santillán tomó a don Luis de Céspedes Oviedo," in AGI, Justicia, legajo 253. This document includes innumerable references to caciques y pueblos of the year 1569. It is an essential complement to source 1.

7. Roys, *The Political Geography*. This pioneering work in its field offers an enormously helpful guide to locating the pre-Hispanic "pueblos" (not actually pueblos in the colonial sense, but rather señoríos or batabilob). It also charts the lineage succesion of the cacicazgos and the gobernatura and contains an outstanding topographical index.

8. *Códice de Calkiní*. This fundamental source for any study of the Canul lineage provides the patronymics of a large part of the batabob constituting this lineage.

9. "Francisco Palomino, protector de los naturales de la provincia de Yucatán contra la ciudad de Mérida y encomenderos sobre que no se carguen los indios," in AGI, Justicia, legajo 1016. A list of some twenty caciques appears in connection with a 1575 legal dispute regarding Indian porters.

10. "Información hecha en el pueblo de Homún sobre la idolatría de los indios (1562)," in *DDQAMY*, 1:135–62.

11. "Información hecha por el doctor Diego Quijada en los pueblos de Homún, Maní y Tacul (1564)," in *DDQAMY*, 1:138–46.

12. "Declaraciones de algunos testigos sobre las investigaciones de las idolatrías de los indios hechas por fray Diego de Landa y sus compañeros (1562)," in *DDQAMY*, 1:32–46.

13. "Proceso contra los indios idólatras de Sotuta, Kanchunup, Mopilá, Sacaba, Yaxcabá, Usil y Tibolón (1562)," in *DDQAMY*, 1:71–129.

14. "Diligencias hechas por el provincial fray Diego de Landa y el obispo fray Francisco de Toral en el asunto de la idolatría de indios (1562)," in *DDQAMY*, 1:189–232.

15. "Fe dada por fray Pedro de Ciudad Rodrigo, guardián de Maní, acerca de una criatura muerta que le trajeron y las señas que tenía (1562)," in *DDQAMY*, 1:179–80.

16. "Carta de los caciques de aquella provincia al rey solicitando envíe nuevo obispo (1580)," in AGI, Audiencia de México, legajo 104, ramo 1. This document offers a short list of some pueblos located in the peninsular northwest.

17. "Relación de Mama," in *RHGY*, 1:116.
18. "Relación de Tahdziú," in *RHGY*, 1:389.
19. "Relación de Chuburná," in *RHGY*, 1:300–401.
20. "Relación de Citilcum," in *RHGY*, 1:180.
21. "Relación de Izamal," in *RHGY*, 1:304.
22. "Relación de Tekal," in *RHGY*, 1:443.
23. "Relación de Tekantó," in *RHGY*, 1:214.
24. "Relación de Titzal," in *RHGY*, 1:238.
25. "Relación de Hocabá," in *RHGY*, 1:133.
26. "Relación de Dzan," in *RHGY*, 1:253.
27. "Relación de Tiab," in *RHGY*, 1:318.
28. "Relación de Tekit," in *RHGY*, 1:285.
29. "Relación de Motul," in *RHGY*, 1:269.
30. "Relación de Cacalchén," in *RHGY*, 1:338.
31. "Relación de Sotuta," in *RHGY*, 1:146–47.
32. "Relación de Tihotzuc," in *RHGY*, 2:198.
33. "Relación de Dzitnup," in *RHGY*, 2:60.

34. "Relación de Xocén," in *RHGY*, 2:226.

35. "Relación de Yalcón," in *RHGY*, 1:335.

36. "Francisco Palomino, defensor de los indios de Yucatán, sobre la querella criminal que don Guillén de las Casas, gobernador de la provincia, por haberle enviado preso a estos reynos (1580)," in AGI, Justicia, legajo 183, ff. 57–69. This document includes a small list of caciques.

37. "Probanza de el capitán don Juan Chan cacique y señor natural de los pueblos de Chancenote y sus sujetos (1622)," in AGI, Audiencia de México, legajo 140.

38. "Proceso de Francisco Manrique sobre haber desposeído don Guillén de las Casas, gobernador de Yucatán, cierta encomienda de indios (1579)," in AGNM, Civil, vol. 2302, expediente 2.

39. "Diligencias que se hicieron sobre junta y pláticas de algunos indios que se denunció parecían que se alteraban (1607)," in AGI, Audiencia de México, legajo 3048.

40. "Proceso hecho por el gobernador de Yucatán sobre quedar vacos la encomienda de Isabel de Lara (1596)," in AGI, Escribanía de Cámara, legajo 304B, ff. 670, 868. This document offers a short listing of the gobernadores of the villages located near Hocabá in the late 1500s.

41. "Información efectuada por Luis de Céspedes Oviedo sobre los excesos de fray Alonso Toral (1567)," in AGI, Audiencia de México, legajo 359.

42. Roys et al., "Census and Inspection," 195.

43. "Título de gobernador a don Luis Pech (1571)," in AGI, Audiencia de México, legajo 3077, ff. 3v–5.

44. Ortiz Yam y Quezada, *Visita de Diego García*, 98, 91, 86, 103.

45. "Visita y cuenta del pueblo de Espita y del pueblo de Tzabcanul (1583)," in AGNM, Tierras, vol. 2726, expediente 6, f. 64.

46. Landa, *Relación*, 24.

47. Roys, *The Titles of Ebtun*, tables 1 and 2.

48. "Relación de Nabalam," in *RHGY*, 2:186.

49. "Relación de Sodzil," in *RHGY*, 2:125–26.

50. "Relación de Dzicab," in *RHGY*, 2:205.

51. "Relación de Kikil," in *RHGY*, 2:267.

52. "Relación de Popolá," in *RHGY*, 2:216

53. "Relación de la villa de Valladolid," in *RHGY*, 2:37.

54. Barrera Vásquez, *Documento núm. 1*.

55. Roys, *The Indian Background*, 192–94, figs. 19–20.

56. Relación de Ekbalam," in *RHGY*, 2:139.

57. "Residencia de don Luis de Céspedes Oviedo," in AGI, Justicia, legajo 250. f. 505.

58. "Relación de Chauac-há," in *RHGY*, 2:245.

59. "Relación de Ichmul," in *RHGY*, 2:299.

60. "Relación de Dzonot," in *RHGY*, 2:83.

61. "Relación de Pixoy," in *RHGY*, 2:51.

62. "Proceso contra Melchor y Francisco Pacheco (1565)," in AGI, Justicia, legajo 248. ff. 3025–62.

63. Fernández de Oviedo, *Historia general*, 2: 121, 126.

64. Francisco López de Gómara, *Historia de la conquista*, (Mexico City: Pedro Robredo, 1943), 1: 67–69, 76.

65. "Crónica de Yaxkukul," 6–7, 21, 26.

66. *Calepino maya*, 123.

67. "Relación de Kanpocolché (1579)," in *RHGY*, 2:321.

68. "Tasaciones de los pueblos de la provincia de Yucatán hechas por la Audiencia de Guatemala (febrero de 1549)," in *ENE*, 5:103–81.

69. "Información hecha por el doctor Quijada contra el obispo fray Francisco de Toral (Mérida, 18 de septiembre de 1562)," in *DDQAMY*, 1:175.

70. Relación de Tabi," in *RHGY*, 2:164.

APPENDIX C

Major Spanish Urban Centers and Their Jurisdictions (1565)

Because two different villages bear the same name in several instances, this appendix includes a parenthetical reference to indicate the pre-Hispanic capital on which the village depended. Asterisks (*) designate place names that cannot be located on existing maps.

JURISDICTION OF THE CITY OF MÉRIDA

Acanceh	Haltuniche	Oxkutzcab
Bolonpoxché	Hocabá	Panabchén
Buctzotz	Hoctún	Pencuyut
Cacalchén	Huhí	Peto
Calotmul (Calotmul)	Hunactí	Pixilá
Caltunpuhuy*	Hunucmá	Pomolché
Caucel	Izamal	Pustunich
Cauich	Kantunil	Sacalum
Chalanté	Kimbilá	Sahcabá*
Chaltún	Kinchil	Sahcabá (Hocabá)
Chuburná	Kiní	Sahcabá (Sotuta)
Citilcum	Kuncheil	Sal
Dzan	Mama	Samahil
Dzemul	Maní	Sanahcat
Dzidzantún	Mopilá	Sihunché
Ekmul*	Motul	Sitilpech
Euán	Oxcum	Sotuta

175

Sudzal	Ticul	Tzucacab
Suma	Tikunché (Mérida)	Ucí
Suyhuá	Timucuy	Uitzil
Tahdziú	Tiscanbanchel	Umán
Teabo	Tixbecyá	Usil
Tecal	Tixcacaltuyú	Xacabá (Sotuta)
Tecoh (Dzidzantún)	Tixcanchunup	Xanabá
Tecoh (unknown)	Tixcochoh	Xocchel
Tekax	Tixculum	Yabacú*
Tekit	Tixiol*	Yaxá (Maní)
Temax	Tixtual*	Yaxá (Sotuta)
Tepakán (Dzidzantún)	Tocbadz*	Yicman*
Teya	Tunkás	
Tibolón	Tzeme	

JURISDICTION OF THE VILLA OF VALLADOLID

Aculemax*	Ebtún	Sucopó
Cachí	Ecab	Tahcab
Calotmul (unknown)	Ekpedz	Tahmuy
Canpocolch	Espita	Tekay
Cehac*	Hunabkú	Tekom
Chancenote	Ichmul	Temaza*
Chauac-há	Kantunilkín	Temozón
Chemax	Kanxoc	Tepip*
Chibxul	Kaua	Tesoc
Chichimilá	Loché	Tesul*
Chikindzonot	Mexcitán	Tibatún*
Chocholá	Nabalam	Tihosuco
Chuinchén*	Pixoy	Tikuch
Conil	Polbalam*	Timul
Cuncunul	Popolá	Tinum
Dzitás	Sabán	Tiscacauché
Dzitnup	Sacalaca	Tixcacalcupul
Dzonotaké	Sisal	Tixcancal
Dzonotchuil	Sodzil	Tixholop*

Tixhualahtún
Tixmucul
Tixol*
Tizimín

Uayma
Xoccén
Yalcobá
Yalcón

Yalsihón
Yaxcabá
Yocchec
Zamá

JURISDICTION OF THE VILLA OF CAMPECHE

Bécal
Calkiní
Champotón
Dzitbalché
Halachó
Hecelchakán
Kinlacam

Kukab*
Maxcanú
Mopilá (Calkiní)
Nohcacab*
Nunkiní
Panbilchén
Pocboc

Pomuch
Salacum*
Sihó
Tenabo
Tepakán (Calkiní)
Tikunché (Calkiní)

APPENDIX D

Sixteenth-Century Governors of Yucatán

A Chronological List
Relating Names, Titles, and Tenure

Francisco de Montejo, Adelantado de Yucatán, December 8, 1526 until 1539, when he delegated his powers to his son

Francisco de Montejo the Son ("El Mozo"), teniente de gobernador and capitán general, 1539 until December 25, 1546, when his father, El Adelantado, arrived in Campeche

Francisco de Montejo, Adelantado de Yucatán, December 25, 1546 to May 13, 1549

Blas Cota, oidor of the Real Audienca de los Confines and juez de residencia del Adelantado, May 13, 1549 to September 3, 1549

Francisco de Herrera, oidor of the Real Audiencia de México, September 3, 1549 to late 1550 or early 1551

Gaspar Juárez de Avila, alcalde mayor, late 1550 or early 1551 to June 13, 1552

Tomás López de Medel, oidor of the Real Audiencia de los Confines, and visitador de la provincia, June 13, 1552 to 1553

Francisco de Montejo the Son, and Francisco Tamayo Pacheco, alcaldes ordinarios de Mérida, they governed until an alcalde mayor arrived from Guatemala, 1553

Alvaro de Carvajal, alcalde mayor, 1554 to 1556

Alonso Ortiz Delgueta, alcalde mayor, 1556 to 1558

Juan de Paredes, alcalde mayor, 1558 to May or June of 1560

García Jofre de Loaysa, oidor of the Real Audienca de los Confines, and visitador de la provincia, May or June of 1560 to June of 1561

Diego Quijada, alcalde mayor, June of 1561 to November 13, 1565

Luis de Céspedes y Oviedo, governador, November 13, 1565 to March 12, 1571

Diego de Santillán, gobernador, March 12, 1571 to September 16, 1573

Francisco Veláques Gijón, gobernador, September 16, 1573 to September 27, 1577

Guillén de las Casas, gobernador, September 16, 1571 to September 16, 1573

Francisco de Solís, gobernador, September 28, 1582 to April of 1583

Diego García de Palacios, oidor of the Real Audienca de México and visitador de la provincia, April of 1583 to April of 1585

Francisco de Solís, gobernador, April of 1585 to October 25, 1586

Antonio de Vozmediano, gobernador, October 25, 1586 to July 30, 1593

Alonso Ordoñez de Nevares, gobernador, July 30, 1593 to his death in Mérida on May 26, 1595

Pablo Higueras de la Cerda, gobernador interino, May 26, 1595 to June 15, 1596

Carlos de Sámano de Quiñones, gobernador interino, June 15, 1596 to late 1597

Diego Fernández de Velasco, gobernador, 1597

Martín de Palomar, teniente de gobernador, 1597 to May of 1598

Diego Fernández de Velasco, gobernador, May of 1598 to August 11, 1604

Notes

List of Abbreviations

AGI	Archivo General de Indias, Sevilla
AGNM	Archivo General de la Nación, México
ASAY	Archivo Sacramental del Arzobispado de Yucatán
DDQAMY	*Don Diego Quijada alcalde mayor de Yucatán, 1561–1565*
DHY	*Documentos para la historia de Yucatán, 1550–1560*
ENE	*Epistolario de Nueva España, 1505–1818*
RHGY	*Relaciones histórico-geográfica de la gobernación de Yucatán*

Introduction

1. Bernardo García Martínez, *Los pueblos de la Sierra: El poder y el espacio entre los indios del norte de Puebla hasta 1700* (Mexico City: Colegio de Mexico, 1987), 75–76.

2. Hildeberto Martínez, "Teucyotl. El gobierno señorial de Tecamachalco, Pueblo, siglo XVI," in *Formas de voto, prácticas de las asambleas y toma de decisiones. Un acercamiento comparativo*, ed. Victor Manuel Franco Pellotier, Danièle Dehouve, and Aline Hémond (Mexico City: Centro de Investigaciones y Estudios en Antropología Social, 2011), 102.

3. Bernardo García Martínez, "Jurisdicción y propiedad: Una distinción fundamental en la historia de los pueblos de indios del México colonial," *Revista europea de estudios Latinoamericanos y del Caribe* 53 (December 1992): 47. This work is without doubt one of the most important and complete reflections on the concept of jurisdiction and the principle of personal association in Mexican colonial villages. See also Rik Hoekstra, "A Different Way of Thinking: Contrasting Spanish and Indian Social and Economic Views in Central Mexico (1550–1600)," in Alij Ouweneel and Simon Miller, eds. *The Indian Community of Colonial Mexico: Fifteen Essays on Land Tenure, Corporate Organizations, Ideology and Village*

Politics (Amsterdam: Centre for Latin American Research and Documentation, 1990), 70–75.

4. René García Castro, *Indios, territorio y poder en la provincia de Matlatzinca: La negociación del espacio político de los pueblos otomianos, siglos XVI–XVII* (Mexico City: Intituto Nacional de Antropología e Historia, Colegio Mexiquense, Centro de Investigaciones y Estudios en Antropología Social, 1999), 37.

5. García Martínez, *Los pueblos de la Sierra*, 66–78; García Castro, *Indios, territorio y poder*, 35–36.

CHAPTER 1

1. Ralph L. Roys, "Traditions of Caste," in *The Book of Chilam Balam of Chumayel*, ed. and trans. Ralph L. Roys (Washington, DC: Carnegie Institution of Washington, 1933), 188–91; Ralph L. Roys, *The Titles of Ebtun* (Washington, DC: Carnegie Institution of Washington 1939) 43–44; Ralph L. Roys, "Personal Names of the Mayas of Yucatan," *Contribution to American Anthropology and History* 6 (1940): 39–40; and Ralph L. Roys, *The Indian Background of Colonial Yucatan*, (Washington, DC: Carnegie Institution of Washington, 1943; Norman: University of Oklahoma Press, 1972), 59–63. Following these works, all of Roys's publications repeated the original idea; for example, see Ralph L. Roys, "Lowland Maya Native Society at Spanish Contact," in *Handbook of Middle American Indians*, Vol. 3, ed. Gordon Willey (Austin: University of Texas Press, 1965), 669–70.

2. Ralph L. Roys, *The Political Geography of the Yucatan Maya* (Washington DC: Carnegie Institution of Washington, 1957), 13, 35, 55, 63, 81, 95, 104, 114, 137, and 156.

3. Roys, *The Political Geography*, 1–17.

4. Charles Suhler, et al., "The Rise and Fall of Terminal Classic Yaxuna, Yucatán, México," in *The Terminal Classic in the Maya Lowlands: Collapse, Transition, and Transformation*, ed. Arthur A. Demarest, Prudence M. Rice, and Don S. Rice (Boulder: University Press of Colorado, 2004), 456.

5. See Joyce Marcus, "Ancient Maya Political Organization" in *Lowland Maya Civilization in the Eighth Century AD*, ed. Jeremy A. Sabloff, and John S. Henderson (Washington, DC: Dumbarton Oaks Research Library and Collection, 1993), 157–62. Alfonso Lacadena García-Gallo and Andrés Ciudad Ruiz reproduce the maps of the regional states that Richard L. Adams proposed for the Late Classic period, and the map that Peter Mathews advanced for the political organization of the Maya lowlands for the period around 790 AD. See Lacadena García-Gallo and Ciudad Real, "Reflexiones recientes sobre la estructura política maya clásica," in *Anatomía de una civilización: Aproximaciones interdisciplinarias a la cultura maya*, ed. Andrés Ciudad Real, et al.(Madrid: Sociedad Española de Estudios Mayas, 1998), 36–37.

6. Simon Martin and Nikolai Grube, *Chronicle of the Maya Kings and Queens: Deciphering the Dynasties of the Ancient Maya* (London: Thames and Hudson Ltd., 2000), 163.

7. Roys, *The Political Geography*, 7; Michael D. Coe, "A Model of Ancient Community Structure in the Maya Lowlands," *Southwestern Journal of Anthropology* 21, no. 2 (1965): 105; Alfonso Villa Rojas, "La tenencia de la tierra entre los mayas de la antigüedad," in *Estudios etnológicos: los mayas*, ed. Alfonso Villa Rojas (Mexico City: Universidad Nacional Autónoma de México, 1985), 33; and Nancy M. Farriss, *Maya Society Under Spanish Rule. The Collective Enterprise of Survival* (Princeton: Princeton University Press, 1984), 163.

8. Roys, *The Political Geography*, 7–8.

9. Tsubasa Okoshi Harada, "Los canules: Análisis etnohistórico del códice de Calkiní" (Ph.D. diss. Universidad Nacional Autónoma de México, 1992) 209.

10. Antonio de Ciudad Real, *Calepino maya de Motul* (Mexico City: Plaza y Valdés Editores, 2001), 125.

11. *Diccionario de autoridades* (Madrid: Editorial Gredos, 1969) 3:125; Ciudad Real, *Calepino maya*, 125.

12. Regarding the word *cuchul*, Ciudad Real, *Calepino maya*, 125, states directly, "The same as *cuchteel*."

13. *Documento núm. 1 del deslinde de tierras en Yaxkukul [Yucatán]*, trans. Alfredo Barrera Vásquez (Mexico City: Instituto Nacional del Antropología e Historia, 1984), 22. See also pages 25, 26, 27, and 30–31. This source, p.56, observes that *kuchteilob*, according to the orthography adopted for writing Maya, should be written with "c" instead of "k."

14. Okoshi Harada, "Los canules," 45, 86, 107, 130, and 139.

15. Daniel G. Brinton, ed., *The Maya Chronicles* (Philadelphia: D. G. Brinton, 1882), 202. See also Juan Martínez Hernández, trans., *Crónicas mayas* (Mérida: Talleres de la Compañía Tipográfica Yucateca, 1928), 11. For the use of *cuchul*, see Alfredo Barrera Vásquez and Sylvanus G. Morley, "The Maya Chronicles," in *Contribution to American Anthropology and History* 48 (1949): 26; this source states, "*yetel holon chan tepeu yetel u cuchulob*: and Holon Chan Tepeu and his subjects." For additional references regarding the context of cuchul, see Brinton, *The Maya Chronicles*, 199, 211, and 212; and Martínez Hernández, *Crónicas mayas*, 28, 29.

16. See *Diccionario de autoridades*, 2:334. Under the entry on "jurisdicción" this text offers as a third definition: "Faculty or power granted for government, for deciding legal cases."

17. Anthony P. Andrews, "The Fall of Chichén Itzá: A Preliminary Hypothesis," *Latin American Antiquity* 1, no. 3 (1990): 267.

18. According to the historical sources, the Itzá presence in the northern lowlands dates from the period of 415–435 AD, when they conquerered Bacalar, which they governed until sometime between 475 and 495. Between 435 and 455 these same people "discovered" Chichén Itzá and occupied it until sometime between 495 and 515. They governed there for some 200 years, and between 692 and 711 they relocated to Chakanputún, for reasons unknown. They remained there until 968, at which date they uprooted yet again and wandered for twenty

years until they came once more to Chichén Itzá under the leadership of Kukulcán. Here the Itzá erected a great political hegemony that lasted until between 1185 and 1204, when the city was destroyed by Hunac Ceel of Mayapán. See *El libro de los libros de Chilam Balam,* trans. Alfredo Barrera Vásquez and Silvia Rendón (Mexico City: Fondo de Cultura Económica, 1963), 35–40.

19. In "Traditions of Caste," 193, Roys suggests that the Xiu were of Nahua origin. According to Indian traditions they came from Tulapan Chiconautla, from which they departed under the leadership of Holon Chan Tepeu; they wandered for eighty years until settling somewhere to the west of Suyuá (either Xicalango, or in all likelihood, a mythic locale) around 849. There they remained until sometime between 928 and 948, when they began their march to Chacnobitón, where they arrived 81 years later, led by Ah Mekat Tutul Xiu. They remained there for almost a century, until sometime between 1086 and 1106.

Juan de Torquemada reports the following concerning the Cocom: "It was said that this [Kukulkán], that the kings of Yucatán descended from him; they were called Cocomes, which means 'oidores.'" See Torquemada, *De los veinte y un libros rituales y monarquía indiana, con el origen y guerra de los indios occidentales, de sus poblazones, descubrimiento, conquista, comercio y otras cosas maravillosas de la misma tierra,* 7 vols. (Mexico City: Universidad Nacional Autónoma de México, 1975–1983), 3:87.

20. Martin and Grube, *Chronicle of the Maya Kings and Queens,* 20, states, "Political expansion, where it occurred, was not an acquisition of territory per se, but rather an extension of these elite networks. The most powerful dynasties brought rival 'divine lords' under their domination, with ties often reaching far outside their immediate region. The bonds between lords and their masters were highly personal and remained in effect even after the death of one party." T. Patrick Culbert is of the opinion that armed warfare among the Maya was "driven by goals of economic and territorial conquest." See Culbert, "La guerra y el estado segmentario," in *La guerra entre los antiguos mayas: Memoria de la primera mesa redonda de Palenque,* ed. Silvia Trejo (Mexico City: Instituto Nacional de Antropología e Historia, 2000), 44.

In Barrera Vásquez and Morley, "The Maya Chronicles," 34, we read that the halach uinicob of Uxmal, Chichén Itzá, and Mayapán reigned between 987 and 1185. Roys, *The Indian Background,* 129, literally translated "halach uinic" as "true man." In this book I have adopted the term "overlord" to designate this personage. In this regard, see "Proceso contra los indios idólatras de Sotuta, Kanchunup, Mopilá, Sahcabá, Yaxcabá, Usil and Tibolón (agosto de 1562)," in *DDQAMY* 1:107.

21. For a discussion of the bellicose spirit and military order that arose during Chichén Itzá's hegemony, see the analysis of Roys, "Toltec Military Orders in Yucatan," in *The Book of Chilam Balam of Chumayel,* 196–200.

22. *RHGY* contains countless references to the fact that Chichén Itzá's power reached all the way to Mexico, Guatemala, and Chiapas; see "Relación de Izamal,"

1:305; "Relación de Kizil," 1:200; and "Relación de Tekantó," 1:216, among others. Fernando Robles Castellanos and Anthony P. Andrews argue that archaeological evidence, contrary to historical sources, suggests that Chichén's influence was more limited, since in his conquests the halach uinic of Chichén Itzá met resistance and was incapable of imposing his jurisdiction on the lords situated between Yaxuná and Cobá. See Robles Castellanos and Andrews, "A Review and Synthesis of Recent Postclassic Archaeology in Northern Yucatán," in *Late Lowland Maya Civilization: Classic to Postclassic*, ed. Jeremy A. Sablof and E. Wyllys Andrews (Albuquerque: University of New Mexico Press, 1986), 84–86.

23. Rafael Cobos states: "the tenth century AD marked the expansion of Chichén Itzá in northern Yucatán when it arose as a regional capital. This regional capital controlled small cities located at its periphery, secured an area between the north coast and central Yucatán, established and controlled its own trade port in the northern coast, and expanded its realm along the eastern and western coasts of the Yucatán peninsula." See Cobos, "Chichen Itzá: Settlement and Hegemony During the Terminal Classic Period," in *The Terminal Classic in the Maya Lowlands: Collapse, Transition, and Transformation*, ed. Arthur A. Demarest, Prudence M. Rice, and Don S. Rice (Boulder: University Press of Colorado, 2004), 531–33.

24. In Maya, ah tepal translates as "lord or sovereign; it was used to refer to kings or lords, and even more appropriately to God. It denotes majesty"; see Ciudad Real, *Calepino maya*, 56. The term is actually a Maya-Nahuatl hybrid. *Ah* expressed the idea of superiority, while in Nahuatl, *tepeua* means "to conquer"; see Barrera Vásquez y Rendón, *El libro de los libros*, 154 (note 1). In Maya, *tepeual* or *tepual* means "to reign." In this same language, *tepal* can be used to indicate "to reign," "to order while reigning," "to be lord," and also the "reign," "command," and "these lordship"; see Ciudad Real, *Calepino maya*, 541.

Numerous references attest to Chichén Itzá as the seat of a centralized power. Operating from the perspective of territorially based power, the Spanish reported that during the hegemony of Chichén Itzá, "all the land was under the dominion of one lord"; see "Relación de Izamal, in *RHGY* 1:305; "Relación de Kizil," 1:200; and "Relación de Tekantó," 1:216.

25. "The Chronicle of Chac-Xulub-Chen," in *Maya Chronicles*, ed. Daniel G. Brinton (Philadelphia: D. G Brinton, 1882), 210.

26. Andrews, "The Fall of Chichén Itzá," 260, working from epigraphic evidence, indicates that a new power structure arose in that city, one characterized by an inclusive ruling class, possibly under the control of a group of governors. This resulted in the rise of a complex new political entity to state power.

27. Michael D. Coe, *The Maya* (New York: Praeger Publishers, 1966), 123, indicates that the political and religious elite were incorporated into the new power structure.

28. Abundant references attest to the fact that all the lords of Yucatán were tributaries and that the lords of Mexico, Guatemala, Chiapas, and other "provinces"

sent presents as a sign of peace and friendship. See "Relación de Izamal," in *RHGY* 1:305; "Relación de Kizil," 1:200; and "Relación de Tekantó," 1:216.

29. Robles Castellanos and Andrews, "A Review and Synthesis," 88.

30. Chichén Itzá's most representative deity was Kukulkán. We also find essentially Mexican gods such as Tezcatlipoca, Tláloc, Chicomecóatl, y Tlalchitonatiuh; see Muriel Weaver, *The Aztecs, Maya and Their Predecessors*, 2nd ed. (New York: Academics Press, 1981), 397.

31. "Relación de Citilcum," in *RHGY* 1:182.

32. The religious influence of Kukulkán was of such a magnitude that even after Mayapán's fall in the mid-fifteenth century, festivities in the month of *xul* were still conducted in honor of that deity. William M. Ringle, "On the Political Organization of Chichen Itza," *Ancient Mesoamerica* 15, no. 2 (2004): 1–5, 7–10, 47–48, argues that in Chichén Itzá the cult of Quetzalcóatl, known in Yucatán as Kukulcán, encompassed beliefs, imagery, and practices tightly linked to an ideology of leadership. A detailed analysis of the architectural and iconographic evidence suggests that the Great Ball Court in particular served as a space where the ruling elites were invested with political power through rituals with pronounced military overtones. "Initiates" assumed Kukulcán's persona in a symbolic ceremony in which the main administrators participated in order to establish a broad, flexible network of political ties. The primary source on this matter is Diego de Landa, *Relación de las cosas de Yucatán*, 10th ed. (Mexico City: Editorial Porrúa, 1973), 98.

33. Roys, "The Hunac Ceel Episode," in *The Book of Chilam Balam of Chumayel*, 177–181. Recent archaeological research suggests that Chichén Itzá began its decline in the late tenth or early eleventh century, in conjunction with the rise of Mayapán; and that while monumental construction and other elite activities ceased, the Itzá probably continued to wield considerable economic and political influence for some years more. See Anthony P. Andrews, E. Wyllys Andrews, and Fernando Robles Castellanos, "The Northern Maya Collapse and its Aftermath," *Ancient Mesoamerica* 14, no. 1 (2003): 151–52.

34. Ralph L. Roys, "Literary Sources for the History of Mayapán," in *Mayapán, Yucatan, Mexico*, ed. H. E. D. Pollock (Washington DC: Carnegie Institute of Washington, 1962), 32–37; Landa, *Relación*, 18; "Probanza del capitán don Juan Chan, cacique y señor natural de los pueblos de Chancenote y sus sujetos" (1622), in AGI, *Audiencia de México*, legajo 140, ramo 2, f. 3v. In Barrera Vásque and Morley, "The Maya Chronicles," 38, the term "multepal" appears in association with Mayapán. And just like the ah tepal, it is a hybrid term composed of two morphemes. The first is *mul*, which means various things in Maya, the most notable of which is, "to do something as a community or as common labor, even if only two people." See Ciudad Real, *Calepino maya*, 415. Concerning the definition of tepal, see note 24 above. Multepal can thus be interpreted as to rule jointly or to govern collectively.

35. David Freidel suggests that the power and superiority of the Cocom were limited, and based on the good will of their vassals. See Freidel, "Lowland Maya Political Economy: Historical and Archaeology Perspectivas in Lights of Intensive Agriculture," in *Spaniards and Indians in Southeastern Mesoamerica: Essays on the History of Ethnic Relations*, ed. Murdo J. Macleod and Robert Wasserstrom (Lincoln: University of New Mexico Press, 1983), 47.

36. Roys, "Literary Sources," 32–37.

37. Tatiana Proskouriakoff, "Mayapán: The Last Stronghold of a Civilization," *Archaeology* 7, no. 2 (1954): 98.

38. Bryan M. Carlo argues that in Yucatec Maya society in the Late Postclassic period, the prominent lineages used two different forms of corporate government. The first was what Carlo refers to as the "brother strategy" of governance, in which the lords on the council of ruling elites belonged to a single lineage entailing concepts of dual rulership. The second variety was the multepal; as described by Ralph L. Roys, it consisted of "joint rule" or "joint governance," and is best characterized as a confederation of territorial lords governing jointly through a particular polity. See Carlo, "Political Decentralization in the Maya Lowlands: An Examination of the Origins of Multepal or Joint Governance" (thesis, Southern Illinois University Carbondale, 2006), 118–22, 169–74. Conversely, William M. Ringle and George J. Bey III distance themselves from Roys's definition of the multepal, and instead suggest that it was a type of court composed of powerful "vassals"—warlords—who, while recognizing a supreme ruler, nonetheless retained numerous rights and prerogatives. See Ringle and Bey, "Post-Classic and Terminal Classic Courts of the Northern Maya Lowlands," in *Royal Courts of the Ancient Maya: Data and Case Studies*, ed. Takeshi Inomata and Stephen D. Houston (Boulder: Westview Press, 2001), 2:273–75.

39. Landa, *Relación*, 13, indicates that since the fall of the ah tepal, the overlords divided up "the pueblos, giving to each one according to his personal importance and the antiquity of his lineage."

40. In Ciudad Real, *Calepino maya*, 80, the word "batab" is translated as "cacique." However, in Landa, *Relación*, and both volumes of *RHGY* contain innumerable references to the ways in which Spaniards used these terms. One conquistador wrote, "They have lords and those who they so recognize are called *batabes*, which is the same as lords." See "Relación de Sinanché," in *RHGY* 1:123.

41. Farriss, *Maya Society*, 73–74, states that "Such movements were long-established Maya habit dating from well before the Spanish conquest, which itself displaced many people. Native chronicles and oral traditions record a number of pre-Columbian migrations within region."

42. Almost nothing is known of the multepal's structure. The clearest feature is that each halach uinic appointed a functionary known as the *caluac* to collect tributes. Landa, *Relación de las cosas de Yucatán*, 14, states that "as a symbol they carried a short, stout cane . . . and this mayordomo kept accounts on the villages

and the individuals who governed them, and these same mayordomos received notice of what was lacking in the lord's house, be it fowl, corn, honey, salt, fish, game, clothing, or other items."

43. Landa, *Relación*, 17.

44. Lisa Lucero, *Water and Ritual: The Rise and Fall of Classic Maya Rulers* (Austin: University of Texas Press, 2006), 34–37, notes that during the late Classic period the vast majority of farmers lived near fertile lands in family units composed of residences sharing a common patio. These residences were to be found dispersed through the territory, and even in zones adjacent to political-administrative centers. Lucero also points out that many farmers resided far from their homes during the agricultural season, and that they relocated to ever greater distances in search of new and cultivable lands, according to the pressures of population growth and increasing competition for resources.

45. See "Relación de la ciudad de Mérida," in *RHGY* 1:71. Cristóbal Sánchez states, "The villages of Tekantó and Tepakan . . . consist of seven or eight villages and at present all these villages are gathered into the aforementioned two." See "Relación de Tekantó," in *RHGY* 1:213.

46. Alonso Julián, encomendero of Sal, stated that the Indians lived "in a land that was leve but rocky, deep in the surrounding monte." See "Relación e Titzal," *RHGY* 1:238.

47. Roys, *The Titles of Ebtun; RHGY* vols. 1 and 2; and Tsubasa Okoshi Harada, *Códice de Calkiní* (Mexico City: Universidad Nacional Autónoma de México, 2009), among others, are sources that offer a huge number of toponyms for places where residential clusters were located. It is a mistake to characterize this clusters as cuchteelob or barrios, as Roys did, since as discussed in the first section of this chapter, Maya texts never associate the word "cuchteel" with a toponym, but rather with a lord.

48. Friar Lorenzo de Bienvenida stated that each household included a father who was the head of family; see Bienvenida's letter (February 10, 1548), in *Cartas de Indias* (Madrid: Imprenta de Manuel G. Hernández, 1877), 1: 74, 78. Ralph L. Roys, et al, state that the family head was called the *ah cuch nal*; see Roys, France V. Scholes, and Eleanor B. Adams, "Census and Inspection of the Town of Pencuyut, Yucatan, in 1583 by Diego García de Palacio, oidor of the Audiencia of Guatemala," *Ethnohistory* 6, no. 3 (1959): 195–225.

49. See the letter of friar Lorenzo de Bienvenida (February 10, 1548), in *Cartas de Indias*, 1:74. Censuses from the sixteenth century to the present day confirm Bienvenida. On this same point, see Inés Ortiz Yam and Sergio Quezada, *Visita de Diego García de Palacio a Yucatán, 1583* (Mexico City: Universidad Nacional Autónoma de México, 2007), 47–50, 86–88, 90–94, 96–98, 100–102, 199–203, 225–27; and Ralph L. Roys, France V. Scholes, and Eleanor B. Adams, "Report and Census of the Indians of Cozumel, 1570," in *Contribution to American Anthropology and History* 30 (1940),:18–21.

50. William A. Haviland, "Ancient Lowland Maya Social Organization," *Archaeological Studies in Middle America* (New Orleans: Middle American Research Institute, 1970), 103; Landa, *Relación*, 19.

51. Richard Pipes advances a clear and precise explanation regarding the difference between possession and property. See Pipes, *Propiedad y libertad: Dos conceptos inseparables de la historia*, (México City: Fondo de Cultura Económica, 2002), 19–20. The testaments from the community of Ixil make it clear that one family group's rights to the monte ended where those of another such group began. The testament of Juan de la Cruz Cobá provides a good example. He left his son a monte that bordered on the south with that of Agustín Aké, on the north with that of Juan Matú, and on the east with the lands of Nicolás Cobá. See "Will of Juan de la Cruz Coba (November 12, 1766)," in Matthew Restall, *Life and Death in a Maya Community: The Ixil Testaments of the 1760s* (Lancaster: Labyrinthos, 1995), 109. For this reason Restall observes that the Ixil testaments make no reference to land measurements. See Restall, *The Maya World. Yucatec Culture and Society, 1550–1850* (Stanford: Stanford University Press, 1997), 193–94.

52. See Roys, *The Titles of Ebtun; RHGY* vols. 1 and 2; and Okoshi Harada, *Códice de Calkiní*, among others.

53. Inés Ortiz Yam, "Los montes yucatecos: La percepción de un espacio en las fuentes coloniales," in *Text and Context: Yucatec Maya Literature in a Diachronic Perspective*, ed. Antje Gunsenheimer, Tsubasa Okoshi Harada, and John F. Chuchiak (Aachen: Bonn Americanist Studies, 2009), 188.

54. In the mental world of the Yucatec Maya, the concept of "monte" entails three elements. The first is the totality of available resources (land, trees, cenotes, stones, animals, and so forth). The second is the immediate cosmos (climate cycles, lunar phases, winds, and the mysteries of the caves). The third element consists of the numerous sounds, both natural (animals, winds) and inexplicable that the Indian perceives in his daily travels through the monte. See Jorge Flores Torres, *Los mayas yucatecos y el control cultural: Etnotecnología, mayaeconomía y pensamiento político de los pueblos centro-orientales de Yucatán* (Mexico City: Universidad Autónoma de Chapingo, and Universidad Autónoma de Yucatán, 1997), 52–56; Alejandra García Quintanilla, "El dilema del *ah kimsah k'ax*, 'el que mata al monte': Significados del monte entre los mayas milperos de Yucatán," *Mesoamérica* 39 (2000): 282–85. The Spanish vision of the Yucatecan milpa was simplistic. Landa, *Relación*, 40, reports: "In working the land they did nothing more than collect the bramble and burn it before planting." In general, when speaking of milpa one thinks of the act of planting corn, beans, chile, squash, and cotton, and like Landa, of the minimum human energy necessary to carry it out. Juan de Magaña, encomendero of Sotuta, remarked, "The grain currently used for producing bread throughout this entire country is corn, and it is possible to produce a great deal with little effort. . . . They also produce beans, chile, and cotton . . . and all of this costs them scant labor, since they do not plow the

earth nor dig in it; nor could they if they wanted to, since this entire land is one monstrous rock." See "Relación de Sotuta," in *RHGY* 1:148. Other entries in the two volumes of *RHGY* support this opinion.

55. In the same fashion, the Maya developed an extensive knowledge about varieties of corn. *Peeu* was "small yellow corn that matures in forty days and quite early." *Kan kan nal* and *mehen chac chob* "were strains of corn that grew and ripened in ninety days." *Zac ixim* was "corn with large white kernels that grows in six months." See Ciudad Real, *Calepino maya*, 133, 491; Cristina Alvarez, *Diccionario etnolingüístico del idioma maya yucateco colonial* (Mexico City: Universidad Nacional Autónoma de México, 1980–1994), 1:224.

56. Alfonso Villa Rojas, *The Maya of East Central Quintana Roo* (Washington DC: Carnegie Institution of Washington, 1943), 111–12, writes that:

> When the milpero chooses a portion of the virgin bush for his milpa, he contracts his first obligation to the gods. On the land selected he must set up a small cross and place before it three or five gourds of zaca [corn gruel]. Then, in shouts loud and prolonged, so that they will be heard over the entire tract to be cultivated, he invites the yuntzilob [field gods] to come and receive the offering. In this way he informs the kuil-kaaxs, or guardians of the bush, that the land is about to be occupied by one who is their friend, so that they will immediately drive out all snakes and other harmful animals and see that the trees about to be felled will put up no resistance and do no harm to the milpero. . . . The next rite . . . is to ask the Cichcelem Yum [roughly, God the Son] to send the whirlwind, kakal-mozon-ik, to fan the flames so that they will run over the whole breadth of the milpa. The help of this wind is very important, for without it the milpa will burn badly and therefore be difficult to plant. When the wind is weak, or delayed in arriving the milpero calls to it with a whistle similar to the one used by the Maya of Chan Kom. . . . The sowing also is accompanied by ritual acts, performed by the milpero in his milpa without the participation of the h-men [modern Maya priest, literally, "he who does"]. The offerings are placed on a small altar, erected on the east side of the field. Seven dishes of zaca, on this occasion sweetened with honey, must be offered on each of the first seven days of the sowing. . . . The offering is commonly referred to as u-hanli-chaacob (the dinner of the rain gods).

57. Landa, *Relación*, 40, states, "They plant in many places, so that if one planting fails, another can compensate." We find abundant references to the same point in both volumes of *RHGY*.

58. Landa, *Relación*, 35, 40, 57. Indigenous society made use of various terms to capture the idea of cooperation. As stated in Alfredo Barrera Vásquez, et al., *Diccionario Maya Cordemex* (Mérida: Ediciones Cordemex, 1980), 539, "*Mul cabtah*: to work as a community, or everyone united in the same task, helping one

another; *mul mentah*: to make something communally or among many; *mul menyah*: community labor." Numerous references to the same phenomenon exist in sixeenth-century sources. See "Relación de Hocabá," in *RHGY* 1:135; "Relación de Sotuta," in *RHGY* 1:148–49. Isaura Inés Ortiz Yam, "Los pueblos del noroeste yucateco hacia 1580" (thesis, Universidad Autónoma de Yucatán, 1998), 81–88, offers a new analysis of *mulmenyah*.

59. Landa, *Relación*, 40.
60. Ibid., 57.
61. "Relación de Muxupip," in *RHGY*:381; "Relación de Chahuac-ha," in *RHGY* 2:246.
62. Regarding dogs, Landa, *Relación*, 39, mentions that, "they do not know how to bark or to do harm to men, and in the hunt they are known for pursuing quails and other birds. They follow the deer tirelessly, and some are superb trackers."
63. The Maya language contains other terms for the same process. Ciudad Real, *Calepino maya*, 403, states, "*Max*: an Indian woman divides her tufts of cotton among many other women, giving each one half an arm's length, in order that they spin it, and when that is done, she joins with other women in spinning someone else's cotton, and then the cotton of yet another, until all have worked their way through the wheel. *Max lam kuch*: to divide cotton to be spun among many women, and afterwards the cotton of another, until all have passed through the wheel."
64. Although definitive evidence is lacking, we can assume the possibility that in some cases blood relatives were vassals of different lords.
65. In Roys, *The Titles of Ebtun*, 73–80, we find various examples of the existence of groups of family chiefs recognizing different batabob. For additional evidence, see Okoshi Harada, "Los canules," 75–85; see also, Barrera Vásquez, *Documento núm. 1*, 17–18.
66. Barrera Vásquez, et al., *Diccionario Maya*, 40, states, "*batabil winik*: Indian cacique who comes from high social rank; *batabil winik talki u chibal Juan*: the indigenous cacique Juan who derives from a lineage."
67. In Barrera Vásquez, *Documento núm. 1*, 17, states, "*Cu yahaulil [Macan Pech] ti batabil*," which Barrera Vásquez translates in the following manner: "[Macan Pech] governed in his 'batabilado.'" Although he consciously hispanicizes the term "batabil" since he was unable to find a term that expressed its precise content, he proposed that the idiomatic rendering of the sentence should be: "[Macan Pech] reigned as batab," that is, in his capacity as lord. Considerable evidence on this point is to be found in *RHGY* vols. 1 and 2. See also, Ciudad Real, *Calepino maya*, 80; and *Diccionario de las autoridades*, 1:38.
68. Landa, *Relación*, 35, 40.
69. Writing from an archaeological perspective, Diane Z. Chase questions those models that posit a terminal post-Classic indigenous society divided exclusively between "nobles" and "plebians." Instead, she proposes the existence of another social group made up of *acmen uinic*, that is, of people of intermediate

social status. See Chase, "Postclassic Maya Elites: Ethnohistory and Archaeology," in *Mesoamerican Elites: An Archaeological Assessment*, ed. Diana Z. Chase and Arlen F. Chase (Norman: University of Oklahoma Press, 1992), 120–21, 131–34. If indeed this idea is correct, it is it is necessary to warn that with the exception of Ciudad Real, *Calepino maya*, 31, early colonial Maya documents contain no evidence that Maya scribes employed this term. Nor did they use the term *yalba uinic* to refer to indigenous plebians or commoners (excepting, once again, Ciudad Real, *Calepino maya*, 287). Put another way, whether or not the terms "acmen uinic" and "yalba uinic" designated two specific social categories is something that should be settled with concrete evidence and not simply assumed on the basis of those terms' existence.

70. "Relación de Sinanché," in *RHGY* 1:123. In regard to his functions, the ah cuch cab can be compared to the Mexica *calpizque* and with the Tarascan *ocámbecha*. The former possessed such obligations as collecting tribute and organizing his barrio's labor force for projects of public construction. See Alfredo López Austin, *Tarascos y mexicas* (Mexico City: Secretaría de Educación Pública, 1981), 123; see also, Pedro Carrasco, "Economía política en el reino tarasco," in *La sociedad indígena en el centro y occidente de México*. ed. Pedro Carrasco (Mexico City: El Colegio de Michoacán, 1986), 76.

71. All evidence seems to suggest that in the cúuchcabalob of Hocabá, Sotuta, and Calotmul, the holpop was what gave the señorío its cohesion. Melchor Pacheco, one of the most famous of the conquistadors, declared that the halach uinic of Hocabá "ruled and governed his people . . . with his caciques, whom were called *holpop*." Juan de Magaña writes in this same tenor regarding Nachí Cocom, the halach uinic of Sotuta when he states, "In olden times they were governed by their caciques, whom they called *holpop*." See "Relación de Hocabá," in *RHGY* 1:134; and "Relación de Sotuta," in *RHGY* 1:146. Regarding the cúuchcabal of Calotmul, see "Relación de Tahdziú," in *RHGY* 1:390.

72. Landa, *Relación*, 34–35.

73. Concerning the *levas*, or military conscriptions, see "Relación de Hocabá," in *RHGY* 1:133; and "Relación de Sotuta," in *RHGY* 1:146.

74. "Relación de Motul," in *RHGY* 1:269.

75. "Relación de Tekantó," in *RHGY* 1:216; "Relación de Dzan," in *RHGY* 1:252; "Relación de Izamal," in *RHGY* 1:306. Additional references on this same point occur throughout both volumes of the same source.

76. John V. Murra offers a broad explanation of labor organization in the peasant community, and of community obligations to the *curaca* (cacique). See Murra, *La organización económica del estado inca* (Mexico City: Siglo XXI Editores, 1980). A comparative reading of this work alongside evidence from sixteenth-century Yucatán helps us to understand labor arrangements and responsibilities for Maya peoples in the period immediately following the Spanish invasion.

77. In 1584 Gonzalo Chuil stated that "to the caciques of the villages here in the seat of Tezemi they maintain a milpa for each one through communal effort

... and the communities always construct the caciques' homes cooperatively, as well as the homes of the principales ... and they assist one another." See Ortiz Yam and Quezada, *Visita de Diego García*, 122.

78. Tsubasa Okoshi Harada, "Tenencia de la tierra y territorialidad: conceptualización de los mayas yucatecos en vísperas de la invasión española," in *Conquista, transculturación y mestizaje: raíz y origen de México*, ed. Lorenzo Ochoa (Mexico City: Universidad Nacional Autónoma de México, 1995), 86–88.

79. See the letter from friar Francisco de Toral, Bishop of Yucatán, to Felipe II (Mérida, 1 March 1563), *DDQAMY*, 2:39. According to friar Gerónimo de Mendieta, *Historia eclesiástica indiana* (Mexico City: Editorial Salvador Chávez Hayhoe, 1945), 4: 157, 168, Bishop Toral was "the first to evangelize the Popoluca nation" and "the first to learn the Popoluca language ... and also the Mexican [i.e., Nahuatl] and to work in both tongues ... in the province and region of Tecamachalco." Eustaquio Celestino Solís and Luis Reyes García, *Anales de Tecamachalco, 1398–1590* (Mexico City: Centro de Investigaciones y Estudios Superiores en Antropología Social, and Fondo de Cultura Económica, and Gobierno de Estado de Puebla, 1992), reports that Toral lived in that area between 1543 and 1561, at which point he was named Bishop of Yucatán. Seen thus, Toral's observation carries much weight, since he knew the system of property and land rental in Tecamachalco.

80. Unless otherwise indicated, material for this section is drawn from appendices A and B.

81. Frances V. Scholes and Ralph L. Roys, *The Maya Chontal Indians of Acalan-Tixchel: A Contribution to the History and Ethnography of the Yucatan Peninsula* (Norman: University of Oklahoma Press, 1968), 67–73; Alfonso Villa Rojas,"Los quejaches: tribu olvidada del antiguo Yucatán," in *Estudios etnológicos: Los mayas*, ed. Alfonso Villa Rojas (Mexico City: Universidad Nacional Autónoma de México, 1985, 447–63); and Grant D. Jones, *Maya Resistance to Spanish Rule: Time and History on a Colonial Frontier* (Albuquerque: University of New Mexico, Press, 1989), 98.

82. Okoshi Harada, *Códice de Calkiní*, 36.

83. Sergio Quezada, "El linaje Xiu," in *Dos décadas de investigación en historia económica comparada en América Latina: Homenaje a Carlos Sempat Assadourian*, ed. Margarita Menegus Bornemann (Mexico City: El Colegio de México, and Centro de Investigaciones y Estudios Superiores en Antropología Social, and Instituto Doctor José María Luis Mora, and Centro de Estudios sobre la Universidad, and Universidad Nacional Autónoma de México, 1999), 113–14.

84. "Relación de Popolá," in *RHGY* 2:215–216; "Relación de Ekbalam," in *RHGY* 2:139; "Relación de Sodzil," in *RHGY* 2:125–126; and "Relación de Dzitnup," in *RHGY* 2:60.

85. Landa, *Relación*, 18.

86. "Probanza del capitán don Juan Chan. ..." (1622), in AGI, Audiencia de México, legajo 140, ramo 2.

87. "Relación de Motul," in *RHGY* 1:269; "Relación de Tekit," in *RHGY* 1:285.

88. Tsubasa Okoshi Harada was the first Mayanist to realize that the term "cúuchcabal" always seems to be associated with a historic place name in the period following the fall of Mayapán. See Okoshi Herada, "Kokotenki Kokishumatzu no mayahokubuteichi no ryoikikozo," *Revista Histórica de la Universidad de Gakushuin* 23 (1985): 26–44.

89. Ciudad Real, *Calepino maya*, 94.

90. Okoshi Harada, "Los canules," 252–55, offers an extensive discussion of the Maya concept of "pueblo."

91. Maya peoples tend toward concrete and descriptive terms, not abstract concepts; that is, they could not speak of a cúuchcabal without refering to a specific case. Put otherwise, this word meant nothing when not accompanied by a noun, and in this case a place name. "Al" is the equivalent of the Spanish preposition "de" ("of," in English). Thus, "u cúuchcabal Maní" translates as "the cúuchcabal of Maní." Personal communication of Tsubasa Okoshi Harada, December 5, 2007.

92. In Ciudad Real, *Calepino maya*, 123, "cúuchcabal" means "land, region, partido, or visita subject to some cabecera, or region. Thus, '"U cúuchcabal Maní, Mutul' means the province or region of Maní, Motul.'"

93. "Relación de Hocabá," in *RHGY* 1:133; "Relación de Sotuta," in *RHGY* 1:146; "Relación de Tabi," in *RHGY* 1:165.

94. Landa, *Relación*, 19–20; Barrera Vásquez y Rendón, *El libro de los libros*, 41.

95. William Gates, trans., *Yucatan Before and After the Conquest by Friar Diego de Landa* (New York: Dover Publications, 1978), 122.

96. We do not know to which lineages the lords of Suyuá and Tabi, the other señoríos of the cúuchcabal of Sotuta, belonged.

97. Appendices A and B of this text explore the cases of Nacahum Cochua and Nadzul Iuit, respectively halach uinicob of Tihosuco and Hocabá.

98. Landa, *Relación*, 98; "Relación de la villa de Valladolid," in *RHGY* 2: 29, 35.

99. "These Indians also had another individual whom they obeyed, a kind of priest who in their language is called *ah kin*. He informed them of the time in which they should plant . . . and they asked him . . . if they were going to have a good year and if it would rain . . . and in the regions where they governed, these same ah kines had books with drawings that indicated the best times for planting and harvesting, and also for hunting." See "Relación de Dzonot," in *RHGY* 2:86.

100. It is important to explain that this list is based on the names of the capitals, and ignores the association that first the Spaniards and later, researchers themselves, made with the word "provincia."

101. Juan de Urrutia reported that his encomiendas, Chauac-há and Chancenote, were cabeceras de provincia; see "Relación de Chauac-há," in *RHGY* 2: 245, 249.

102. In Ciudad Real, *Calepino maya*, 123, we read, "u cúuchcabal Maní, Mutul; la provincia o comarca de Maní, Motul."

103. Okoshi Harada, *Códice de Calkiní*, 63, mentions "tu cuchcabal San Luis Calkiní."

104. According to Antonio Méndez, encomendero of Tihosuco, "a cacique named Nacahum Cochuah ruled this province in the days of the heathens, and his residence and seat of authority was in Tihosuco"; see "Relación de Tihosuco," in *RHGY* 2:198.

105. The encomendero Diego de Sarmiento de Figueroa said that Popolá had thirteen dependent villages, and that when the Spanish arrived in Yucatán, these same villages were ruled by Nadzul Cupul; see "Relación de Popolá," in *RHGY* 2:215–16.

106. Juan Farfán, encomendero of Kanpocolché, claimed that he had taken part in the conquest of the Uaymiles "which is otherwise known as the province of Chetumal." See "Relación de Kanpocolché," in *RHGY* 2:320.

107. The "Crónica de Yaxkukul" refers to the "cúuchcabal Sací" and the "cúuchcabal Chichén Itzae," which Juan Martínez Hernández respectively translates as "the partido of Valladolid' and "the province of Chichén Itzá"; see Martínez Hernández "Crónica de Yaxkukul," in *Crónicas mayas*, ed. Juan Martínez Hernández (Mérida: Talleres de la Compañía Tipográfica Yucateca, 1926), 21, 26. See also, "Relación de Ichmul," in *RHGY* 2:296.

108. Juan Gutiérrez Picón stated that, "this Cupul was lord of Ekbalam for a long time. He ruled and dispensed justice in his province, and was known as its lord." See "Relación de Ekbalam," in *RHGY* 2:139.

109. In *RHGY* vol. 1 and *DDQAMY* vol. 1 we find innumerable references to Maní, Hocabá, Sotuta, and Dzidzantún as political centers where a halach uinic resided.

110. Gonzalo Fernández de Oviedo y Valdés reports that when Juan de Grijalva reached the island of Cozumel, "he had the interpreter tell [the Indians] that he wanted . . . to speak with the cacique . . . and they replied that they would be happy to arrange it, and that the *calachuni* [halach uinic], that is to say, the king or cacique, would be delighted to receive them." See Fernández de Oviedo, *Historia general y natural de las Indias, Islas y Tierra Firme del mar océano* (Madrid: Ediciones Atlas, 1959), vol. 2, chap. 121. Regarding Can Pech, Oviedo (2:126) recounts that when Grijalva reached that port, he sought water from its "*calachuni*, for as I have said this is how they call their cacique or main lord."

111. Roys, *The Political Geography*, 77, supposes that Calotmul was a dependent pueblo of the cúuchcabal of Maní. Quite possibly he reached this conclusion since at the time of Spanish arrival

Calotmul was ruled Ah Kukul Xiu. Spaniards thus referred to the area as the province of Calatamud; see "Residencia de Diego de Quijada" (1565), in AGI, Justicia, legajo 245, ff. 1112v–43v, where an account of his señoríos appear.

112. Ciudad Real, *Calepino maya*, 63.

113. Tsubasa Okoshi Harada, "Mito, historia y legitimación del poder entre los mayas posclásicos de Yucatán," in *Yucatán a través de los siglos* ed. Ruth

Gubler and Patric Martell (Mérida: Universidad Autónoma de Yucatán, 2001), 213–19.

114. Okoshi Harada, "Mito, historia y legitimación," 221, 224–25.

115. Tsubasa Okoshi Harada, "La historia de los Cocom: Una lectura de la *Relación* de fray Diego de Landa," in *Texto y contexto. La literatura maya yucateca en perspectiva diacrónica*, ed. Antje Gusenheimer, Tsubasa Okoshi Harada, and John F. Chuchiak IV (Bonn: Estudios Americanistas de Bonn, 2009), 147–53.

116. Landa, *Relación*, 18–19.

117. "Relación de Tiab," in *RHGY* 1:318; "Relación de Izamal," in *RHGY*, 1:305. All this appears to indicate that as in the center of Mexico, it is only possible to speak of lineages among the Maya nobility, not the commoners; see Pedro Carrasco, "Los linajes nobles del México antiguo," in *Estratificación social en la mesoamerica preshispánica*, ed. Pedro Carrasco and Johanna Broda (Mexico City: Centro de Investigaciones Superiores del Instituto Nacional del Antropología e Historia, 1976), 20.

118. "Probanza de don Juan Kauil (1618)," in *The Maya Chronicles* ed. Daniel G. Brinton (Philadelphia: D. G. Brinton, 1882), 114–16.

119. Landa, *Relación*, 41.

120. For Robert M. Carmack, Suyuá is Xicalango; see *The Quiché Mayas of Utatlán: The Evolution of a Highland Guatemala Kingdom* (Norman: University of Oklahoma Press, 1981), 46. However, in this context said toponym seems to indicate a mythical location. In the same vein, it is worth noting that the origin point of the Canul is also identified as being the west of Suyuá; see Okoshi Harada, "Los canules," 158–59.

121. *Códice Pérez*, trans. Ermilo Solís Alcalá (Mérida: Liga de Acción Social, 1949), 264–67; Barrera Vásquez y Morley, "The Maya Chronicles," 27.

122. Landa, *Relación*, 16. A traditional narrative recorded by Juan Bote states: "it is said that the first of them [i.e., the Tutul Xiu] was called Hunuuikil Chac [Hun Uitzil Chac], lord of Uxmal, a very ancient city and blessed with lovely buildings." See "Relación de Tiab y Tiek," in *RHGY* 1:319.

123. For a more detailed examination of this individual, see Sergio Quezada and Tsubasa Okoshi Harada, *Papeles de los Xiu de Yaxá* (Mexico City: Universidad Nacional Autónoma de México, 2001), 21–27.

124. "Relación de Teab," in *RHGY* 1:319.

125. "Probanza de don Juan Kauil (1618)," 114–116.

126. "Relación de Motul," in *RHGY* 1:269.

127. Landa, *Relación*, 35. See also, Quezada and Okoshi Harada, *Papeles de los Xiu*, 55.

128. See Ciudad Real, *Calepino maya*, 205. Spaniards used the term "principal" in reference to Indian nobility. Nevertheless, the nobles preferred the term "almehen" when speaking of themselves.

129. For a broad discussion of the origin of Suyuá, its philological significance, and its use among the indigenous nobility, see Argelia Segovia Liga,

"Los indios de Mariscal: Revision de un manuscrito yucateco del siglo XVII" (thesis, Universidad Nacional Autónoma de México, 2008), 24–29.

130. One example states, "Go to join for me the mats from the bottom of the cenotes, two white ones and two yellow ones, for I want to eat them." In the coded language of Suyuá, the "mats of the cenotes" thus requested are jícamas, two white and two yellow. See Barrera Vásquez y Rendón, *El libro de los libros*, 132–34; see also, Roys, *The Book of Chilam Balam*, 88–98.

131. The well known Xiu genealogical tree is an example of the lineage as both parental institution and political group. Frans Blom presents a detailed analysis of of the family ties and the responsibilities they entailed; see Blom, "Gaspar Antonio Chi, Interpreter," *American Anthropologist* 28, no. 2 (1928): 255–57. Another example concerns the Iuit. Don Francisco Namon Iuit, possibly the son of Nadzul Iuit, was the halach uinic of Hocabá, and his brothers served as rulers of Hoctún, Huhí, and Tiscanbanchel; see Roys, *The Political Geography*, 58, 60. In reference to the pueblos governed by the Chel lineage, Cristóbal de San Martín, encomendero of Cansahcab, stated, "and thus issued the descendents of said Mo Chel, and they have governed, and at present are governing, those villages of Cansahcab, Dzidzantún and Yobaín"; see "Relación de Cansahcab," in *RHGY* 1:95.

132. Roys, "Traditions of Caste," 192.

133. Barrera Vásquez y Rendón, *El libro de los libros*, 135.

134. Landa, *Relación*, 42. Although succession rules were complicated, this rank usually passed along the father's line, and was the lineage's patrimony. One example of these often confusing arrangements concerns Ah Dzulub Xiu, the halach uinic of Maní who was assassinated around 1536. Despite the fact that his own son survived him, Ah Dzlulub Xiu was in fact succeeded by Ah Kukum Xiu, the second son of Ah Ziyan Xiu, his second cousin; see Roys, "Traditions of Caste," 189–90.

135. Unless otherwise indicated, the material for this section appears in Robert S. Chamberlain, *The Conquest and Colonization of Yucatán, 1517–1550* (Washington, DC: Carnegie Institute of Washington, 1948). Chamberlain's classic book remains the most important work written over the the topic. Beyond his erudition, the author's greatest achievement was to establish with precision that the Spaniards had made two previous attempts to submit the Maya prior to eventual success. The first of these lasted from 1527 to 1529, and the second from 1529 to 1535. Chamberlain's principal contribution consists in analyzing the causes for their failures, as well as identifying the circumstances that facilitated Spanish conquest of the Maya between 1541 and 1547.

136. Jones, *Maya Resistance*, 41–43.

137. For an account of these events, see Chamberlain, *The Conquest*, 241–52.

138. Landa, *Relación*, 4. By "Lacandón," Landa possibly refers to the region stretching along the south, southeast, and east of the Gulf of Honduras. By "Taiza" he means the region of the Guatemalan Petén inhabited by the Itzaes; its political

center was Tayasal, located on an island then called Noh Petén and today known as the island of Flores, of Lake Petén Itzá.

Chapter 2

1. Stella María González Cicero offers an analysis of how the Franciscans organized their provincia in Yucatán. See González Cicero, *Perspectiva religiosa en Yucatán, 1517–1571* (Mexico City: El Colegio de México, 1978), 77–108.

2. By the terms of the *Capitulaciones de Granada*, once the land had been pacified, don Francisco de Montejo became the captain general and governor for life of Yucatán. It is well known that he was unable to lead his soldiers during the invasion's final stage, and named his son lieutenant commander-in-chief. With the foundation of Mérida, the son, representing his father, asumed office as lieutenant governor. See Chamberlain, *The Conquest*, 20–34, 204.

3. Chamberlain, *The Conquest*, 275–306, provides a detailed discussion of the overall and particular causes that motivated the Crown to remove the Adelantado from the governorship of Yucatán, and an examination of the quarrels between Montejo and the Audiencia de Guatemala that brought about the former's removal from power.

4. Estimates of the indigeous population in the period before the Spanish invasion present an authetic study in contrast. Helmut Wagner estimates between 8 and 10 million inhabitants; Jakeman suggests 1.375 million; Frederick W. Lange states 2.285 million; Morley argues for 1.600 million; Sanders says between 535 thousand and 592 thousand; Solano and Pérez Lila prefer 700 thousand; and finally, Cook and Borah calculate 800 thousand. See Manuela Cristina García Bernal, *Población y encomienda en Yucatán bajo las Austrias* (Sevilla: Escuela de Estudios Hispano-Americanos de Sevilla, 1978), 28–29.

5. "Relación de Dzan," in *RHGY* 1:253; Landa, *Relación*, 11, states: "This land is divided into provinces."

6. *RHGY* vols. 1 and 2 contain countless examples of how the Spanish employed the term "provincia" in the ways descibed here. See also, Landa, *Relación*, 11. Roys's proposed typology over political organization at the time of invasion is based on the ways that the Spanish deployed "province." See Roys, *The Indian Background*, 11.

7. "Ayuda de costa a Juan May, cacique de Yaxkukul (7 de septiembre de 1563)," in AGI, Justicia, legajo 253, f. 1029; "Cédula de encomienda a Jorge Hernández (1543)," in AGNM, Civil, vol. 648, expediente 1, ff. 73v–74; and "Relación de Sinanché," in *RHGY* 1:123.

8. "Relación de Citilcum," in *RHGY* 1:179–80. For additional references concerning use of the term "pueblo" as a residential clustering, see "Relación de ciudad de Mérida," in *RHGY* 1:71; "Relación de Sinanché," in *RHGY* 1:124; "Relación de Kizil," in *RHGY* 1:197–98; "Relación de Tepakán," in *RHGY* 1:213; "Relación de Izamal," in *RHGY* 1:303; and "Relación de Temul," in *RHGY* 2:102.

9. For an analysis of the use of the term "pueblo" in central Mexico, see Bernardo García Martínez, *Los pueblos de la Sierra: El poder y el espacio entre los indios del norte de Puebla hasta 1700* (Mexico City: El Colegio de México, 1987), 78 and note 23.

10. In Spanish sources the terms "parcialidad" or "barrio" are used interchangeably to refer to a cluster of Indian residences. During the colonial period the term "parcialidad" denoted a distinct pueblo congregated with other pueblos in the same place. See "Ayuda de costa a Juan May, cacique de Yaxkukul (7 de septiembre de 1563)," in AGI, Justicia, legajo 253, f. 1029; "Cédula de encomienda a Jorge Hernández (1543)," in AGNM, Civil, vol. 648, expediente 1, ff. 73v–74; Ortiz Yam and Quezada, *Visita de Diego García*, 85, 90, 96, and 99. For further discussion of these terms, see Farriss, *Maya Society*, 163–64.

11. "Ayuda de costa a Juan May . . . (7 de septiembre de 1563)," in AGI, Justicia, legajo 253, f. 1029; "Cédula . . . a Jorge Hernández (1543)," in AGNM, Civil, vol. 648, expediente 1, ff. 73v–74v; "Relación de Citilcum," in *RHGY* 1:181; "Relación de Tekantó," in *RHGY* 1:215; "Relación de Dzan," in *RHGY* 1:252; "Relación de Motul," in *RHGY* 1:269; "Cédula de encomienda a Melchor Pacheco (28 de noviembre de 1542)," in AGI, Justicia, legajo 215, ff. 17, 19–20.

12. Regarding the use of the term "cacique" to refer to the halach uinic, see "Relación de Hocabá," in *RHGY* 1:133; and "Relación de Sotuta," in *RHGY* 1:146. Regarding the use of the term "batab" to refer to a lord or señor, see "Relación de Citilcum," in *RHGY* 1:182; and "Relación de Dzan," in *RHGY* 1:252.

13. Juan de Solórzano y Pereira, *Política indiana* (Madrid: Editorial Atlas, 1972), vol. 2, chap. 27, no. 4.

14. With the imperial policy of limiting Maya elites' social and economic power, the use of the term "señor" in the 1700s came to lack the political content that had so troubled the Crown during the sixteenth century. See Quezada and Okoshi Harada, *Papeles de los Xiu*, 112–13; Delfina E. López Sarrelangue, *La nobleza indígena de Pátzcuaro en la época virreinal* (Mexico City: Universidad Nacional Autónoma de México, 1965), 86.

15. During his visita of the province, don Tomás López Medel began to use the word "cacique" as much for "halach uinic" as for "batab." See "Ordenanzas de Tomás López (1552)," in Diego López Cogolludo, *Historia de Yucatán* (Mexico City: Academia Literaria, 1957), 293–395.

16. "Proceso contra los indios idólatras de Sotuta, Kanchunup, Mopilá, Sacabá, Yaxcabá, Usil y Tibolón (agosto de 1561)," in *DDQAMY*, 1:75, 107, 120, and 123. This volume contains innumerable references to the increasingly liberal usage of honorific terms among colonial Maya.

17. Silvio Zavala, *La encomienda indiana*, 2nd ed. (Mexico City: Editorial Porrúa, 1973), 40–73. This work, dedicated to the evolution of the encomienda in the Americas, explores how it involved assigning a cacique to a conquistador. See also, Silvio Zavala,"Los primeros títulos de encomienda en Nueva España," in *Memoria del Colegio Nacional* 7, no. 1 (1970): 11–19; and García Martínez, *Los pueblos de la Sierra*, 79.

18. An encomienda title issued by Montejo the Son underscores this peculiar characteristic: "By reason of this document, the lords and naturales of Taculuté, Nunkiní, Cicilché, and Temuco . . . are entrusted to you, Jorge Hernández . . . with all their barrios and estancias and milpas attached to said villages, anexos, and their surrounding territories." See "Cédula . . . a Jorge Hernández (1543)," in AGNM, Civil, vol. 648, expediente 1, ff. 73–74.

19. By 1549, for example, two different encomenderos shared the tribute from Chalanté, Sotuta, and Tekom (among other pueblos). See "Tasaciones de los pueblos de la provincia de Yucatán hechas por la Audiencia de Santiago de Guatemala (febrero de 1549)," in *ENE*, 5: 132, 142, 170, and 173.

20. See appendix A of this book; see also "Residencia de Diego de Quijada (1565)," in AGI, Justicia, legajo 245, ff. 1001–1526. Excluding the "Tasaciones de 1549," which is the oldest tabulation of encomenderos and of the pueblos that they controlled, the Quijada residency provides the most complete listing, and one where it is possible to find a linking of encomendero with the cacique(s) under his authority. The appendices presented by García Bernal ilustrate the extraordinary importance of this relationship from the mid-sixteenth to the early eighteenth centuries. See Manuela Cristina García Bernal, *La sociedad de Yucatán, 1700–1750* (Sevilla: Escuela de Estudios Hispano-Americano de Sevilla, 1972), 137–67; and García Bernal, *Población y encomienda*, 479–533.

21. Chamberlain, *The Conquest*, 199; "Carta de fray Lorenzo de Bienvendia a S. A. (10 de febrero de 1548)," in *Cartas de Indias*, 1:74.

22. Chamberlain, *The Conquest*, 303.

23. "Tasaciones de los pueblos . . . (febrero de 1549)," in *ENE* 5:103–81.

24. Chamberlain, *The Conquest*, 238, notes that during the early colonial years in Yucatán, the Spanish considered their encomiendas semifeudal gifts that they could govern like their own possessions.

25. "María de Solórzano contra Francisco Quiroz sobre las encomiendas de ciertos pueblos de la provincia de Yucatán," in AGNM, Civil, vol. 648, expediente 2, f.155v.

26. "Carta de fray Luis de Villalpando, fray Diego de Béjar y fray Miguel de Vera a su Majestad, dando relación de cosas tocantes al bien de los naturales y españoles de la provincia de Yucatán (29 de julio de 1550)," in *DHY* 1:1–4; "Carta de fray Lorenzo . . . (10 de febrero de 1548), in *Cartas de Indias*, 1:70–82.

27. In 1532 the Crown decided that the encomendero had no direct dominion over his Indians, since this right belonged exclusively to the King. For a discussion of the evolution of the debate regarding this jurisdiction, see Zavala, *La encomienda*, 41–63. Concerning the Yucatecan case, see García Bernal, *Población y encomienda*, 227–31.

28. The legal and economic evolution of the tasaciones, along with other groups of royal decrees regarding tribute, are explored in depth in one of Zavala's classic works, *La encomienda*, and in José Miranda, *El tributo indígena en la Nueva España durante el siglo XVI* (Mexico City: El Colegio de México, 1952).

29. In early 1547 friar Juan de la Puerta, a commissary of the Franciscan order, requested that the King assign tasaciones to tribute so that the Indians would know what they were to give. See "Carta de fray Juan de la Puerta al Consejo de Indias (Mérida, 1 de febrero de 1547)," in *Cartas de Indias*, 1:68. The Franciscans' protests persisted, and one year later friar Lorenzo de Bienvendia composed a review of all the many abuses that the Spanish had inflicted on the indigenous population. In his telling, the 1546–1547 rebellion had originated from encomendero excesses and the unending demand for tribute and personal services. See "Carta de fray Lorenzo . . . (10 de febrero de 1548)," in *Cartas de Indias* 1: 70–82.

30. For a broad examination of the quarrels that sprang up among groups of Spaniards, and the Crown's decision to remove the Adelantado from his position as governor of Yucatán and impose its own authority, see Chamberlain, *The Conquest*, 292–310.

31. Chamberlain, *The Conquest*, 272–310, provides an extensive discussion of Yucatán's problematic politics and the Crown's attempts to gain the upper hand with encomendero interests.

32. "The Chronicle of Chac-Xulub–Chen," 194.

33. "Nombramiento e instrucciones al Licenciado Tomás López oidor de la Audiencia de Guatemala, para la visita de las provincias de Yucatán, Cozumel y Tabasco (9 de enero de 1552)," in *DHY*, 1:17; "Tasaciones del pueblo de Motul (1549–1560)," in *DDQAMY* 2:111–13.

34. "Tasaciones . . . de Motul (1549–1560)," in *DDQAMY* 2:111–12; Sergio Quezada, "Los sistemas de trabajo en Yucatán, 1541–1561," *Boletín de la Escuela de Ciencias Antropológicas de la Universidad de Yucatán* 9, no. 44 (1980): 64.

35. Chamberlain, *The Conquest*, 203, 213, 225, 229, and 234.

36. It is essential to point out that in this context, the term "jurisdiction" was used in the following sense: "boundary or limit of one place next to another, or of one province beside another, in which one's dominion is circumscribed from that of another." See *Diccionario de Autoridades*, 2:334.

37. "Relación de la villa de Valladolid," in *RHGY* 2:33. See appendix C regarding the division of pueblo boundaries.

38. Until March 24, 1600, the Crown granted the alcaldes ordinarios of the four major Spanish settlements' cabildos the power to assume gubernatorial control of their districts or jurisdictions during those periods when the larger province lacked a governor. See Jorge Ignacio Rubio Mañé, *Notas y acotaciones a la Historia de Yucatán de fray Diego López Cogolludo* (Mexico City: Academia Literaria, 1957), 459.

39. From the beginning Yucatán was part of the Audiencia of México, but in 1543, with the creation of the Audiencia de los Confines, the Crown transferred the peninsula to Confines's jurisdiction. In 1548 Yucatán was returned once more to Mexico, and then, two years later, back to la Audiencia de los Confines. Finally, in 1560, the Crown issued its final decision and placed Yucatán under

Mexico's authority, where it stayed for the remainder of the colonial period. See Peter Gerhard, *The Southeast Frontier of New Spain* (Princeton: Princeton University Press, 1979), 15; Scholes, "Introducción," in *DDQAMY* vol. 1, chap. 7–8; "Real cédula para que las provincias de Yucatán, Cozumel y Tabasco sean del distrito de la Audiencia de los Confines (7 de julio de 1550)," in *DHY* 1:6–7; "Real cédula para que las provincias de Yucatán, Cozumel y Tabasco sean sujetas a la Audiencia de la Nueva España (9 de enero de 1560)," in *DHY* 1:8–9. For a discussion of the factors that led the Crown to make these many jurisdictional changes, see Jorge Ignacio Rubio Mañé, "Las jurisdicciones de Yucatán: La relación de la plaza de teniente del rey en Campeche. Año de 1744," *Boletín del Archivo General de la Nación* 7, nos. 3–4 (1966): 551–56.

40. Rubio Mañé, "Las jurisdicciones," 556–59.

41. "Real cédula naming Doctor Diego Quijada alcalde mayor de Yucatán (19 de febrero de 1560)," in *DDQAMY* 1:5.

42. In this context, the concept of jurisdiction is understood to mean "the faculty or power that is conceded to the government in order to decide legal conflicts." See *Diccionario de Autoridades*, 2:334.

43. Ciudad Real, *Calepino maya*, 125.

44. González Cicero, *Perspectiva religiosa*, 78–83, discusses the origins of these first Franciscans and the routes through which they came to Yucatán.

45. For additional sources on the first evangelical labors of these Franciscans, see González Cicero, *Perspectiva religiosa*, 83–89; López Cogolludo, *Historia de Yucatán*, 255.

46. López Cogolludo, *Historia de Yucatán*, 256; González Cicero, *Perspectiva religiosa*, 87.

47. López Cogolludo, *Historia de Yucatán*, 267.

48. Ibid., 268–69. It appears that the eastern Maya rebellion of 1546–1547 caused the Franciscans to limit their activities to the north and northeast of Mérida.

49. The organizational evolution of the Franciscan province of San José of Yucatán can be summarized thus: The first seven friars who arrived in Campeche around 1544–1545 created a congregación. In 1549 that congregación evolved into the dependent custodia of the Franciscan province of the Santo Evangelio de México. A decade later, the capítulo general of the Franciscan order voted for the custodia of San José de Yucatán and that of the Santísimo Nombre de Jesús de Guatemala to form a single province, separate from that of Santo Evangelio. Finally, in 1565 the order's capítulo general separated these two custodias into independent provincias. See Scholes, "Introducción," in *DDQAMY* vol. 1, chaps. 12–15; and González Cicero, *Perspectiva religiosa*, 104–106.

50. For additional references over who constituted this second group of Franciscans arriving in Yucatán, and the first steps in setting up a custodia, see González Cicero, *Perspectiva religiosa*, 91, 104–108; and López Cogolludo, *Historia de Yucatán*, 269.

51. Landa, *Relación*, 31.

52. García Martínez, *Los pueblos de la Sierra*, 131–32, states that starting in the second half of the sixteenth century, the lack of friars became all the more acute, owing to the fact that the Crown grew more reluctant to allow new members of the regular orders to go to New Spain. This fact obliged the Francisans, around 1564, to close eight convents, four of which were located in the Puebla sierra.

53. Prior to the arrival of the group of 1560–1561, fifteen friars had come to Yucatán in 1553; see González Cicero, *Perspectiva religiosa*, 93–97, 102–103.

54. Apart from these twenty-two guardianías, by 1582 the secular clergy administered the *vicaría* of Peto and curates of Valladolid and Salamanca de Bacalar, with a total of some forty señoríos. See "Carta de don Guillén de las Casas, gobernador de Yucatán, a Su Majestad con una memoria de los conventos, vicarías y pueblos de la provincia (25 de marzo de 1582)," in *DHY* 2:55–63.

55. Alejandra Moreno Toscano states: "The relationship between the pueblos that were cabeceras de doctrina with the villages that were their sujetos . . . makes one think of a tiny planetary system. Its chief center of attraction, the pueblo cabecera, is surrounded by varying numbers of sujetos-satellites that live, depend and come together around this religious, political, and economic system." See Moreno Toscano, *Geografía económica de México (siglo XVI)* (Mexico City: El Colegio de México, 1968), 102, 110.

56. When the Franciscan commissary, friar Alonso Ponce, visited Yucatán in 1580, his brothers in the order organized a welcome celebration for him in every cabecera de doctrina. For example, in "the pueblo and convent of San Luis de Calkiní, there were innumerable people, who received him with many branches, and with dances of the country, along with dances with tambourines from Castille accompanied by flutes and trumpets. Later the people of that village, along with those of the guardianía (all of whom are Maya Indians) gathered, with offerings of many hens and chickens." See Antonio de Ciudad Real, *Tratado curioso y doctor de las grandezas de la Nueva España* (Mexico City: Universidad Nacional Autónoma de México, 1976), 2:352.

57. By the late 1580s, practically all the casas conventuales founded by the Franciscans were of masonry and completely finished. Ciudad Real, *Tratado*, 2:321–329, furnishes abundant information over the physical state of the Yucatecan conventuals' construction for those years.

58. Ortiz Yam and Quezada, *Visita de Diego Garía*, 51–52, 90–91, 97–98, 102–103, 108–109, 211–12, and 236–73.

59. Fray Bernardo de Lizana, *Devocionario de nuestra señora de Izamal y conquista espiritual de Yucatán* (Mexico City: Universidad Nacional Autónoma de México, 1995), 62–64.

60. Ibid., 88.

61. Ibid., 102–12; López Cogolludo, *Historia de Yucatán*, 310–16.

62. "Carta de don Guillén . . . (25 de marzo de 1582)," in *DHY*, 2:61.

63. Miguel A. Bretos, "Capillas de indios yucatecas del siglo XVI: notas de un complejo formal," in *Cuadernos de Arquitectura de Yucatán* 1 (1987): 8.

64. Ciudad Real, *Tratado*, 2:322.

65. In the early 1580s, for example, friar Pedro de Vergara, guardián of Tizimín convent, asked the caciques of his pueblos de visita for a contribution to buy a *manga de la cruz* (cloth decoration for a cross), Juan Tamay declared that from the villages of Tizimín, Tekay, Dzonotchuil, and Tiscacauchén alone the friar collected four hundred cotton mantas; see Ortiz Yam and Quezada, *Visita de Diego García*, 108–109.

66. Lope de Vega, *El peregrino en su patria* (Madrid: Editorial Castalia, 1973), Book 4, states: "In their customs they differed little from animals, until religion and Spanish custom civilized them." Cf., *Diccionario de Autoridades*, 311. López Medel had a similar idea in mind when he remarked that the Indians of Yucatán lived "separated from one another in the monte."

67. Peter Gerhard, "Congregaciones de indios en la Nueva España antes de 1570," in *Historia mexicana* 24, no. 3 (1977): 347. By the verb "reduce," Spaniards understood the act of converting the Indians to the true religion, and by "reducción," the conversion of an Indian village to Christianity; see *Diccionario de Autoridades*, 533–34. William F. Hanks, *Converting Words: Maya in the Age of the Cross* (Berkeley: University of California Press, 2010), 2–8, proposes a novel interpretation regarding the reducción policy's impact on colonial Maya society. He sees the congregaciones not only as implying a spacial restructuring in which the indigenous population lived under a "temporal policing," but also as bringing with it the transformation and restructuring of indigenous language under Latin patterns and grammatical rules, all part of the missionaries' goal of teaching neophytes Christian tradition and Catholic prayers and practices. The Franciscans' "linguistic reductions" were oriented around what Hanks defines as "linguistic conversion," that is, around the transformation of pagan language and idolatry to a revised and reordered code, one appropriate to the discursive practices of the newly Christian Indians.

68. López Cogolludo, *Historia de Yucatán*, 254, gives an account of the reducción measures of friar Luis de Villalpando and of the places where he carried them out. "The first thing that he did was to reduce those who lived on the plains to convenient locations where it was possible to preach to them, to catechize, and to teach them as he wished, keeping them close at hand, since there were few ministers. In this way he peopled many of the villages that remain today in the district of Campeche, and along the camino real to Mérida." See also, González Cicero, *Perspectiva religiosa*, 84–86.

69. Chamberlain, *The Conquest*, 282.

70. To form an idea of the powers that the Audienca of Guatemala authorized to don Tomás López, see "Nombramiento . . . al licenciado Tomás López . . . (9 de enero de 1552)," in *DHY* 1:13–25.

71. Don Tomás stated that "one of the causes that has obstructed the temporal and spiritual advancement of the naturales of said provinces is that they live far apart from one another in the monte." See López Cogolludo, "Ordenanzas de . . . López, (1552)," in *Historia de Yucatán*, 295.

72. The steps taken by friar Lorenzo de Bienvenida and the involved process whereby this order arrived in Yucatán are well documented. By 1553 some thirty-four Franciscans were already living in the province; see González Cicero, *Perspectiva religiosa*, 93–97.

73. López Medel indicated how the pueblos were to be created. He wrote: "all the naturales . . . are to gather in the villages, and are to make houses together, creating in the form of a village everyone of a parcialidad and caberera, in a single convenient location." See López Cogolludo, "Ordenanzas de . . . López (1552)," 294.

74. Barrera Vásquez, *Documento núm.1*, 39. García Martínez, *Los pueblos de la Sierra*, 156, offers a model for how villages were laid out, and the bulk of existing evidence suggests that his model was the norm. He states that for the most part, "priests would select the best spot for the church, and based on that would plan the plaza and streets, with space reserved for such public construction such as the casa de gobierno, fountains, etc.; and for private homes and orchards, thus establishing a complete blueprint for human settlement."

75. "Relación de Chahuac-há," in *RHGY* 2:247. For other opinions along the same lines, see "Relación de la villa de Valladolid," in *RHGY* II (1579), 40; "Relación de Dzonot," in *RHGY* 2:86; and "Relación de Popolá," in *RHGY* 2: 215, 218.

76. "Relación de Kanpocolché," in *RHGY* 2: 321, 327.

77. "Residencia de . . . Quijada (1565)," in AGI, Justicia, legajo 245. This legajo contains the most complete listing of the pueblos that had come into being as a result of the reducción program. However, many of these early pueblos conformed to the description provided by the Mérida cabildo: "The villages that are now populated are formless, nor do they possess streets, for the houses are of wood covered by straw, and thus, whether great or small, to the eye they amount to nothing more than a collection of huts." See "Relación de la ciudad de Mérida," in *RHGY* 1:71.

78. Roys, *The Titles of Ebtun*, 73–80.

79. "Relación de Tinum," in *RHGY* 2:158. The audiencias, instiutions created by the Spanish Crown, were the highest bodies of justice. The Audiencia de los Confines was founded in 1544 in Gracias a Dios (Honduras), and in 1549 was moved to Santiago de los Caballeros. Its original facade still stands in present-day Gracias.

80. "The Chronicle of Chac-Xulub-Chen," 200, states that when the caciques "recieved the great commissions, they measured the land according to the authorization given by our great prince and king, he who reigns, and our master the first oidor Tomás López." See also Roys, *The Titles of Ebtun*, 72.

81. According to the *Diccionario de Autoridades*, 3:801, the word "frontera" means "the line or limit that separates and divides the Kingdoms, one being the limit of the other." See also, Tsubasa Okoshi Harada and Sergio Quezada, "Vivir con fronteras: Espacios mayas peninsulares del siglo XVI," in *El territorio maya: Memoria de la quinta mesa redonda de Palenque*, coord. Rodrigo Liendo Stuado (Mexico City: Instituto Nacional de Antropología e Historia, 2008), 142.

82. The *Diccionario de Autoridades*, 4:140, holds that "lindero" means: "the limit, path, or road that serves to divide posessions one from another, so that the owners of these know which what belongs to whom." According to Martín Alonso, the word "término" carries the sense of "mojón, permanent symbol the is placed to fix the boundaries of land possessed, its limits and frontiers." See Alonso, *Enciclopedia del idioma. Diccionario histórico y moderno de la lengua española (siglos XII al XX) etimológico, tecnológico, regional e hispanoamericano* (Mexico City: Aguilar, 1998), vol. 3, no. 3932. See also, Okoshi Harada and Quezada, "Vivir con fronteras," 142–43.

83. Quezada and Okoshi Harada, *Papeles de los Xiu de Yaxá*, 56, 58; Okoshi Harada and Quezada, "Vivir con fronteras," 144.

84. Okoshi Harada, *Códice de Calkiní*, 52, states: "*ti yanix u bakaal haaob yetel u ciob*: there was a great deal of chocolate and *balché*." Working from archaeological evidence of the late Classic period, Lisa J. LeCount argues that the consumption of food and beverages during the Maya convites implied a complex dynamic that defined the individual's position within the social order, and that facilitated the reproduction of the social order. LeCount distinguishes between celebrations restricted to the nobility and principales, in which participants consumed sumptuous dishes and exchanged prestigious gifts; and those events in which the people consumed more basic foods, and which promoted equality and solidarity within the pueblo. See "Like Water for Chocolate: Feasting and Political Ritual among the Late Classic Maya at Xunantunich, Belize," in *American Anthropologist* 103, no. 4 (2001): 935–37, 943–46. John F. Chuchiak IV describes the circumstances in which the lords and principales carried out the ritual consumption of balché during the early colonial years; see "It Is Their Drinking that Hinders Them: *Balche* and the Use of Ritual Intoxicants among the Colonial Yucatec Maya, 1550–1780," in *Estudios de cultura maya* 24 (2004): 137–71.

85. Quezada and Okoshi Harada, *Papeles de los Xiu de Yaxá*, 57–59.

86. *Códice Pérez*, 359. When Macan Pech, batab of Yaxkukul, traced out his territory, he wrote: "And then we left and went to the boundaries of the monte, to the places of our empty homes without entering the abandoned homes of strangers." See also, Quezada and Okoshi Harada, *Papeles de los Xiu de Yaxá*, 60–61.

87. Quezada and Okoshi Harada, *Papeles de los Xiu de Yaxá*, 55–65; and *Códice Pérez*, 359.

88. When Macan Pech, batab of Yaxkukul, demarcated the village boundaries, he indicated the importance of the distribution of monte by saying: "We record this information . . . so that it by known by all residents past and future . . . so that they will have the wherewithall to eat; so that they [can] burn the trunks of the trees, so that they be able to plant their corn, so that they can sustain themselves. . ." Barrera Vásquez, *Documento núm. 1*, 34–35.

89. In Barrera Vásquez, *Documento núm.1*, we find the toponyms of sixteen wells and one aguada that served as markers for the territorial boundaries of

the caciques of Yaxkukul, Mocochá, Conkal, Nolo, Euán, and Kuncheil; see also, in Roys, *The Titles of Ebtun*, 106–10, how cenotes functioned as territorial markers.

90. Cases studies of this point can be found in Roys, *Titles of Ebtun*, 82; and in *Códice Pérez*, 363.

91. Despite the Maya's attempts to avoid future conflicts, these conflicts proved unavoidable; see Roys, *The Titles of Ebtun*, 82.

92. García Martínez, *Los pueblos de la Sierra*, 155, states that in the sierra of northern Puebla, "there is no clear evidence to indicate that the original intention was to congregate the entire population of each altepetl in a single location; moreover, in most cases this approach was impossible, all the more so in jagged terrain like that of the sierra, where space for large concentrations of people simply did not exist."

93. López Cogolludo, *Historia de Yucatán*, 227. The earliest evidence on the appearance of barrios comes from the town of Pencuyut; see Ortiz Yam and Quezada, *Visita de Diego García*, 45, 47, 49. By the mid-seventeenth century the pueblo of Teabo consisted of the barrios San Francisco, San Gaspar, San Miguel, San Marcos, San Bernabé, and San Ildefonso. Those of Tekax were Santa Ana, San Pedro, San Miguel, San Francisco, San Ildefonso, San Gaspar, San Juan, San Diego, and San Cristóbal. See "Definitorio de la orden de San Francisco de la provincia de Yucatán (1657)," in AGI, Audiencia de México, legajo 308, ff. 53, 101.

94. Ortiz Yam and Quezada, *Visita de Diego García*, 47–51. García Martínez, *Los pueblos de la Sierra*, 156, states that the reducciones in northern Puebla were accompanied by a "review and modification of toponyms. The cabecera normally assumed the name of the altepetl, a practice possibly corresponding to some previous usage, if within tthe atlepetl's territory there had been some privileged place closely associated to the traditions that atlepetl's origin."

95. López Cogolludo, *Historia de Yucatán*, 233–40.

96. The phenomenon of Indian *cimarronaje*, or illicit flight, made its appearance in regions of refuge, places still free from European dominance. Spanish colonial documents of the seventeenth century refer to those fugitive Indians who never returned to colonially controlled areas as *cimarrones* or *tepches* ("idolaters"). These Indians shed their colonial identities and reassumed their old names, traditions, and forms of dress. Both Spaniards and Indians co-existed with them and even maintained close commercial ties. See "Relación de la villa," in *RHGY* 2:41; "Probanza de el capitán, don Juan Chan cacique y señor natural de los pueblos de Chancenote y sus sujetos (1622)," in AGI, Audiencia de México, legajo 140, ramo 2.

97. "Relación de Citilcum," in *RHGY* 1:180; and "Relación de Kizil," in *RHGY* 1:198.

98. "Residencia de . . . Quijada (1565)," in AGI, Justicia, legajo 245. This legajo contains the names of the pueblos that had been congregated in a single "seat" by 1565. For Farriss, *Maya Society*, 162, the friars' virtue consisted in not violating

preexisting political organization in such a way as to make the reducciones a process that fragmented the cúuchcabalob.

99. "Residencia de ... Quijada (1565)," in AGI, Justicia, legajo 245, f. 1,434v; and "Relación de Izamal," in *RHGY* 1:304.

100. "Residencia de ... Quijada (1565)," in AGI, Jusicia, legajo 245.

101. During the second half of the sixteenth century, some pueblos that served as the seat of these congregaciones (Calkiní, Chancenote, Izamal, Maní, Tekantó, Oxkutzcab, Tizimín, Sotuta, and Hunucmá) were converted into cabeceras de guardianía.

102. "Peticiones de Joaquín de Leguizamo, procurador de la ciudad de Mérida, y otros papeles sobre lo que trató el doctor Quijada en el asunto de cargar los indios con tributos y otras mercancías (1563–1564)," in *DDQAMY* 2:113–37; "Información hecha por el doctor Diego Quijada en los pueblos Homún, Maní y Tacul (enero de 1564)," in *DDQAMY* 2:138–46; "Información hecha en esta ciudad de Mérida y en sus términos por el doctor Diego Quijada sobre los caminos que mandó hacer y limpiar en ellas (abril de 1565)," in *DDQAMY* 2:146–59; and "Residencia de ... Quijada (1565)," in AGI, Justicia, legajo 245, f.294.

103. To avoid repeating the names of Dzonotchuil, Tekay, and Tiscacauchén, all reduced to Tizimín, henceforth the text will simply refer to these four villages as the congregación of Tizimín.

Regarding the importance of space as a factor in postinvasion prosperity, a few cases worth mention. At the beginning of the 1580s, Calkiní, a town on the camino real between Mérida and Campeche, experienced "a large procession of peddlars." And while in clear demographic collapse, Hunucmá, the place to which Sihunchén and Yabacu were resettled, had grown in population; its encomendero attributed this fact to its salubrious location, but could not resist mentioning the matter of Hunucmá's location: "Through said village passes the camino real that runs from the city [Mérida] to the port of Sisal," one of the peninsula's key ports during the second half of the sixteenth century. See "Relación de Chuburná," in *RHGY* 1:400; and "Carta de don Guillén ... (25 de marzo de 1582)," in *DHY* 2:54.

104. Sergio Quezada, *Los pies de la república: Los mayas peninsulares, 1550–1750*, (Mexico City: Centro de Investigaciones y Estudios Superiores en Antropología Social, and Instituto Nacional Indigenista, 1997), 154.

105. According to José Miranda, New Spain's first encomenderos used the returns on their encomienda to launch productive activities. Those active in mining used tribute to acquire slaves, and to cover maintenance costs; the salaries of the miners and the production costs came both from encomienda and from the returns of the enterprise. Mining entrepreneurs acquired tools through barter (either of gold, or of some goods obtained through tribute), or were made by slaves or encomienda Indians. Unlike those empresario encomenderos, the Spaniards in Yucatán only began productive activities when their tribute incomes declined as a result of the tasaciones of 1549, 1552, and 1561, and from the

demographic collapse. See Miranda, *La función económica del encomendero en los orígenes del régimen colonial (Nueva España, 1525–1531)* (Mexico City: Universidad Nacional Autónoma de México, 1965), 10–11. See also, Ortiz Yam and Quezada, *Visita de Diego García*, 26–27.

106. Ortiz Yam and Quezada, *Visita de Diego García*, 26.

107. Quezada, "La presencia española en la agricultura maya, siglo XVI," in *Agricultura indígena: pasado y presente*, ed. Teresa Rojas Rabiela (Mexico City: Centro de Investigaciones y Estudios Superiores en Antropología Social, 1990), 197.

108. "Carta de Francisco Palomino, defensor de los naturales (13 de mayo de 1579)," in AGI, Indiferente General, legajo 1,390.

109. Ortiz Yam and Quezada, *Visita de Diego García*, 27; Quezada, "La presencia española," 199, demonstrates that in 1577 Yucatán contained some forty-eight ingenios, each capitalized at around two to three thousand pesos.

110. Ortiz Yam and Quezada, *Visita de Diego García*, 27.

111. In 1582 Hernando Muñoz Zapata, encomendero of Oxkutzcab, stated that indigo "had so fallen in price that all Spaniards have already forsaken it, because the costs outway the gains." See "Relación de Oxkutzcab," in *RHGY* 1:357; Quezada, *Los pies de la república*, 152.

112. Ortiz Yam and Quezada, *Visita de Diego García*, 28.

113. Ibid., 28.

114. Ibid., 28–29.

115. Ortiz Yam, "Los pueblos del noroeste yucateco," 104–109.

116. For example, when the caciques of Espita and Tzabcanul attended the religious celebrations of Tizimín congregación, they went to the house of Antonio Rodríguez to purchase libations. See Ortiz Yam and Quezada, *Visita de Diego García*, 29–30.

117. Ibid., 30.

118. Solange Alberro "El amancebamiento en los siglos XVI y XVII: un medio eventual de medrar," in *Familia y poder en Nueva España* (Mexico City: Instituto Nacional de Antropología e Historia, 1991), 159–62, 164.

119. Another Spaniard guilty of adultary was Francisco Pinto, who carried on an illicit affair with Ana Be, whose husband Martín Tun was at that moment a fugitive. See Ortiz Yam and Quezada, *La visita de Diego García*, 30–32.

120. "Francisco Palomino, defensor de los naturales, solicita sobrecédula para que no haya alcaldes mayores y corregidores (31 de marzo de 1579)," in AGI, Indiferente Genera, legajo 1390; López Cogolludo, *Historia de Yucatán*, vol. 7, chap. 8; "Testimonio de los autos para la entrega de las instrucciones," in *RHGY* 1:37; "Relación de Mama," in *RGHY* 1:109; and "Relación de Temul," in *RHGY* 2:102.

121. López Cogolludo, *Historia de Yucatán*, 391.

122. "Carta de Don Guillén . . . (25 de marzo de 1582)," in *DHY* 2:55–63. This document provides the names of the Franciscan convents in that year, along with accounts of the visitas. It also lists in detail the villages that had been congregated into a single asiento.

123. Ibid., 55–63.

124. The history of this reducción comes from two of the most important tallies of Yucatecan pueblos in the second half of the sixteenth century. One is from 1565, and as previously indicated, is found in "Residencia de . . . Quijada," while the other is from 1582, and was created by governor don Guillén de las Casas. The two listings are complementary. The first allows us to determine with great precision which reducciones the Franciscans organized as a result of López Medel's visit, while through the second document we observe the process of disintegration those reducciones suffered between 1565 and 1582, along with the new reducciones that appeared.

125. In the listings of 1565 we find the account of the dependent pueblos of Maní physically relocated to that town. See "Residencia de . . . Quijada (1565)," in AGI, Justicia, legajo 245, ff. 1023–1098.

126. Ciudad Real, *Tratado*, 2:367.

Chapter 3

1. "Relación de Kanpocolché," in *RHGY* 2:322; and "Relación de Sucopó," in *RHGY* 2:118. For additional references, see "Relación de Dzonot," in *RHGY* 2:86; and "Relación de Kikil," in *RHGY* 2:267.

2. García Martínez, *Los pueblos de la Sierra*, 99, states: "The cabildos aimed at centralizing the political and administrative functions of every village. First, they concentrated these activities in a single institution, displacing all others at least in legal terms. Second, the instition of cabildo reinforced the principle of a hierarchical pyramid in which caciques received the position of gobernador. Third, the cabildo was ever after associated with a particular place, that is, the cabecera, even though pueblo subdivisions and dependencies, entities that the Spanish knew as barrios or estancias, enjoyed representation through certain of their members, and in particular through the alcaldes."

3. Farriss, *Maya Society*, 468, note 14, states: "The office of *gobernador* had already been introduced by 1552, but the full transition to a Spanish system seems to have taken place between the López *visita* and the García de Palacio *visita*." For her part, Manuela Cristina García Bernal writes that the single issuing of the Ordenanzas of García de Palacio in 1583 "lead us to think that the system of Spanish cabildos had yet to be consolidated among the Mayas . . . if we accept the thesis that the transition to the Hispanic system of municipal government had begun prior to his arrival that is, in the period between the visitas of . . . the oidores [López Medel and García de Palacio]." See García Bernal, "García de Palacio y sus ordenanzas para Yucatán," *Temas americanistas* 5 (1985): 6.

4. Charles Gibson, *The Aztecs Under the Spanish Rule: A History of the Indians of the Valley of Mexico, 1519–1810* (Stanford: Stanford University Press, 1964), 167, writes thus regarding the Valley of Mexico: "The history of municipal offices

held by Indians begins, however, not with cabildos but with the creation of what Indians called *gobernadoryotl.*" García Martínez, *Los pueblos de la Sierra,* 101, observes that the region he studies, the cacique did not necessarily occupy the office of gobernador. Thus, he writes, in 1542 the principales of Xuxupango elected a certain don Francisco, who was without doubt a distinguished principal. For García Martínez, this example is important in that "the appointment the cacique received (or else did not receive) allowed the separation of the administrative functions that were assigned (however poorly defined) from the inherent qualities of rank and lineage."

5. López Cogolludo, "Ordenanzas de Tomás López (1552)," in *Historia de Yucatán,* 293–94.

6. "Residencia de Diego Quijada (1565)," in AGI, Justicia, legajo 245, f. 1178; "Residencia de Luis de Céspedes Oviedo," in AGI, Justicia, legajo 253, f. 284v; and "Información hecha en el pueblo de Homún sobre la idolatría de los indios (septiembre de 1562)," in *DDQAMY* 1:140.

7. Quezada and Okoshi Harada, *Papeles de los Xiu,* 55–57.

8. "Proceso contra los indios idólatras de Sotuta, Kanchunup, Mopilá, Sacabá, Yaxcabá, Usil y Tibolón (agosto de 1562)," in *DDQAMY* 1:89.

9. "Residencia de . . . Quijada (1565)," in AGI, Justicia, legajo 245, ff. 1001–1526. These pages contain the most complete tally of the pueblos with their respective caciques-gobernadores. The information provided therein allows us to trace the rise of the gobernador of the positions of the república, and the conflicts generated by the imposition of imperial policy. Quijada's "Residencia" is a key source and of incalculable value insofar as its information comes from the declarations of the Maya elite and allow us to evaluate with considerable exactitude the initial results of the Spanish policy of creating cabildos throughout the pueblos.

10. "Nombramientos de alcaldes y regidores hechos por Jofre de Loaysa (15 de mayo de 1560), in AGI, Justicia, legajo 246, ramo 1, ff. 5538–39v; and "Ordenanzas efectuadas por don Luis de Céspedes Oviedo en la visita que efectuó en la provincia de Maní (20 de abril de 1567)," in AGI, Justicia, legajo 252, ff. 699v–700.

11. In 1560 Jofre de Loaysa issued the ambiguous ruling that the regidor should see to the welfare of the república, and carry out the responsibilities of his office; see "Nombramientos de alcaldes . . . (15 de mayo de 1560), in AGI, Justicia, legajo 246, ramo 1, ff. 5538–39v.

12. In 1579 Francisco Cimé, principal of Yobaín, was the ah cuch cab of the village and appears to have been responsible for delivering tribute to the encomendero; see "Proceso de Francisco Manrique sobre haber sido desposeído por Guillén de las Casas, gobernador, de su encomienda (1579)," in AGNM, Civil, volume 2302, expediente 2, f. 7.

13. In the documentation generated by Dr. Diego García de Palacio's visita in Yucatán in 1583–1584, the terms "ah cuch cab" and "mayordomo" are used interchangeably to refer to an individual in charge of the cajas de comunidad;

see Ortiz Yam and Quezada, *Visita de Diego García*, 98, 106, 203, 209. Farriss, *Maya Society*, states that "The *regidor* was used interchangeably with *ah cuch cab* in Maya and early Spanish documents." Spanish documents in *RHGY* vol. 2 describe the position as a "regidor," but in reference to the role that individual played in pre-Hispanic political organization, and not in the colonial cabildos; however, Ciudad Real, *Calepino maya*, 38, defines the position as "regidor y jurado." We must bear in mind the Spanish tendency to match certain functionaries of the prehispanic lordship's political hierarchy with the officials of the Spanish cabildos.

14. Ortiz Yam and Quezada, *Visita de Diego García*, 98, 106, 203, 209.

15. Quezada and Okoshi Harada, *Papeles de los Xiu*, 30–31; Barrera Vásquez, *Documento núm. 1*, 17.

16. The gobernador de Yicamán, a dependency of Maní, stated that the two alguaciles of his pueblo had been named by friars; see "Residencia de . . . Quijada (1565)," in AGI, Justicia, legajo 245, f. 1010.

17. Ibid., 1297–98.

18. "Ordenanzas efectuadas por . . . Céspedes Oviedo . . . (20 de abril de 1567)," in AGI, Justicia, legajo 252, ff. 699v–700. By 1565 pueblos such as Sotuta and Tekax had eight and seven alguaciles, respectively, while Tikuch and Tizimín had six each. See "Residencia de . . . Céspedes Oviedo," in AGI, Justicia, legajo 253, ff. 859v, 896v, 937, 1029v–31.

19. "Nombramiento de alguacil del pueblo de Usil (11 de septiembre de 1563), in AGI, Justicia, legajo 253, ff. 1030v–31.

20. Mayas used the hybrid term *ah canan llaves* to refer to the carcelero, or jailer. *Ah canan* translates as "he who guards something. And fixing it to a name or thing, it meant to guard that which the name denotes." See Ciudad Real, *Calepino maya*, 36.

21. Similar petitions came from the gobernadores of the pueblos of Calkiní and Umán; see "Residencia de . . . Quijada (1565)," in AGI, Justicia, legajo 245, ff. 1491v., 1475v., 1498v., 1503v–04, 1520–21v.

22. "Relación de Sotuta," in *RHGY* 1:147; "Relación de Motul," in *RHGY* 1:269; Roys, *The Political Geography*, 51.

23. "Ordenanzas de . . . López (1552)," in López Cogolludo, *Historia de Yucatán*, 295, 304; "Nombramiento de gobernador indígena hecho por Jofre de Loaysa, oidor de la Audiencia de Guatemala (24 de mayo de 1560), in AGI, Justicia, legajo 246, ramo 1, ff. 5537v.–38; "Título de gobernador a Luis Pech (8 de octubre de 1571)," in AGI, Audiencia de México, legajo 3077, ff. 3v–5; Roys, *The Indian Background*, 169–170, and Farriss, *Maya Society*, 232 and 486n.17, compare the functions of the batab with those which appear under the title of gobernador, and conclude that they were analogous regarding the source of power.

24. "Nombramiento de gobernador indígena . . . (24 de mayo de 1560)," in AGI, Justicia, legajo 246, ramo 1, ff. 5537v.–38; "Ordenanzas . . . de López (1552)," in López Cogolludo, *Historia de Yucatán*, 293.

25. "Título de gobernador . . . (8 de octubre de 1571)," in AGI, Audiencia de México, legajo 3077, ff. 3v–5.

26. "Nombramiento de gobernador indígena . . . (24 de mayo de 1560)," in AGI, Justicia, legajo 246, ramo 1, ff. 5537v.–38; "Título de gobernador . . . (8 de octubre de 1571)," in AGI, Audiencia de México, legajo 3077, ff. 3v–5. García Martínez, *Los pueblos de la Sierra*, 100, observes that a phenonenon similar to that of Yucatán in the villages of the northern Puebla sierra. Rodolfo Pastor, *Campesinos y reformas: la mixteca, 1700–1856* (Mexico City: El Colegio de México, 1987), 88, indicates that from 1560 onward, governorship in the Mixteca was an elective office.

27. "Residencia de . . . Quijada (1565)," in AGI, Justicia, legajo 245, f. 1212v.

28. Ortiz Yam and Quezada, *Visita de Diego García*, 252.

29. "Relación de Chauac-há," in *RHGY* 2:245; "Relación de Popolá," in *RHGY* 2:219; "Residencia de . . . Quijada (1565)," in AGI, Justicia, legajo 245, ff. 1551v., 1552v.

30. "Relación de Chauac-há," in *RHGY* 2:247.

31. "Residencia de . . . Quijada (1565)," in AGI, Justicia, legajo 245, f. 1295.

32. Ibid., f. 1298.

33. "Probanza de el capitán don Juan Chan cacique y señor natural de los pueblos de Chancenote y sus sujetos (1622)," in AGI, Audiencia de México, legajo 140, ramo 2, ff. 1–2v. At the beginning of the seventeenth century don Juan Chan Pat had already become the "gobernador de los gobernadores" of the pueblos de su vicaría Chancenote. For a history of this case, see Quezada, "Don Juan Chan."

34. "Relación de Popolá," in *RHGY* 2:215.

35. In 1565 Ekmul and Yaxá, dependent villages of Sotuta, were physically located with their capital. However, sources for the early 1580s provide no information on Ekmul. This suggests that its cacique had fallen under the political sway of Sotuta's gobernador, and that Ekmul had lost the status of pueblo. Regarding Yaxá, documents still place it with its capital in those years. See "Residencia de . . . Quijada (1565)," in AGI, Justicia, legajo 245, f. 1298v; "Carta de don Guillén de las Casas a Su Majestad con una memoria de los conventos, vicarías y pueblos de la provincia de Yucatán (25 de marzo de 1582)," in *DHY* 2:59; and "Relación de Sotuta," in *RHGY* 1:145.

36. Ciudad Real, *Tratado*, vol. 2, 352.

37. "Residencia de . . . Quijada (1565)," in AGI, Justicia, legajo 245, f. 1498v.

38. Ibid., ff. 1348v–404.

39. Farriss, *Maya Society*, 164, based on the examples of Tizimín and Civikal, states that pueblos located in the same place suffered a process of political disintegration and became parcialidades unified under a single administration. For her, the process was uneven, and does not allow us to understand why these pueblos lost their autonomy, or when.

40. For a discussion on this point, see section 5 of Chapter 2, above, including Tables 4 and 5.

41. López Cogolludo, *Historia de Yucatán*, 232–40, offers a list of settlements formed as a result of the second round of reducciones.

42. "Carta de don Guillén . . . (25 de marzo de 1582)," in DHY, 2:63.

43. To trace the places to which the villages were relocated, see Gerhard, *The Southeast Frontier*, 55–146; and Roys, *The Political Geography*. In reality, both authors base their works on the 1582 list that appears in "Carta de don Guillén . . . (25 de marzo de 1582)," in DHY 2:55–63, and in López Cogolludo, *Historia de Yucatán*, 232–40.

44. López Cogolludo, *Historia de Yucatán*, 235–40. The history of the Yucatecan villages' political organization can be traced through the *juicios de residencia*. For the most part, when these juicios began, they were announced through all the villages so that their cabildos and representatives report whether they had suffered any sort of injustice, in order that they receive redress. In Yucatán this announcement was made in Maya, and all the repúblicas had to confirm whether they had been made aware that the process was to begin. Their obligatory formal replies allow a detailed list of the functionaries making up these bodies. This, in turn, allows us to determine whether or not villages gathered in a single location had a single cabildo. See "Residencia de Miguel Francisco Codornio de Sola (1674)," AGI, Escribanía de Cámara, legajo 319c, ff. 38, 41.

45. The fate of Tibatún, another of Chancenote's dependent pueblos, remains unknown; possibly the former's cacique fell under the political influence of the latter's gobernador. See "Carta de don Guillén . . . (25 de marzo de 1582)," in DHY 2:61.

46. In 1582 Tixul was still physically located within Maní; when friar Alonso conducted his visita in 1588, Tixul had already been relocated, and three years later appeared as cabecera de doctrina. See Ciudad Real, *Tratado*, 2:367; López Cogolludo, *Historia de Yucatán*, 235–40.

47. Ciudad Real, *Tratado*, 2:376.

48. "Relación de Dzan," in RHGY 1:253. As indicated in chapter 2 above, this same reducción included Sacalum, a pueblo de visita of Maní.

49. In 1583 the gobernadores of Tizimín, Dzonotchuil, Tekay, and Tiscacauchén were don Juan Huchín, don Juan Chuil, don Pablo Miz, and don Juan Canché, respectively; see Ortiz Yam and Quezada, *Visita de Diego García*, 85, 90, 96, 100.

50. García de Palacio had ordered that in "said pueblos [of Tizimín, Tekay, Tiscacauché, and Dzonotchuil], there must be a gobernador who rules and maintains justice." See Ortiz Yam and Quezada, *Visita de Diego García*, 104.See also "Sobre las heridas que dio fray Luis de Castilla a la mujer de Diego Pérez (1606)," AGI, Audiencia de Lima, legajo 300. Despite its lurid title, which presents the pages within as concerning the case of a friar beating a woman, this misclassified and mislabeled document actually provides a list of the repúblicas of each of the villages incorporated into the Tizimin reducción.

51. Landa, *Relación*, 31, 54.

52. Pedro Sánchez de Aguilar, *Informe contra idolorum cultores del obispado de Yucatán* (Mérida: E. G. Triay e Hijos, 1937), 151.

53. "Petición de don Francisco de Montejo Xiu para hacer una compañía con Joaquín de Leguizamo (1565)," in AGI, Justicia, legajo 245, f. 2784v.

54. Francisco de Montejo Xiu and Francisco Che signed the six-year contract, supposedly representing "the Indians who are . . . in the school of Maní monastery, learning evangelical doctrina," since it was their responsibility to see to the "growth and well being of said school," with the consent of the friars and the alcalde mayor. The implication is that the community funds were being disguised as private property. "Petición de don Francisco de Montejo Xiu . . . (1565)," in AGI, Justicia, legajo 248, ff. 2789v–91v.

55. Ibid., ff. 2795v–805.

56. "Cuenta de la caja de comunidad del pueblo de Homún (7 de septiembre de 1563)," in AGI, Justicia, legajo 253, f. 1027; and "Mandamiento a la caja de comunidad del pueblo de Xanabá (18 de mayo de 1563)," in AGI, Justicia, legajo 253, f. 1028. For the cajas of the villages of Calotmul, Tinum, and Chancenote, see "Residencia de . . . Quijada (1565)," in AGI, Justicia, legajo 245, ff. 544–45, 552, 560.

57. Ortiz Yam and Quezada, *Visita de Diego García*, 133, 122, 128.

58. Ibid., 214.

59. "Ordenanzas efectuadas por . . . Céspedes Oviedo . . . (20 de abril de 1567)," in AGI, Justicia, legajo 252, ff. 700–701; Ortiz Yam y Quezada, *Visita de Diego García*, 89–90, 94–96, 98–99, 103–104.

60. Ortiz Yam and Quezada, *Visita de Diego García*, 121. The one and one half real contribution to the community fund then being imposed in central Mexico at some undetermined point, before 1577, which served as a key source of revenue for the cajas, began to play that role in Yucatán in 1583 with the visita of don Diego García de Palacio. Unlike the case in central Mexico, in the peninsula this oidor established as quota the sum of one real per Indian tributary, that is, per married Indian man. See Miranda, *El tributo*, 140; "Carta del defensor de los indios, Francisco de Palomino, a S. M. (12 de abril de 1585)," in AGI, Audiencia de México, legajo 3048.

61. Ortiz Yam and Quezada, *Visita de Diego García*, 90–91, 102.

62. "Petición de don Francisco de Montejo Xiu . . . (1565)," in AGI, Justicia, legajo 248, f. 2782v.

63. "Cuenta de la caja de . . . Homún (7 de septiembre de 1563)," in AGI, Justicia, legajo 253, f. 1027; Ortiz Yam and Quezada, *Visita de Diego García*, 98.

64. "Cuenta de la caja . . . de Homún (1563)," in AGI, Justicia, legajo 253, f. 1026v.

65. Ciudad Real, *Tratado*, 2:367.

66. In 1552 Tomás López Medel, with the aim of providing for travelers, ordered that mesones be constructed in all the villages; see "Ordenanzas de Tomás López (1552)," in López Cogolludo, *Historia de Yucatán*, 303.

67. Ortiz Yam and Quezada, *Visita de Diego García*, 113, 118–19, 130, 135.

68. This theme receives extensive review in Chapter 4 above. See "Residencia de . . . Quijada (1565)," in AGI, Justicia, legajo 245, ff. 1023–24, 1370v, 1374v, 1380v, 1422.

69. For additional references, see the declarations of Hernando Muñoz Zapata, Juan Insuasti, regidor of the villa of Campeche, and of Alonso de Villanueva,

alcalde of the villa of Valladolid, in "Residencia de . . . Quijada (1565)," in AGI, Justicia, legajo 245, ff. 34, 39, 55, 268, 442; and "Cargos de residencia contra el doctor don Diego Quijada (31 de enero de 1566)," in *DDQAMY* 2:240.

70. In this regard, see the declarations of Feliciano Bravo, escribano mayor, in "Residencia de Diego de Quijada," in AGI, Justicia, legajo 246, ramo 1, f. 5537; and "Cargos . . . contra . . . Quijada (31 de enero de 1566), in *DDQAMY* 2:238.

71. "Residencia de . . . Quijada (1565)," in AGI, Justicia, legajo 245, f. 1148.

72. "Relación de Yalcón," in *RHGY* 2:335.

73. Ortiz Yam and Quezada, *Visita de Diego García*, 127.

74. "Real cédula al virrey de la Nueva España sobre que en los pueblos de indios de la provincia de Yucatán haya alcaldes y regidores (13 de mayo de 1579)," in AGI, Audiencia de México, legajo 2999–D2, f. 193.

75. Scholes, "Introducción," *DDQAMY* 1:xi, states that government by the alcaldes mayores appointed by the audiencias was not totally satisfactory in the eyes of the Crown, not only because of the need to name two visitadores (Tomás Lóez and Jofre de Loaysa), but also because of the sort of petitions that reached Spain.

76. After don Diego, the authorities who came to Yucatán arrived with the responsibilities of governor already designated directly by the King; see Rubio Mañé, "Las jurisdicciones," 559.

77. For a discussion of the process whereby the repartimiento of personal services was set up in Yucatán, see Sergio Quezada, "Los sistemas de trabajo en Yucatán, 1541–1561," *Boletín de la Escuela de Ciencias Antropológicas de la Universidad de Yucatán* 9, no. 44 (1980): 55–69.

78. "Auto del alcalde mayor don Diego de Quijada sobre el asunto de indios de servicio (18 de julio de 1561)," in *DDQAMY* 1:6–7.

79. "Carta del cabildo de la ciudad de Mérida a Su Majestad (Mérida, 6 de octubre de 1561)," in *DDQAMY* 1:13–16.

80. Scholes, "Introducción," *DDQAMY* 1:xxxvi–xxxviii.

81. Ibid., 1:lxxv.

82. "Ordenanzas efectuadas por . . . Céspedes Oviedo . . . (20 de abril de 1567), in AGI, Justicia, legajo 252, ff. 699v–700.

83. In this regard, see "Residencia de . . . Quijada (1565)," in AGI, Justicia, legajo 245, ff. 1542–70.

84. Ibid., f. 1551.

85. "Residencia de Luis de Céspedes de Oviedo (1571)," in AGI, Justicia, legajo 250, f. 587.

86. "Francisco Palomino, defensor de los naturales, suplica se le dé sobrecédula para que no haya alcaldes mayores y corregidores en los pueblos de indios," in AGI, Indiferente General, legajo 1390.

87. It is significant and revealing that in the expedientes thus far discovered of the visita of Diego García de Palacio in Yucatán in 1583, there appear no complaints on the part of los caciques and principales of the pueblos, alleging that

encomenderos or other Spaniards intervened in the villages' internal affairs. This fact gives some idea of how Spaniards advanced their economic activities in the process of colonizing Maya society. In this regard, see Ortiz Yam and Quezada, *Visita de Diego García*, 28–32.

88. "Proceso que hizo el doctor Diego Quijada contra los caciques de la provincia de Maní, sobre decir que se emborracharon (octubre de 1561)," in AGI, Justicia, legajo 248, ff. 2077–78v, 2112–15v.

89. Quezada and Okoshi Harada, *Papeles de los Xiu*, 68.

90. María de Lourdes Villafuerte García, "Relaciones entre los grupos sociales a través de la información matrimonial: Ciudad de México, 1628–1634" (Thesis, Universidad Nacional Autónoma de México, 1998), 31.

91. Landa, *Relación*, 53.

92. López Cogolludo, *Historia de Yucatán*, 182.

93. Ortiz Yam and Quezada, *Visita de Diego García*, 64.

94. Ibid., 225–27.

95. Landa, *Relación*, 55, stated that the women "Wear their hair very long and make a great show of it, parting it in the middle and braiding it in various ways."

96. The *Siete partidas* defined five types of *alcahuetes*, or pimps; and Juan N. Rodríguez San Miguel, *Pandectas hispano-mexicanas* (México City: Universidad Nacional Autónoma de México, 1980), 3:496, lists a typology of four. The first of these are the *"bellacos malos* who guard the whores, who take a part of what the women make." The second are the *"trujamanes* [who go] to the men, pimping the women, who remain in their houses, in exchange for something the men pay." The third are "men who keep captives and servants in their own houses, with the intention of doing evil with their bodies, taking from them what they earn." The fourth is "when the man is so vile that he prostitutes his own wife."

97. Ortiz Yam and Quezada, *Visita de Diego García*, 134.

98. Ibid., 115.

99. Ibid., 60, 78, 112, 118, 123, 135, 140, 216, 221.

100. Ibid., 112, 117, 129.

101. "Tasaciones del pueblo de Motul (1549–1561)," in *DDQAMY* 2:111–113.

102. Gonzalo Chuil, ecribano of Calotmul, stated that, "they have divided said village into three parts, and the third part of the village pay tribute first, then the next third pay the next part, and later the rest." See Ortiz Yam and Quezada, *Visita de Don Diego*, 125.

103. "Carta de Pedro Gómez, tesorero de Yucatán a su majestad enviándole las cuentas de los años desde 1553 hasta fin de 1561 (marzo de 1563)," in *DDQAMY* 2:44. At the end of this same letter the treasurer (*tesorero*) states that at the end of the year "the account that the caciques have brought is produced, and they are made to understand what is lacking, so that they bring it, and returning to their villages and picking up what they must provide requires several days, and it is true that up until now they have not paid the remainder that they owe."

104. "Traslado de la carta que Francisco Palomino escribió a su majestad (28 de marzo de 1573)," in AGI, Justicia, legajo 1016; "Carta de los oficiales reales de Yucatán a su majestad (2 de abril de 1573)," in AGI, Audiencia de México, legajo 365, f. 55.

105. "Respuesta de Francisco de Palomino a las peticiones de Carlos Arellano y Alonso de Herrera (19 de septiembre de 1578)," in AGI, Justicia, legajo 1016, f. 32v.

106. Ortiz Yam and Quezada, *Visita de Diego García*, 56.

107. Landa, *Relación*, 57.

108. "Traslado de la carta que Francisco Palomino . . . (28 de marzo de 1573)," in AGI, Justicia, legajo 1016.

109. Ortiz Yam and Quezada, *Visita de Diego García*, 55, 59, 62, 141, 217, 222, 239, 242.

110. "Los oficiales reales contra el guardián de Motul (1573)," in AGI, Audiencia de México, legajo 3177, ff. 8–9; Ortiz Yam and Quezada, *Visita de Diego García*, 97, 102, 117, 120, 122.

111. Miranda, *El tributo indígena*, 10–12.

112. Ortiz Yam and Quezada, *Visita de Diego García*, 55, 58, 76, 113, 118, 140.

113. Ibid., 113.

114. "Los oficiales reales contra . . . (febrero de 1573)," in AGI, Audiencia de México, legajo 3177, ff. 6–7.

115. Ortiz Yam and Quezada, *Visita de Diego García*, 17–18, 243–53.

Chapter 4

1. For a detailed analysis of the colonial evolution of the Yucatecan nobility as a social group, see Farriss, *Maya Society*, 227–55.

2. See Quezada and Okoshi Harada, *Papeles de los Xiu*, 55–57; "Residencia de Diego de Quijada (1565)," in AGI, Justicia, legajo 245, f.1185v.; and "Información hecha por el doctor Diego de Quijada en los pueblos de Homún, Maní y Tacul (enero de 1564)," in *DDQAMY* 2:138.

3. Toward the mid-1500s the caciques of Homún, Huhí, Tiscanbanchel, Sanahcat, Hoctún, Sahcabá, Yaxcabá, and Tibolón already enjoyed permits to ride horses. See "Residencia de . . . Quijada (1565)," in AGI, Justicia, legajo 245, ff. 1475, 1185v, 1212v, and 1232v.

4. See "Relación de Motul," in *RHGY* 1:272.

5. The two volumes of *RHGY* provide the most complete sources for understanding the process of Yucatec Maya nobility adopting Spanish cultural patterns. In particular, see "Relación de Oxkutzcab," in *RHGY* 1:355–66; "Relación de Titzal," in *RHGY* 1:238; and "Relación de la villa de Valladolid," in *RHGY* 2:40.

6. Farriss, *Maya Society*, 97, writes: "By the end of the seventeenth century, only a handful of the Maya elites, if that many, could communicate with Spanish-speaking officials, although others may have known a smattering of Spanish words."

7. Don Diego de Santillán wrote that in 1571 "a French vessel [arrived] in said port of Sisal and set out on the road that passed through Hunucmá, and as quickly as possible the cacique of that village came in person to Mérida to report the matter and give warning, and because of him they were arrested, imprisoned, and punished, and for that reason they gave the cacique his appointment ... as he showed himself worthy of it." See "Relación de Chuburná," in *RHGY* 1:400. William B. Taylor, *Landlord and Peasant in Colonial Oaxaca* (Stanford: Stanford University Press, 1972), 37–38, reports a similar case for Oaxaca.

8. During the seventeenth century, faced with the need to concentrate the Indian populations that inhabited far-flung and inaccesible zones, the office of captain became common in frontier villages. It was these individuals who began to organize small Maya militias that the Spanish controlled by granting selected privileges. In 1624 Oxkutzcab had a unit of 124 men who enjoyed an exemption from the *holpatán*, a one-real tax that paid the salary of magistrates of the *tribunal de indios*. Nor did they have to contribute the twenty cacao grains for the caja de comunidad, nor provide personal services. Moreover, they enjoyed "all the honors and preeminence and exceptions and liberties . . . that the descendents of the caciques and indigenous lords have." See "Petición de los indios del pueblo de Oxkutzcab (1624)," in AGI, Audiencia de México, legajo 145, ramo 1. It is significant to point out that the importance that these designations acquired and the role that these armed Indians discharged have not received sufficient attention from scholars of colonial Yucatán. See the comments of Farriss, *Maya Society*, 97–89, 175, concerning don Pablo Paxbolón.

9. Farriss, *Maya Society*, 174–75.

10. See Sergio Quezada, "Don Juan Chan, un cacique antiidólatra," *Mayab* 5 (1989): 41–44.

11. López Cogolludo, *Historia de Yucatán*, 261–62.

12. Ibid., 260–66, provides a detailed narrative of the events leading to attempts on the lives of the friars, and of the agreement that friar Luis de Villalpando formed with don Francisco de Montejo the Adelantado, not to execute those involved.

13. See "Ordenanzas de López Medel, (1552)," in López Cogolludo, *Historia de Yucatán*, 299–300.

14. See Ibid., 294.

15. Ibid., 294–95; see also, Farriss, *Maya Society*, 175–76.

16. Don Tomás issued the following order for macehuales: "And if some cacique commits an injury . . . notify the [Spanish authorities] that . . . there must be an investigation." See, "Ordenanzas de López Medel (1552)," in López Cogolludo, *Historia de Yucatán*, 294.

17. López Medel wrote, "We are free men in Jesus Christ, while secular law also declares free those born of free parents. But despite these facts . . . the caciques and principales . . . took possession of free Indians, poor and unprotected orphans, who have no parents, and made them serve as slaves, at times even carrying them elsewhere to sell. I therefore order." See Ibid., 301.

18. Silvio Zavala, *Los esclavos indios en la Nueva España* (Mexico City: El Colegio Nacional, 1967), 107–60, offers a broad discussion of the Crown's antislavery policies.

19. For a discussion of Yucatecan Indian slavery during the early colonial years, see Quezada, "Los sistemas de trabajo," 57.

20. "Ordenanzas de . . . López Medel (1552)," in López Cogolludo, *Historia de Yucatán*, 294–95.

21. John F. Chuchiak IV argues that even as Spanish authorities heightened the offensive to limit the Maya lords' rights and privileges, those same lords continued to hold fast to their traditions. Thus, during the convites of the second half of the sixteenth century, the batabob organized ritual consumption of balché to honor the principales of their lordships, all with an eye to maintaining their own social prestige and upholding thier political ties. See Chuchiak, "It Is Their Drinking that Hinders Them: *Balché* and the Use of Ritual Intoxicants among the Colonial Yucatec Maya, 1550–1780," *Estudios de cultural maya* 24 (2004): 149–51.

22. "Proceso que hizo el doctor Diego Quijada contra los caciques de la provincia de Maní sobre decir se emborracharon (octubre de 1561)," in AGI, Justicia, legajo 248, ff. 2077–78v, 2112–15v.

23. Ibid., ff. 2071v, 2079–80.

24. "Memorial de fray Diego de Landa (undated)," in *DDQAMY* 2:417. For an appraisal of the Franciscans' mission work from the arrival in Yucatán to the inquisitional trials, see González Cicero, *Perspectiva religiosa*, 119–24.

25. For an extensive treatment of the inquisitorial trials of 1562, of the political and religious context in which they played out, and of the participation of friar Diego de Landa, don Diego de Quijada, the bishop, and the encomenderos, see Scholes, "Introducción," *DDQAMY* 1:v–cvii.

26. Beyond soliciting the intervention of the alcalde mayor, friar Diego de Landa set in motion the inquisition by naming Francisco Orozco and Bartolomé Bohorques as respective notary and alguacil of the Holy Office. See "Declaraciones de algunos testigos de la investigación de las idolatrías de los indios hechas por fray Diego de Landa y sus compañeros (1562)," in *DDQAMY* 1: 25–26, 35.

27. In addition to don Gaspar Che of Sacalum, the list of those arrested included don Francisco de Montejo Xiu of Maní, don Diego Uz of Tekax, and the caciques of Hunactí, Mama, Pencuyut, Tekit, Tahdziú, Tikunché, and Oxkutzcab. See Ibid., 26, 32–35. These pages contain a list of the the Indian principales so detained.

28. "Respuesta de fray Diego de Landa a los cargos hechos por fray Francisco de Guzmán (undated)," in *DDQAMY* 2:416.

29. "Residencia . . . de Quijada (1565)," in AGI, Justicia, legajo 245, f. 1215. The *collera* was a chain of prisoners that walked tied one to another so that they could not escape.

30. "Petición que presentó fray Diego de Landa ante el doctor Quijada, pidiendo el auxilio del brazo seglar para llevar presos a la ciudad de Mérida

algunos indios culpados en el asunto de la idolatría (julio de 1562)," in *DDQAMY* 1:70.

31. "Testimonios de algunos españoles sobre las idolatrías de los indios (1562)," in *DDQAMY* 1:165; "Información hecha en el pueblo de Homún sobre la idolatría de los indios (septiembre de 1562)," in *DDQAMY* 1:146–47; and "Declaraciones de algunos testigos . . . (1562)," in *DDQAMY* 1:53–54.

32. In Ciudad Real, *Calepino maya*, 117, "coyol" is translated as "token or sign."

33. "Testimonios de algunos españoles . . . (1562)," in *DDQAMY* 1"165; "Información hecha en el pueblo de Homún sobre la idolatría de los indios (septiembre de 1562)," in *DDQAMY* 1:146–47; "Declaraciones de algunos testigos . . . (1562)," in *DDQAMY* 1:53–54.

34. "Diligencias hechas por el provincial fray Diego de Landa y el obispo fray Francisco de Toral en el asunto de las idolatríás de los indios (1562–1563)," in *DDQAMY* 1:193–94.

35. Scholes, "Introducción," *DDQAMY* 1:il.

36. "Declaraciones de algunos testigos . . . (1562)," in *DDQAMY* 1: 27, 29. The sanbenito is the ensignia of the Inquisition, placed over the chest and shoulders of the penitent; it takes the form of a yellow capote, or sleeveless tunic, adorned with a red cross. The coroza is a type of conical paper hat like a dunce cap placed on the penitent as a symbol of punishment.

37. Ibid., 48–49.

38. Ibid., 49.

39. González Cicero, *Perspectiva religiosa*, 163. In early 1563 Toral wrote: "since the Indians are such novices in faith, and since we must root them in that faith through sermons, confessions, and saintly admonitions so that they may know what is necessary for their salvation, and on their own may extirpate and uproot their idolatries and other sins. And it is not appropriate to harrass them, as the friars in essence have done." See "Probanza hecha a pedimento del obispo fray Francisco de Toral sobre la manera en que fray Diego de Landa y otros religiosos usaron la jurisdicción eclesiástica en la provincia de Yucatán (1563)," in *DDQAMY* 1:250.

40. Scholes, "Introducción," *DDQAMY* 1:lxiv–lxv, notes that the sentence that friar Francisco de Toral meeted out to the caciques and principales was to receive lashes "or some other benign form of punishment," and that once their crimes of idolatry had been explained to them, and they had been punished, they were sent back to their villages. See also, Landa, *Relación*, 33.

41. Hildeberto Martínez lists the wealth of the lords of Tepeaca; see *Tepeaca en el siglo XVI: Tenencia de la tierra y organización de un señorío* (Mexico City: Ediciones de La Casa Chata, 1984), 80–90. For other examples, see Gibson, *The Aztecs*, 263–77; García Martínez, *Los pueblos de la Sierra*, 186, 191–92; and Delfina E. López Sarrelangue, "El caso de un gobernador michoacano en el siglo XVI," *Relaciones* 6, no. 22 (1985): 24–26.

42. "Proceso . . . contra los caciques la provincia de Maní (1561)," in AGI, Justicia, legajo 248, ff. 2077–78.

43. The individual who carried out the inventory of Chan's belongings described his house thus: "And after proceeding through said house, we found no other possessions than a chair. That house is a hut of straw and cane poles with plastered and finished walls, and includes a kitchen." The description of the goods of Juan Nic and Gaspar Queb, principales of Maní, has much the same tenor; see "Proceso . . . contra los caciques de la provincia de Maní (1581)," in AGI, Justicia, legajo 248, ff. 2077–78.

44. Revelatory in this regard are the testimonies of the caciques of Huhí, Sahcabá, Tibolón, Tibatún, and Pocboc; see "Residencia of . . . Quijada (1565)," in AGI, Justicia, legajo 245, ff. 1185v., 1202v., 1320, 1206v., and 1198. For additional references, see "Residencia de Luis de Céspedes Oviedo, in AGI, Justicia, legajo 253, ff. 944, 951.

45. Around 1565 the caciques of Chaltún, Timucuy, Tixiol, and Acanceh declared that they had observed these regulations when obtaining Indian services to repair their own homes. See "Residencia de . . . Quijada (1565)," in AGI, Justicia, legajo 245, ff. 1542, 1544, 1546, and 1548. García Martínez, *Los pueblos de la Sierra*, 195, notes that this tendency also prevailed among the caciques of the northern sierra of Puebla; see also, Gibson, *The Aztecs*, 156–57.

46. "Ordenanzas efectuadas por don Luis de Céspedes Oviedo en la visita que efectuó en la provincia de Maní (20 de abril de 1567)," in AGI, Justicia, legajo 252, ff. 698–701.

47. Isaura Inés Ortiz Yam, "Los pueblos del noroeste yucateco" (Thesis, Universidad Autónoma de Yucatán, 1998), 111.

48. Prior to the reform of García de Palacio in 1583, Indian tributaries gave blankets, chickens, wax, corn, beans, chile, honey, fish, salt, pitchers, pots, griddles, and rope. See "Tasaciones del pueblo de Motul (1549–1560)," on *DDQAMY*, 2:111–12.

49. Moreover, García de Palacio incorporated unmarrieds and widows of both sexes as half-tribute payers. This reform, together with the individual *capitación*, or tax payment responsibility, soon became common practice and remained in effect until the end of the eighteenth century, when Yucatecan encomiendas were swept back by the Crown. See García Bernal, *Población y encomienda*, 385–86; López Cogolludo, *Historia de Yucatán*, 401. Miranda, *El tributo*, 138, states that this tributary reform was implemented in the viceregal center from 1560 onward.

50. Miranda, *El tributo*, 175, summarized the importance of this fiscal reform in terms of cacique power over the distribution of tribute. He affirms that from 1560 onward an inversion took place in the arrangements of tasación. That is, "before [1560] it began with a fixed general sum, determined by one authority [the audiencia], to arrive at the individual amount, determined by another authority [the cacique]; but now [after 1560], one authority [the audiencia] worked from the individual amount—that is, the quota of each tributary—to reach a general amount by multiplying that sum by the number of total tributaries. Before, the general amount determined tasación; now, it was settled by the individual payers." It should be remembered that in Yucatán, owing to the tasaciones

of 1549, caciques dealt out the tribute assignments among their people. These same caciques used the measure of dividing households into groups of three, regardless of how many people made up each household, so that each third be responsible for one of the three tribute collections that took place each year. García Martínez, *Los pueblos de la Sierra*, 194–95, states that at the root of this reform, "the caciques and officials of the república continued to be responsible for collecting tribute, but saw restrictionts or limitations in their power to determine that amount that each person or family head should pay."

51. Ortiz Yam and Quezada, *Visita de Diego García*, 243–44.

52. It is important to emphasize that by the mid-seventeenth century the privileges of the caciques scarcely differed from those set forth by don Diego de Quijada; see Quezada and Okoshi Harada, *Papeles de los Xiu*, 73–106. García Martínez, *Los pueblos de la Sierra*, 192, notes that as a result of the royal decree (cédula) of January 31, 1552, the wealth of the caciques remained linked to the development of their administrative ability. Similarly, this same text states that once the funds for the caja de comunidad had been set aside (these being responsibility of the cabildo), the income of the cacique remained separate from those of the gobernador, whether these were separate individuals or united in a single person. These same observations apply to the Yucatecan lords. It is essential to point out that since the economic prerogatives that Spanish power allocated to the caciques consisted in control of forced labor, the benefit of this arrangement does not appear in the accounts of the cajas de comunidad.

53. This review of the evolution from cacicazgo to governorship is supported by Appendix B above, and all information comes from that source unless otherwise noted. It is well known that in central Mexico there were no fixed rules for the passing of paternal surnames. The Yucatecan case differs significantly in that, since the Franciscans began to impose Christian names, the pre-Hispanic patronymic took the place of the Spanish surname. The appendices provide abundant evidence of this point. For example, *Batab* Uz, whose name was more an indication of hierarchical ranking, became Diego Uz under the Franciscans. Similarly, Ah Kukum Xiu was baptized as Francisco de Montejo Xiu. This policy was accompanied by a general tendency to transmit last names from father to son. Breaks in succession are thus fairly easy to detect. Bautismal books of Yucatecan villages confirm the persistence of Indian patronymics in the Western style. See "Libro de bautizos del pueblo de Conkal (1586–1773)," in ASAY. There were also cases of Indian hidalgos who adopted Spanish surnames, but the practice remained the exceptions that proved the rule.

54. It is important to remember the observation of Farriss, *Maya Society*, 239, that the criterion for succession of señorío disappeared within a few generations, and that it was replaced by a system defined as hereditary access to government, an arrangement that preserved the basic concept of rule of heredity by adapting it to colonial circumstances.

55. Abundant and angry comments on the part of the caciques attest to this Spanish practice. For example, see "Residencia de . . . Quijada (1565)," in AGI, Justicia, legajo 245, ff. 1011–562.

56. One case was that of don Hernando Cupul, cacique of Espita. Being a widower, he began a relationship with María Itzá, wife of Francisco Homa, and had a son with her. When governor Guillén de las Casas (1577–1582) learned of the affair in 1580, he suspended Cupul from his cacicazgo; the disgraced cacique only recovered his office when he married María Xol. See Ortiz Yam and Quezada, *Visita de Diego García*, 205, 215.

57. Chamberlain, *The Conquest*, 232–36, narrates in detail the severe repression that the conquistadors employed to submit the region of Tihosuco's cúuchcabal.

58. "Residencia de Luis de Céspedes Oviedo," in AGI, Justicia, legajo 253, f. 655.

59. At the time of the Spanish invasion, the Tzeh governed the pre-Hispanic capital of Chancenote, but also the villages of Tibatún, Tixcancal, and Tixmucul. See appendix B above.

60. The third section of chapter 3 above presents the history of the successions of Chancenote.

61. "Residencia de . . . Céspedes Oviedo," in AGI, Justicia, legajo 253, f. 663.

62. Gibson, *The Aztecs*, 167–68, states, "But the significant fact for Indian government was that the office of gobernador came to be differentiated from that of tlatoani, with the two offices held by different persons." For Gibson, "It was a deliberate viceregal policy in the sixteenth century to take advantage of such opportunities to introduce the desired Hispanic institution and simultaneously to reduce the powers of hereditary caciques." See also, García Martínez, *Los pueblos de la Sierra*, 198–99.

63. "Residencia de . . . Quijada (1565)," in AGI, Justicia, legajo 245, ff. 1370v–71.

64. Ibid., ff. 1381.

65. Don Diego de Quijada possibly did the same with the successor of don Tomás Tun of the village of Usil. Up until 1561 don Tomás appeared as cacique-gobernador, and one year later Pedro Yah was gobernador. See appendix B above.

66. These villages were Mama, Teabo, Yicmán, and Tekax, all dependencies of Maní; Mopilá and Tepakán of Calkiní; Citilcum and Tekantó of Dzidzantún; Xocchel of Hocabá; Tibolón of Sotuta; Tzucacab of Calotmul; and finally, the independent villages of Chocholá and Sihó. See appendix B above.

67. Don Francisco Cocom was the son of Nachí Cocom, the halach uinic of Sotuta. Upon the latter's death, most likely in the 1550s, his son was still not old enough to assume the title. Rather, it was occupied by his uncle don Lorenzo, who came to be known as the halach uinic of Sotuta province. He was tried for idolatries, and around 1563, imprisoned by the inquisitorial authorities, he hung himself. In these same years don Francisco attained his majority and succeeded his uncle. See "Procesos contra los indios idólatras de Sotuta, Kanchunup, Mopilá, Yaxcabá, Sahcabá, Usil y Tibolón (agosto de 1562)," in *DDQAMY*, 1: 73n24, 73n80;

"Relación de Sotuta," in *RHGY* 1:147. A similar case was that of Melchor Pech, either the son or brother of Naum Pech, the last halach uinic of Motul. This latter died shortly after the conquest; the former succeeded him, since he appears as cacique and governor of that capital at least until 1567. See "Relación de Motul," in *RHGY* 1:269; and Roys, *The Political Geography*, 51.

68. Sherburne F. Cook and Woodrow Borah, *Ensayos sobre historia de la población: México y el Caribe* (Mexico City: Siglo XXI Editores, 1977), 2:120–21; García Bernal, *Población y encomienda*, 66–67. In this latter work (53, 85) the author calculates that between the mid-sixteenth and early seventeenth century the Indian population had fallen from 232,576 to 164,064. For a different view of the demographic changes of this period, see Cook and Borah, *Ensayos*, 2: 71, 75.

69. Roys, *The Political Geography*, 77.

70. Don Diego de Santillán named Gaspar Antonio as lieutenant governor for the entire province of Maní; see "Probanza de Gaspar Antonio para una ayuda de costa (1579)," in AGI, Audiencia de México, legajo 104, f. 10. For one of Francisco Palomino's accusations, see the transcription of his letter to the King of Spain (March 28, 1573), in AGI, Justicia, legajo 1061.

71. In the village of Dzan, a dependent of Maní, it may have been don Luis de Céspedes Oviedo who appointed Miguel Cuyoc as governor. See Appendex 2 below. Recent studies have shown that once they were removed from their lordships, many of the Maya nobles and traditional caciques retained their prestige by occupying the important post of village escribano, a post that often entailed lifetime appointment. For evidence on this point, see John F. Chuchiak IV, "Writing as Resistance: Maya Graphic Pluralism and Indigenous Elite Strategies for Survival in Colonial Yucatán, 1550–1750," *Ethnohistory* 57, no. 1 (2010): 87–116.

72. Regarding this point we must consider the interpretation that Farriss, *Maya Society*, 243, advances concerning Xiu political evolution during the seventeenth century. Based on this example, she suggests that the resurgence of the lineages resulted from a compromise between the indigenous concept of legitimacy based on hereditary claims and the Spanish desire to reduce the power of the lineage governors.

73. Despite the fragmentary nature of the evidence regarding the Chel, this ruling lineage appears to have felt the effects of the demographic collapse in the succession of Dzilam and Yobaín, since in 1567 in the former and 1579 in the latter we find Juan Can and Juan Chan acting as respective gobernadores. Regarding Cansahcab, together with the pre-Hispanic capital of Dzidzantún, there is no reference to their indigenous rulers after 1569, and in both pueblos the Chel governed in that year. There is also the governing lineage of the Cochuah. As previously mentioned, the various Spanish invasions caused them to lose control of the pre-Hispanic capital of Tihosuco. Some time later, in 1563, in the face of don Diego de Quijada's campaign to purge caciques from governorships, he named Alonso Cupul as gobernador of Ekpedz, despite the fact that don Melchor

Cochuah served as batab. The historical record only tracks Agustín Cochuah, cacique of Ichmul, until 1569, the year that he was serving as both cacique and governor of his village. See appendix B above.

74. Farriss, *Maya Society*, 245, states that these lineages, by reason of their exceptionally large size, did not disappear altogether from public office.

75. "Título de gobernador a Luis Pech (8 de octubre de 1571)," in AGI, Audiencia de México, legajo 3007, ff. 3v–5.

76. All evidence indicates that the caciques of the Pech lineage, ruling in the pueblos of Telchac, Dzemul, Sitpach, and Tixiol, were caught unawares by the demographic collapse. But their successors managed to maintain rule over those villages. Regarding the Canul lineage—or at least the heirs of don Pedro of Hecelchakán, of don Juan de Hunucmá, and of another don Juan of Nunkiní—they retained their governorships until 1576, 1580, and 1595, respectively. The story was much the same for the Cupul lineage: only the descendents of the caciques of Nabalam and Ekbalam hung on to their offices, the former until 1571, an the latter until 1579. See appendix B above.

77. The ruling lineage of the Cupul was also displaced in Chalanté, Tinum, and Tisacacauché, where Francisco Tepal, Francisco Cantun, and Juan Canché began to serve as governors, the first two in 1569 and the third in 1580. The Canul lineage also suffered the loss of the governorship in Tepakán, Dzibilkil, and Yabacú. See appendix B above.

78. See Ortiz Yam and Quezada, *Visita de Diego García*, 52–53, 104–106, 205–206.

79. García de Palacio stated that "in the election of governor for this pueblo, he is to remain here, and cannot be removed without just cause and after having fulfilled the period for which he was named." See Ortiz Yam and Quezada, *Visita de Diego García*, 243.

80. Ibid., 104–106.

81. García de Palacio established a salary of twelve *cargas* of corn annually for the alcaldes. He did not do the same for the income of the regidores; while those of Tizimín, Tecay, Dzonotchuil and Tiscacauché were paid eight cargas of corn, those of Espita received only ten. See Ibid., 104–106, 205–206.

82. See Ortiz Yam and Quezada, *Visita de Diego García*, 52–53, 104–106, 205–206.

83. "Averiguación que fray Luis de Cifuentes y Sotomayor, obispo de la provincia hace en virtud de la real cédula de S. M., en razón de inquirir y saber los agravios que reciben los indios naturales de estas provincias (1670)," in AGI, Escribanía de Cámara, legajo 318 A, f. 222v.

84. "Residencia del doctor Frutos Delgado (1673)," in AGI, Escribanía de Cámara, legajo 319b, ff. 63, 65, 70, 79, 80, 83, 90, 94, 97; Roys, *The Indian Background*, 137–41. García Martínez, *Los pueblos de la Sierra*, 200, notes that for the decade of 1580, "the concept of cacicazgo became looser and at the same time less conflictive, and as a consequence the title of cacique could be used even by individuals who had been nothing more than principales, perhaps far removed from the direct descent of those originally recognized as *tlahtoque*."

Glossary

adelantado (Span.)   roughly, "pioneer" or "trailblazer"; in Yucatecan parlance, the honorific term for the eldest Francisco Montejo

aguada (Span.)   rain-fed temporary wetlands found in the south of the Yucatán peninsula

ah cuch cab (Maya)   individual responsible for enforcing a batab's decisions in the lordship

ah kin (Maya)   a pre-Christian Maya priest; literally, "sun priest"

ah tepal (Maya)   sovereign atop a pyramid of personal relationships; in Early Postclassic Yucatán, used to refer to the "king" of Chichén Itzá

alcabala (Span.)   volume-based royal sales tax

alcalde mayor (Span.)   royal Spanish officials appointed to govern the Yucatecan colony

alguacil (Span.)   sheriff or legal enforcer

almehen (Maya)   nobleman

almojarifazgo (Span.)   tax on products entering or leaving a port

altepetl (Nahuatl, pl., *altepeme*)   lordship, señorío, the basic unit of Nahuat society

anexo (Span.)   residential cluster

arroba (Span.)   measure of weight equalling approximately eleven kilograms

audiencia (Span.)   court of law

avencindado (Span.)   resident of a pueblo

227

ayuntamiento (Span.)   a governing town council, either of a Spanish city or villa; also known as *cabildo*

balché (Maya)   a ritual and mildly alcoholic beverage composed of honeyed water and fermented bark of a tree of the same name
barrio (Span.)   see *parcialidad*
batab (Maya)   village headman; cacique
batabil (Maya)   lordship, señorío
bienes de comunidad (Span.)   community property, usually in the form of tools, livestock, or constructions

cabecera (Span.)   head town, either in a religious or secular districting
cabecera de doctrina (Span.)   Franciscan-supervised community where a *guardián* lived, and where a convent had been constructed
cabildo (Span.)   a governing town council, either of a Spanish city or villa; or of a Maya pueblo (in this latter usage, synonymous with *república*)
cacicazgo (Taíno)   the rank or status of cacique
cacique (Taíno)   headman of an Indian village
caja de comunidad (Span.)   "Community Chest"; municipal treasury
calmulna (Maya)   community house where women were forced to weave cloth
calzas atadas (Span.)   literally, "tied pants," a common form of dress for men in the sixteenth century
canto llano (Span.)   mass conducted in the form of singing
cantor (Span.)   singer
capitán general (Span.)   title of military leadership awarded to the eldest Francisco de Montejo
capítulo (Span.)   Chapter, a governing junta of a Franciscan *custodia*, or Province, celebrated every three years
carcelero (Span.)   jailer
casta (Span.)   generic term for an individual of racially mixed background
cédula (Span.)   royal order or decree
cenote (Maya, orig. *ts'ono'ot*)   natural limestone well common in Yucatán
chirimía (Span.)   wooden flute similar to a recorder
chuccabal (Maya)   conquistador of señoríos

chuntan (Maya)   see *almehen*
ciudad (Span.)   city; more specifically, in Spanish parlance the largest of three types of settlements, followed by *villas* and *pueblos*
coadjutor (Span.)   assistant, usually in administrative matters of the church or of village affairs
colación (Span.)   residential cluster
congregación (Span.)   Franciscan practice of concentrating Indian villages into a single location; the community formed from said practice
convite (Span.)   a banquet
copal (Nahuatl)   incense derived from the berry of an indigenous tree
coroza (Span.)   "dunce cap" used in an auto-da-fé
corregidor (Span.)   local Spanish official with judicial, administrative, and fiscal duties
coyol (Maya)   flag or banner
cuchteel (Maya)   individual who stands in a subordinate relationship with someone else; a subject or vassal; a parishioner; a *parcialidad*
cuchul (Maya)   a vassal
cuerpos de república   see *cabildo*
custodia (Span.)   a Franciscan district secondary in size
custodio (Span.)   chief administrator of a Franciscan *custodia*
cúuchcabal (Maya)   political alliance headed by a *halach uinic*

defendor de indios (Span.)   also, protector de naturales
definidor (Span.)   Franciscan appointed during the chapter elections to provide counsel on religious or administrative matters in the province; these officials served three-year terms and were selected during the Franciscan chapter meetings held every three years
distrito (Span.)   see *jurisdicción*
doctrina (Span.)   district or territory under the responsibility of a priest of the Franciscan order

encomendero (Span.)   holder of tributary rights
encomienda (Span.)   tributary rights
escribano (Span.)   town clerk charged with record-keeping
estancia (Span.)   residential cluster; also, small property used for commercial production of some commodity

fanega (Span.)   measure of volume equaling 55.5 liters
feligrés (Span.)   parishioner
fiscal (Span.)   Indian official responsible for teaching Christian doctrine

gobernador (Span.)   after 1550, title given to the Indian official responsible for a pueblo or province
guardián (Span.)   chief administrator of a Franciscan *guardianía* who had administrative and judicial power over his assigned convent region
guardianía (Span.)   a Franciscan mission district consisting of a cabecera de doctrina and all of its subsidiary visita towns administratively controlled by a Franciscan official called a *guardián*

halach uinic (Maya)   a Maya overlord, above the level of batab
holpatán (Maya)   colonial-era contribution paid by Indians to underwrite the cost of Indian courts
holpop (Maya)   an office of undetermined character, apparently similar to "cacique"

indígena (Span.)   an Indian
ingenio (Span.)   a mill; most commonly refers to a sugar mill, but in this study the term applies to a place for processing indigo

juez de residencia (Span.)   official who conducts a *juicio de residencia*
juicio de residencia (Span.)   administrative review of one's predecessor in office
junta (Span.)   see *congregación*
jurisdicción (Span.)   one of the four major Spanish administrative divisions of Yucatán: Mérida, Campeche, Valladolid, and Bacalar

katún (Maya)   a twenty-year cycle that formed an integral part of the Maya pre-Hispanic calendar
kuil-kaxob (Maya)   spirits believed to guard the monte

licenciado (Span.)   a bachelor's degree; in colonial times, the title functioned to designate a lettered person qualified for the legal professional

GLOSSARY 231

limosna (Span.)   literally, "alms"; in Yucatecan colonial usage, Indian tribute paid to support the Church

macehual (Nahuatl)   Indian commoner
maestro de doctrina (Span.)   teacher of basic religious matters
maestro de escuela (Span.)   school teacher
mandamiento (Span.)   in colonial Yucatecan usage, the royal order authorizing use of Indian *repartimiento* labor
manga de la cruz (Span.)   popular cloth adornment for altars
mayordomo (Span.)   see *ah cuch cab*
mesón (Span.)   a publicly maintained inn
milpa (Nahuatl)   cornfield cultivated by means of slash-and-burn agriculture
milpa caña (Nahuatl-Span.)   milpa field in its first year of planting
milpa rosa (Nahuatl-Span.)   milpa field in its second year of planting
milpería (Nahuatl)   residential cluster
milpero (Nahuatl)   milpa farmer
mojonera (Span.)   stone or stones used to mark a boundary
monte (Span.)   forest or overgrown, uncultivated land
mulmenyah (Maya)   collective labor
multepal (Maya)   a form of government in which Maya leaders took decisions as a group; associated with the city of Mayapán

naborío (Taino)   Indian unattached to a pueblo, usually urban servants of the Spaniards
naguatato (Nahuatl)   interpreter
natural (Span.)   an Indian
noria (Span.)   water wheel

oidor (Span., literally, "listener")   representative or agent of an audiencia, assigned to hear cases
ordenanza (Span.)   legal or administrative instruction

parcialidad (Span.)   subdivision of a *congregación*, one in which families loyal to a batab organized their homes close to his place of residence
pierna de manta (Span.)   bolt of cloth the length of a human leg

pozole (Nahuatl)   beverage made of coarsely ground corn
principal (Span.)   Maya nobleman, *almehen*
provincia (Span.)   Province, a Franciscan mission territory comprised of numerous smaller convent jurisdictions called *guardianías*
provincial (Span.)   supervisor of a Franciscan Province, or *provincia*
pueblo (Span.)   village
pueblo de visita (Span.)   in Franciscan parlance, a secondary town governed by periodic visits of a friar from the *cabecera*
pueblo pasajero (Span.)   village located along the *camino real*

reducción (Span.)   see *congregación*
regidor (Span.)   official of the indigenous *república*
rejollada (Span.)   natural stone basin used to collect rain water
repartimiento de indios (Span.)   administrative technique whereby a Spanish official temporarily allocated Indians for encomienda service
repartimiento de mercancía (Span.)   administrative technique whereby a Spanish official, usually the *alcalde mayor*, advanced payments of cash or goods, payments which Indian recipients where then expected to redeem through any of a variety of services
rueda (Span.)   see *mulmenyah*

sahal (Maya)   role or obligation assumed by an Indian noble
saplam saplam (Maya)   system of collective cotton spinning used by Maya women
señorío (Span.)   *batabil*, lordship
sujeto (Span.)   in administrative terms, a town of secondary importance, subordinated to a *cabecera*

tameme (Nahuatl)   porter, freight carrier
tanda (Span.)   see *mulmenyah*
tasaciones (Span.)   Crown- or court-appointed limits or quotas on Indian tributary demands
teniente de alcalde (Span.)   assistants to the *alcalde mayor*, each assigned to one of the four *jurisdicciones*
terrazguero (Span.)   sharecropper
teuctli (Nahuatl)   lord of a seigniorial house

tlahtoani (Nahuatl; plural, *tlahtoque*)   governor of an altepetl
tomín (Span.)   one eighth of a *peso*, or the equivalent of one *real*
tostón (Span.)   one quarter of a Spanish *peso*, equal to four *reales*, or a half-*peso*
tupil (Nahuatl)   enforcer of village law

vecino (Span.)   in most usages, a non-Indian resident of a city or town
vicaria (Span.)   district or territory under the jurisdiction of a priest of the secular order
villa (Span.)   a mid-sized Spanish urban settlement
visita (Span.)   inspection made by a *visitador*; a priest's or friar's visit to an outlying community within his religious jurisdiction; a pueblo that receives such visits or inspections
visitador (Span.)   inspector equipped with broad powers of review and reform

xoth (Maya)   group of women who spin cotton using the *mulmenyah* system

zaragüelles (Span.)   baggy pants tied at the waist and ankles, popular in early colonial times

Bibliography

Archival Sources

AGI   Archivo General de Indias, Sevilla.
AGNM   Archivo General de la Nación, México.
ASAY   Archivo Sacramental del Arzobispado de Yucatán.

Secondary and Published Primary Sources

Alberro, Solange. "El amancebamiento en los siglos XVI y XVII: Un medio eventual de medrar." In *Familia y poder en Nueva España*, 155–66. Mexico City: Instituto Nacional de Antropología e Historia, 1991.

Alonso, Martín. *Enciclopedia del idioma: Diccionario histórico y moderno de la lengua española (siglos XII al XX) etimológico, tecnológico, regional e hispanoamericano*. 3 vols. Mexico City: Aguilar, 1998.

Álvarez, Cristina. *Diccionario etnolingüístico del idioma maya yucateco colonial*. 3 vols. Mexico City: Universidad Nacional Autónoma de México, 1980–94.

Andrews, Anthony P. "The Fall of Chichén Itzá: A Preliminary Hypothesis." *Latin American Antiquity* 1, no. 3 (1990): 258–67.

Andrews, Anthony P., E. Wyllys Andrews, and Fernando Robles Castellanos. "The Northern Maya Collapse and its Aftermath." *Ancient Mesoamerica* 14, no. 1 (2003): 151–56.

Barrera Vásquez, Alfredo. *Diccionario Maya Cordemex*. Mérida: Ediciones Cordemex, 1980.

———, trans. *Documento núm. 1 del deslinde de tierras en Yaxkukul Yucatán*. Mexico City: Instituto Nacional del Antropología e Historia, 1984.

Barrera Vásquez, Alfredo, and Silvia Rendón, trans. *El libro de los libros de Chilam Balam*. Mexico City: Fondo de Cultura Económica, 1963.

Barrera Vásquez, Alfredo, and Sylvanus G. Morley. "The Maya Chronicles." *Contribution to American Anthropology and History* 48 (1949): 1–85.
Blom, Frans. "Gaspar Antonio Chi, Interpreter." *American Anthropologist* 28, no. 2 (1928): 250–62.
Bretos, Miguel A. "Capillas de indios yucatecas del siglo XVI: Notas de un complejo formal." *Cuadernos de Arquitectura de Yucatán* 1 (1987): 1–12.
Brinton, Daniel G., ed. *The Maya Chronicles.* Philadelphia: Daniel G. Brinton, 1882.
Carlo, Bryan M. "Political Decentralization in the Maya Lowlands: An Examination of the Origins of Multepal or Joint Governance." Master's thesis, Southern Illinois University, Carbondale, 2006.
Carmack, Robert M. *The Quiché Mayas of Utatlán: The Evolution of a Highland Guatemala Kingdom.* Norman: University of Oklahoma Press, 1981.
Carrasco, Pedro. "Los linajes nobles del México antiguo." In *Estratificación social en la mesoamerica preshispánica,* 19–36. Edited by Pedro Carrasco and Johanna Broda. Mexico City: Centro de Investigaciones Superiores del Instituto Nacional del Antropología e Historia, 1976.

———. "Economía política en el reino tarasco." In *La sociedad indígena en el centro y occidente de México,* 63–102. Edited by Pedro Carrasco. Mexico City: El Colegio de Michoacán, 1986.

Cartas de Indias. 2 vols. Madrid: Imprenta de Manuel G. Hernández, 1877.
Celestino Solís, Eustaquio, and Luis Reyes García. *Anales de Tecamachalco, 1398–1590.* Mexico City: Centro de Investigaciones y Estudios Superiores en Antropología Social, and Fondo de Cultura Económica, and Gobierno de Estado de Puebla, 1992.
Chamberlain, Robert S. *The Conquest and Colonization of Yucatán, 1517–1550.* Washington, D.C.: Carnegie Institute of Washington, 1948.
Chase, Diane Z. "Postclassic Maya Elites: Ethnohistory and Archaeology." In *Mesoamerican Elites: An Archaeological Assessment,* 118–34. Edited by Diana Z. Chase and Arlen F. Chase. Norman: University of Oklahoma Press, 1992.
"The Chronicle of Chac-Xulub-Chen." In *The Maya Chronicles,* 189–259. Edited by Daniel G. Brinton. Philadelphia: D. G. Brinton, 1882.
Chuchiak, John F. IV. "It Is Their Drinking That Hinders Them. *Balche* and the Use of Ritual Intoxicants among the Colonial Yucatec Maya, 1550–1780." *Estudios de cultura maya* 24 (2004): 137–71.

———. "Writing as Resistance: Maya Graphic Pluralism and Indigenous Elite Strategies for Survival in Colonial Yucatán, 1550–1750." *Ethnohistory* 57, no. 1 (2010): 87–116.

Ciudad Real, Antonio de. *Calepino maya de Motul.* Mexico City: Plaza y Valdés Editores, 2001.

———. *Tratado curioso y doctor de las grandezas de la Nueva España.* 2 vols. Mexico City: Universidad Nacional Autónoma de México, 1976.

Cobos, Rafael. "Chichen Itza: Settlement and Hegemony During the Terminal Classic Period." In *The Terminal Classic in the Maya Lowlands: Collapse, Transition, and Transformation*, 517–44. Edited by. Arthur A. Demarest, Prudence M. Rice, and Don S. Rice. Boulder: University Press of Colorado, 2004.

Códice Pérez. Translated by Ermilo Solís Alcalá. Mérida: Liga de Acción Social, 1949.

Coe, Michael D. "A Model of Ancient Community Structure in the Maya Lowlands." *Southwestern Journal of Anthropology* 21, no. 2 (1965): 97–114.

———. *The Maya*. New York: Praeger Publishers, 1966.

Cook, Sherburne F., and Woodrow Borah. *Ensayos sobre historia de la población: México y el Caribe*. 3 vols. Mexico City: Siglo XXI Editores, 1977.

"Crónica de Yaxkukul." In *Crónicas mayas*. Edited by Juan Martínez Hernández. Mérida: Talleres de la Compañía Tipográfica Yucateca, 1926.

Culbert, Patrick. "La guerra y el estado segmentario." In *La guerra entre los antiguos mayas: Memoria de la primera mesa redonda de Palenque*, 41–52. Edited by Silvia Trejo. Mexico City: Instituto Nacional de Antropología e Historia, 2000.

Diccionario de Autoridades. 3 vols Madrid: Editorial Gredos, 1969.

Documentos para la historia de Yucatán, 1550–1560. Edited by France V. Scholes. 3 vols. Mérida: Publicaciones Carlos R. Menéndez, 1936–38.

Don Diego Quijada alcalde mayor de Yucatán, 1561–1565. Edited by Francisco V. Scholes and Eleanor B. Adams. 2 vols. Mexico City: Editorial Antigua Librería Robredo de José Porrúa e Hijos, 1938.

Epistolario de Nueva España, 1505–1818. Edited by Francisco del Paso y Troncoso. 16 vols. Mexico City: Antigua Librería Robredo de José Porrúa e Hijos, 1939–42.

Farriss, Nancy M. *Maya Society Under Spanish Rule: The Collective Enterprise of Survival*. Princeton: Princeton University Press, 1984.

Fernández de Oviedo y Valdés, Gonzalo. *Historia general y natural de las Indias, Islas y Tierra Firme del mar océano*. 5 vols. Madrid: Editorial Atlas, 1959.

Flores Torres, Jorge. *Los mayas yucatecos y el control cultural: Etnotecnología, mayaeconomía y pensamiento político de los pueblos centro-orientales de Yucatán*. Mexico City: Universidad Autónoma de Chapingo, and Universidad Autónoma de Yucatán, 1997.

Freidel, David. "Lowland Maya Political Economy: Historical and Archaeology Perspectivas in Lights of Intensive Agricultura." In *Spaniards and Indians in Southeastern Mesoamerica: Essays on the History of Ethnic Relations*, 40–63. Edited by Murdo J. Macleod y Robert Wasserstrom. Lincoln: University of New Mexico Press, 1983.

García Bernal, Manuela Cristina. "García de Palacio y sus ordenanzas para Yucatán." *Temas americanistas* 5 (1985): 1–12.

———. *La sociedad de Yucatán, 1700–1750*. Sevilla: Escuela de Estudios Hispano-Americano de Sevilla, 1972.

———. *Población y encomienda en Yucatán bajo las Austrias*. Sevilla: Escuela de Estudios Hispano-Americanos de Sevilla, 1978.

García Castro, René. *Indios, territorio y poder en la provincia de Matlatzinca: La negociación del espacio político de los pueblos otomianos, siglos XVI–XVII*. Mexico

City: Insitituto Nacional de Antropología e Historia, Colegio de México, Centro de Investigaciones y Estudios en Antropología Social, 1999.

García Martínez, Bernardo. "Jurisdicción y propiedad: una distinción fundamental en la historia de los pueblos de indios del México colonial." *European Review of Latin American and Caribbean Studies* 53 (1992): 47–60.

———. *Los pueblos de la Sierra: El poder y el espacio entre los indios del norte de Puebla hasta 1700*. Mexico City: El Colegio de México, 1987.

García Quintanilla, Alejandra. "El dilema del *ah kimsah k'ax*, 'el que mata al monte.' Significados del monte entre los mayas milperos de Yucatán." *Mesoamérica* 39 (2000): 255–86.

Gates, William, trans. *Yucatan Before and After the Conquest by Friar Diego de Landa*. New York: Dover Publications, 1978.

Gerhard, Peter. "Congregaciones de indios en la Nueva España antes de 1570." *Historia mexicana* 24, no. 3 (1977): 347–95.

———. *The Southeast Frontier of New Spain*. Princeton: Princeton University Press, 1979.

Gibson, Charles. *The Aztecs Under the Spanish Rule: A History of the Indians of the Valley of Mexico, 1519–1810*. Stanford: Stanford University Press, 1964.

González Cicero, Stella María. *Perspectiva religiosa en Yucatán, 1517–1571*. Mexico City: El Colegio de México, 1978.

Hanks, William F. *Converting Words: Mayas in the Age of the Cross*. Berkeley: University of California Press, 2010.

Haviland, William A. "Ancient Lowland Maya Social Organization." In *Archaeological Studies in Middle America*, 26. Nueva Orleans: Middle American Research Institute, 1970.

Hoekstra, Rik. "A Different Way of Thinking: Contrasting Spanish and Indian Social and Economic Views in Central Mexico (1550–1600)." In, *The Indian Community of Colonial Mexico: Fifteen Essays on Land Tenure, Corporate Organizations, Ideology and Village Politics*, 69–86. Edited by Alij Ouweneel and Simon Miller. Amsterdam: Centre for Latin American Research and Documentation, 1990.

Jones, Grant D. *Maya Resistance to Spanish Rule. Time and History on a Colonial Frontier*. Albuquerque: University of New Mexico, Press, 1989.

Lacadena García–Gallo, Alfonso, and Andrés Ciudad Real. "Reflexiones recientes sobre la estructura política maya clásica." In *Anatomía de una civilización: Aproximaciones interdisciplinarias a la cultura maya*, 31–64. Edited by Andrés Ciudad Real, Yolanda Fernández, José Miguel García Campillo, María Josefa Iglesias Ponce de León, Alfonso Lacadena García-Gallo, and Luis T. Sanz Castro. Madrid: Sociedad Española de Estudios Mayas, 1998.

Landa, Diego de. *Relación de las cosas de Yucatán*. 10th ed. Mexico City: Editorial Porrúa, 1973.

LeCount, Lisa J. "Like Water for Chocolate: Feasting and Political Ritual among the Late Classic Maya at Xunantunich, Belize." *American Anthropologist* 103, no. 4 (2001): 935–53.

Lizana, Fray Bernardo de. *Devocionario de nuestra señora de Izamal y conquista espiritual de Yucatán*. Mexico City: Universidad Nacional Autónoma de México, 1995.

López Austin, Alfredo. *Tarascos y mexicas*. Mexico City: Secretaría de Educación Pública, 1981.

López Cogolludo, Diego. *Historia de Yucatán*. Mexico City: Academia Literaria, 1957.

López de Gómara, Francisco. *Historia de la conquista de Mexico*. 2 vols. Mexico City: Pedro Robredo, 1943.

López Sarrelangue, Delfina E. "El caso de un gobernador michoacano en el siglo XVI." *Relaciones* 6, no. 22 (1985): 21–30.

———. *La nobleza indígena de Pátzcuaro en la época virreinal*. Mexico City: Universidad Nacional Autónoma de México, 1965.

Lucero, Lisa. *Water and Ritual: The Rise and Fall of Classic Maya Rulers*. Austin: University of Texas Press, 2006.

Marcus, Joyce. "Ancient Maya Political Organization." In *Lowland Maya Civilization in the Eighth Century AD*, 111–83. Edited by Jeremy A. Sabloff, and John S. Henderson. Washington, D.C.: Dumbarton Oaks Research Library and Collection, 1993.

Martin, Simon, and Nikolai Grube. *Chronicle of the Maya Kings and Queens: Deciphering the Dynasties of the Ancient Maya*. London: Thames and Hudson Ltd., 2000.

Martínez Hernández, Juan, trans. *Crónicas Mayas*. Mérida: Talleres de la Compañía Tipográfica Yucateca, 1928.

Martínez, Hildeberto. *Tepeaca en el siglo XVI: Tenencia de la tierra y organización de un señorío*. Mexico City: Ediciones de La Casa Chata, 1984.

———. "Teucyotl: El gobierno señorial de Tecamachalco, Puebla, siglo XVI." In *Formas de voto, prácticas de las asembleas y toma de decisiones: Un acercamiento comparativo*, 101–38. Edited by Victor M. Franco Pellotier, Danièle Dehouve, and Aline Hémond. Mexico City: Centro de Investigaciones y Estudios en la Antropología Social, 2011.

Mendieta, Gerónimo de. *Historia eclesiástica indiana*. 4 vols. Mexico City: Editorial Salvador Chávez Hayhoe, 1945.

Menegus Bornemann, Margarita. "El cacicazgo en la Nueva España." In *El cacicazgo en la Nueva España y Filipinas*. Edited by Margarita Menegus Bornemann and Rodolfo Aguirre Salvador, 13–69. Mexico City: Universidad Nacional Autónoma de México, Plaza y Valdés Editores, 2005.

Miranda, José. *El tributo indígena en la Nueva España durante el siglo XVI*. Mexico City: El Colegio de México, 1952.

———. *La función económica del encomendero en los orígenes del régimen colonial (Nueva España, 1525–1531)*. Mexico City: Universidad Nacional Autónoma de México, 1965.

Moreno Toscano, Alejandra. *Geografía económica de México (siglo XVI)*. Mexico City: El Colegio de México, 1968.

Murra, John V. "El control vertical de un máximo de pisos ecológicos en la economía de las sociedades andinas." In *Formaciones económicas y políticas del mundo andino*, 59–115. Edited by John V. Murra. Lima: Instituto de Estudios Peruanos, 1975.

———. *La organización económica del estado inca*. Mexico City: Siglo XXI Editores, 1980.

Okoshi Harada, Tsubasa. *Códice de Calkiní*. Mexico City: Universidad Nacional Autónoma de México, 2009.

———. "Kokotenki Kokishumatzu no mayahokubuteichi no ryoikikozo." *Revista Histórica de la Universidad de Gakushuin* 23 (1985): 26–44.

———. "La historia de los Cocom. Una lectura de la *Relación* de fray Diego de Landa." In *Texto y contexto: La literatura maya yucateca en perspectiva diacrónica*, 139–58. Edited by Antje Gusenheimer, Tsubasa Okoshi Harada, and John F. Chuchiak IV. Bonn: Estudios Americanistas de Bonn, 2009.

———. "Los canules. Análisis etnohistórico del códice de Calkiní." PhD diss. Universidad Nacional Autónoma de México, 1992.

———. "Mito, historia y legitimación del poder entre los mayas posclásicos de Yucatán." In *Yucatán a través de los siglos*, 213–28. Edited by Ruth Gubler and Patric Martell. Mérida: Universidad Autónoma de Yucatán, 2001.

———. "Tenencia de la tierra y territorialidad: conceptualización de los mayas yucatecos en vísperas de la invasión española." In *Conquista, transculturación y mestizaje: raíz y origen de México*, 67–94. Edited by Lorenzo Ochoa. Mexico City: Universidad Nacional Autónoma de México, 1995.

Okoshi Harada, Tsubasa, and Sergio Quezada. "Vivir con fronteras: Espacios mayas peninsulares del siglo XVI." In *El territorio maya. Memoria de la quinta mesa redonda de Palenque*, 137–49. Coord. Rodrigo Liendo Stuado. Mexico City: Instituto Nacional de Antropología e Historia, 2008.

Ortiz Yam, Isaura Inés. "Los montes yucatecos: La percepción de un espacio en las fuentes coloniales." In *Text and Context. Yucatec Maya Literature in a Diachronic Perspective*. Edited by Antje Gunsenheimer, Tsubasa Okoshi Harada, and John F. Chuchiak. Aachen: Estudios Americanistas de Bonn, 2009.

———. "Los pueblos del noroeste yucateco." Master's thesis, Universidad Autónoma de Yucatán, 1998.

Ortiz Yam, Isaura Inés, and Sergio Quezada. *Visita de Diego García de Palacio a Yucatán, 1583*. Mexico City: Universidad Nacional Autónoma de México, 2007.

Pastor, Rodolfo. *Campesinos y reformas: la mixteca, 1700–1856*. Mexico City: El Colegio de México, 1987.

Pipes, Richard. *Propiedad y libertad: Dos conceptos inseparables de la historia*. México City: Fondo de Cultura Económica, 2002.

"Probanza de don Juan Kauil (1618)." In *The Maya Chronicles*, 114–16. Edited by Daniel G. Brinton. Philadelphia: D. G. Brinton, 1882.

Proskouriakoff, Tatiana. "Mayapán: The Last Stronghold of a Civilization." *Archaeology* 7, no. 2 (1954): 96–103.

Quezada, Sergio. "Don Juan Chan, un cacique antiidólatra." *Mayab* 5 (1989): 41–44.

———. "El linaje Xiu." In *Dos décadas de investigación en historia económica comparada en América Latina: Homenaje a Carlos Sempat Assadourian*, 113–121. Edited by Margarita Menegus Bornemann. Mexico City: El Colegio de México, and Centro de Investigaciones y Estudios Superiores en Antropología Social, and Instituto Doctor José María Luis Mora, and Centro de Estudios sobre la Universidad, and Universidad Nacional Autónoma de México, 1999.

———. "La presencia española en la agricultura maya, siglo XVI." In *Agricultura indígena: Pasado y presente*, 107–201. Edited by Teresa Rojas Rabiela. Mexico City: Centro de Investigaciones y Estudios Superiores en Antropología Social, 1990.

———. *Los pies de la república: Los mayas peninsulares, 1550–1750*. Mexico City: Centro de Investigaciones y Estudios Superiores en Antropología Social, and Instituto Nacional Indigenista, 1997.

———. "Los sistemas de trabajo en Yucatán, 1541–1561." *Boletín de la Escuela de Ciencias Antropológicas de la Universidad de Yucatán* 9, no. 44 (1980): 55–69.

Quezada, Sergio, and Tsubasa Okohsi Harada. *Papeles de los Xiu de Yaxá*. Mexico City: Universidad Nacional Autónoma de México, 2001.

Relaciones histórico-geográfica de la gobernación de Yucatán. Edited by Mercedes de la Garza, Ana Luisa Izquierdo, María del Carmen León, and Tolita Figueroa. 2 vols. Mexico City: Universidad Nacional Autónoma de México, 1983.

Restall, Matthew. *Life and Death in a Maya Community: The Ixil Testaments of the 1760s*. Lancaster: Labyrinthos, 1995.

———. *The Maya World: Yucatec Culture and Society, 1550–1850*. Stanford: Stanford University Press, 1997.

Ringle, William M. "On the Political Organization of Chichen Itza." *Ancient Mesoamerica* 15, no. 2 (2004): 167–218.

Ringle, William M., and Bey, George J., III. "Post-Classic and Terminal Classic Courts of the Northern Maya Lowlands." In *Royal Courts of the Ancient Maya: Data and Case Studies*, 2:266–307. Edited by Takeshi Inomata and Stephen D. Houston. Boulder: Westview Press, 2001.

Robles Castellanos, Fernando, and Anthony P. Andrews. "A Review and Synthesis of Recent Postclassic Archaeology in Northern Yucatán." In *Late Lowland Maya Civilization: Classic to Postclassic*, 53–98. Edited by Jeremy A. Sablof and Wyllys Andrews V. Albuquerque: University of New Mexico Press, 1986.

Rodríguez de San Miguel, Juan N. *Pandectas hispano-mexicanas*. Vol. 3. México City: Universidad Nacional Autónoma de México, 1980.

Roys Ralph L., ed. and trans. *The Book of Chilam Balam of Chumayel*. Washington, D.C.: Carnegie Institution of Washington, 1933.

———. "The Hunac Ceel Episode." In *The Book of Chilam Balam of Chumayel*, 177–81. Edited and translated by Ralph L. Roys. Washington, D.C.: Carnegie Institution of Washington, 1933.

———. *The Indian Background of Colonial Yucatan*. Washington, D.C.: Carnegie Institution of Washington, 1943.

———. "Literary Sources for the History of Mayapán." In *Mayapán, Yucatan, Mexico*, 25–86. Edited by. H. E. D. Pollock. Washington, D.C.: Carnegie Institute of Washington, 1962.

———. "Lowland Maya Native Society at Spanish Contact." In *Handbook of Middle American Indians*. 3:659–78. Edited by Gordon Willey. Austin: University of Texas Press, 1965.

———. "Personal Names of the Mayas of Yucatan." *Contribution to American Anthropology and History* 6 (1940): 31–48.

———. *The Political Geography of the Yucatan Maya*. Washington, D.C.: Carnegie Institution of Washington, 1957.

———. "Traditions of Caste and Chieftainship among the Maya." In *The Book of Chilam Balam of Chumayel*, 188–95. Edited and translated by Ralph L. Roys. Washington, D.C.: Carnegie Institution of Washington, 1933.

———. "Toltec Military Orders in Yucatan." In *The Book of Chilam Balam of Chumayel*, 196-200. Edited and translated by Ralph L. Roys. Washington, D.C.: Carnegie Institution of Washington, 1933.

———. *The Titles of Ebtun*. Washington, D.C.: Carnegie Institution of Washington, 1939.

Roys, Ralph L., France V. Scholes, and Eleanor B. Adams. "Report and Census of the Indians of Cozumel, 1570." In *Contribution to American Anthropology and History* 30 (1940): 5–30.

Roys, Ralph L., France V. Scholes, and Eleanor B. Adams. "Census and Inspection of the Town of Pencuyut, Yucatan, in 1583 by Diego García de Palacio, oidor of the audiencia of Guatemala." *Ethnohistory* 6, no. 3 (1959): 195–225.

Rubio Mañé, Jorge Ignacio. "Las jurisdicciones de Yucatán: La relación de la plaza de teniente del rey en Campeche. Año de 1744." *Boletín del Archivo General de la Nación* 7, nos. 3–4 (1966): 549–631.

———. *Notas y acotaciones a la Historia de Yucatán de fray Diego López Cogolludo*. Mexico City: Academia Literaria, 1957.

Sánchez de Aguilar, Pedro. *Informe contra idolorum cultores del obispado de Yucatán*. Mérida: E. G. Triay e Hijos, 1937.

Scholes, France V., and Ralph L. Roys. *The Maya Chontal Indians of Acalan-Tixchel: A Contribution to the History and Ethnography of the Yucatan Peninsula*. Norman: University of Oklahoma Press, 1968.

Segovia Liga, Argelia. "Los indios del Mariscal: Revisión de un manuscrito yucateco del siglo XVII." Thesis, Universidad Nacional Autónoma de México, 2008.

Solórzano y Pereira, Juan de. *Política indiana*. Madrid: Editorial Atlas, 1972.

Suhler, Charles, Traci Ardren, David Freidel, and Dave Johnstone. "The Rise and Fall of Terminal Classic Yaxuna, Yucatán, México." In *The Terminal Classic in the Maya Lowlands: Collapse, Transition, and Transformation*, 456–84. Edited

by Arthur A. Demarest, Prudence M. Rice, and Don S. Rice. Boulder: University Press of Colorado, 2004.
Taylor, William B. *Landlord and Peasant in Colonial Oaxaca*. Stanford: Stanford University Press, 1972.
Torquemada, Juan de. *De los veinte y un libros rituales y monarquía indiana, con el origen y guerra de los indios occidentales, de sus poblazones, descubrimiento, conquista, comercio y otras cosas maravillosas de la misma tierra*. 7 vols. Mexico City: Universidad Nacional Autónoma de México, 1975–1983.
Vega, Lope de. *El peregrino en su patria*. Madrid: Editorial Castalia, 1973.
Villa Rojas, Alfonso. *The Maya of East Central Quintana Roo*. Washington, D.C.: Carnegie Institution of Washington, 1943.
———. "Los quejaches: tribu olvidada del antiguo Yucatán." In *Estudios etnológicos: los mayas*, 447–66. Edited by Alfonso Villa Rojas. Mexico City: Universidad Nacional Autónoma de México, 1985.
———. "La tenencia de la tierra entre los mayas de la antigüedad." In *Estudios etnológicos: los mayas*, 23–45. Edited by Alfonso Villa Rojas. Mexico City: Universidad Nacional Autónoma de México, 1985.
Villafuerte García, María de Lourdes. "Relaciones entre los grupos sociales a través de la información matrimonial: Ciudad de México, 1628–1634." Master's thesis, Universidad Nacional Autónoma de México, 1998.
Weaver, Muriel. *The Aztecs, Maya and Their Predecessors*. 2nd ed. New York: Academics Press, 1981.
Zavala, Silvio. *La encomienda indiana*. 2nd ed. Mexico City: Editorial Porrúa, 1973.
———. "Los primeros títulos de encomienda en Nueva España." In *Memoria del Colegio Nacional 7*, no. 1 (1970): 11–19.
———. *Los esclavos indios en la Nueva España*. Mexico City: El Colegio Nacional, 1967.

INDEX

Acanceh, as reducción, 65, 74
Aguadas, 16
Ah cuch cab. See *Principales*
Ah kin (sun priest), 21, 113
Ah tepal, 12
Alcabala, 70
Alcalde (indigenous office), 79
Alcalde mayor, 47–48
Alguacil (indigenous office), 80
Almehenob. See *Principales*
Almojarifazgo, 70
Atlepetl, 4
Audiencia, administrative functions, 40; naming of *alcaldes mayores*, 91–92; support for Franciscans, 49, 59; and Tomás López Medel's *visita* to Yucatán, 56

Bacalar, Salamanca de, 36, 97; established as city, 42, 46–47
Balché, 60
Barrera Vásquez, Alfredo, 9
Batab: and *cabeceras*, 42–43; and *cabildos*, 94–99; and *cúuchcabal*, 23–27; Diego de Landa's persecutions of, 105–109; as dispenser of justice, 19–21; and early Franciscans, 57; and *encomienda*, 44–45; and family chieftains, 18–19; older interpretation of, 3–4, 6–7; after Mayapán collapse, 24; as preconquest lineage governors, 27–32; reduction of authority, 117–122; retitled as *señores*, 43; and slavery, 103; and Spanish territoriality, 41. See also *Cacique; Cacique-Gobernador*
Batabil: decline of, 83–84; early nature of, 18–19, 20–21; misconception as territorially based, 6–7; and natural resources, 16–17; older interpretation of, 3–4; reorganization under early Spanish colonialism, 59–63
Bécal, as reducción, 74
Bienes de comunidad, 88–89
Book of Chilam Balam, 12

Cabecera, as Spanish settlement term, 42–43, 47
Cabeza de doctrina, 51
Cabildo (indigenous), 75; and *caja de comunidad*, 87–88; and *congregación*, 82–86; and demographic collapse, 96–97; displacement of batabs, 81–82; opposition to, 89–94; origins, 76–77; power in the early villages, 94–99
Cabildo (Spanish), 45, 47
Cacique, 85–86, 87–88; ambiguity of term, 94–95; and colonial land measurement, 60–61; early privileges of, 101–102; exploitation of villages, 97–98; final reduction of

245

Cacique, continued
  power, 109–122; and slavery, 103; support for pastoral visits, 51; See also *Batab, Cacique-Gobernador*
Cacique-Gobernador, 77, 81; and *cabildos*, 78–82, 94–99; defense of authority, 90–91; and demographic collapse, 96–97; introduction of term, 78; and slavery, 94–95. See also *Cacique*
Caja de comunidad, 77, 79, 86–89
Calepino maya, 19, 23, 48
Calkiní, 25, 35, 60, 84, 85, 115; as reducción, 64, 66, 61, 73
Calkiní Codex, 9, 10
Calotmul, 117, 118, as reducción, 74
Camino real, 66
Campeche, 33, 36, 49, 50, 92, 97, 103; establishment as city, 42, 46–48; as reducción, 56
Canché lineage, 26
Canul lineage, 22, 25, 119
Caucel, as reducción, 65
Cehache, 22, 38, 116
Céspedes Oviedo, Luis de, 83, 93, 111, 116
Chac Xib Chac, *al tepal* of Chichén Itzá, 13
Champotón, 34, 35, 80, 97, 115
Chancenote, 23, 83; as reducción, 64, 66, 73
Chel lineage, 25–26
Chetumal, 33, 34, 35,
Chi, Gaspar Antonio, 16
Chichén Itzá, 7, 22, 30, 33, 34; period of hegemony, 11–14
Chichimilá, as reducción, 65, 74
Chuyubchuén, as reducción, 74
Ciudad, as Spanish settlement term, 42
Ciudad Real, Antonio de, 9–11, 18, 48
Cochuah lineage, 113–114
Cocom lineage, 12, 25, 38, 100–101
Congregación, 55–59, 61; spatial distribution of, 63–75
Conkal, evangelized, 49, 50
Convite, 60
ACrónica de Chac-Xulub-Chen,@ 9
Cuchteel, 8–9, 24, 31
Cupul lineage, 22, 25, 38, 119

Custodia, as Franciscan administrative unit, 49
Cúuchcabal, 40; creation of, 21–27; defined, 23

Dávila, Alonso, 34
Defensor de los naturales, 91
Distrito, as administrative unit, 47
Doctrina, 77, 80, 86, 96
Documento núm. 1, 9
Don, as honorific title, 101–102
Dzilam, 33
Dzidzantún, 35, 52, 78, 84; evangelization, 49; as reducción, 64, 73
Dzonotaké, as reducción, 65, 74
Dzuluinicob, 22, 27, 35, 38, 116

Ekbalam, 22, 35
Encomendero, 68–69, 79; defined, 43–46; and halach uinicob, 20
Encomienda, 39; defined, 43–46
Escribano (indigenous office), 80
Espita, 88; as reducción, 74

Franciscans, 39; and *cacique* power, 94; establishment of *congregaciones*, 63–75; initial operations in Yucatán, 48–59

García de Palacio, Diego, 6, 82, 77, 86, 99, 111–112, 121
Gobernador, 78–79
Guardianía, 39, 51

Halach uinic: after 1560, 78–79; and *cabeceras*, 42–43; and *cúuchcabal*, 23–27; Diego de Landa's persecutions of, 105–109; during Early Postclassic period, 12–14; as dispenser of justice, 19–21; and *encomienda*, 45–46; before Mayapán collapse, 12–13; older interpretation of, 6–7; reordering of authority after Mayapán collapse, 14–15; retitled as *señores*, 43; rites of appointment, 31–32; and slavery, 103; and Spanish concepts of territory, 41; under Mayapán *multepal*, 14–15. See also *Cacique*

Hocabá, 20, 35, 44, 78, 94, 107, 108, 115, 118, 119
Hoctún, 44, 82, 118, 119
Homún, 89, 90; as reducción, 73
Huhí, 44, 78, 118, 119
Hunac Ceel, *halach uinic* of Mayapán, 13
Hunucmá, 102; as reducción, 65, 71, 74

Ichmul, 113
Izamal, 7, 49, 66; evangelization of, 49; and pilgrimages, 52

Juez de residencia, 95
Juicio de residencia, 90, 92
Junta: See *Congregación*
Jurisdicción, as administrative concept, 47

Kauil lineage, 30–31
Kikil, as reducción, 74
Kinchil, as reducción, 65, 74
Kukulkán, 13; and annual rituals, 27

Landa, Diego de, 14, 17, 19, 20, 30, 31, 36–37, 52, 92–93; anti-idolatry campaign of, 106–109
Loaysa, García Jofre de, 48, 78, 79, 91, 94, 114
López de Cogolludo, Diego, 61, 71
López Medel, Tomás, 45, 46, 48, 56, 58, 77–78, 89, 91, 94, 103–105, 119
Lord: See *Batab*
Lordship: See *Batabil*

Macehual, 69, 70, 108
Maestro de escuela, 70, 108
Maní, 22, 50, 78, 80, 86, 87, 89, 94, 105, 108, 110, 115; as encomienda of Francisco de Montejo, 44; evangelization of, 49; as reducción, 64, 66, 71–72, 73; religious persecutions of Diego de Landa, 106–109; as scene of rituals, 27
Maya of Yucatán, 1546–1547 uprising, 36, 49, 56, 104; and adultery, 95–96; cabildos, 78–82; and church music, 86; collective labor and land access, 16–18; colonial community resources, 86–89; concentration under Spanish rule, 39; and *cúuchcabal*, 23–24; decline of lineages, 100–101; early Postclassic period, 11–14; effects of colonial policy, 82–86; after fall of Mayapán, 14–15; imposition of territorial limits, 59–63; and lineages, 27–32; and *reducciones*, 63–75; reduction of indigenous nobility, 112–22; resistance to *congregación*, 63; resistance to Spanish invasion, 35; southern exodus, 22–24
Mayapán, 31, 37, 38; fragmentation of power, 22–23; and halach uinicob, 12–13; *multepal* of, 14–15; resentment over collapse of, 29
Mérida, 35, 50, 56, 66, 67, 81, 87, 97, 99, 103, 107, 108; establishment as city, 44, 46–48; evangelization of, 49
Mesón, 69
Milpa farming, and Maya land tenure, 16–17
Mojonero, 59–60
Montejo, Francisco de (Adelantado, the father), 34, 40, 44, 47, 49, 76; organization of conquest of Yucatán, 32–33; removal as governor, 45
Montejo, Francisco de (the Nephew), 34, 35
Montejo, Francisco de (the Son), 34, 35, 48
Motul, 31, 35, 49, 50, 81
Mulmenyah, 17–18, 20
Multepal, creation of, 14–15; fragmentation of, 21–27

Nachí Cocom, 25, 26, 35, 81, 115
Naguatato, 70
New Laws (1542), 103

Okoshi Harada, Tsubasa, 8
Overlord. See *Halach uinic*
Oxkutzcab, 24, 71, 72

Pacheco, Gaspar, 35–36
Panabá, as reducción, 65, 74
Parcialidad, and *Cuchteel*, 9
Pech lineage, 25–26, 31, 119–20
Popolá, 22, 84
Principales, 19–20, 21, 27–28, 94

Provincia, introduction of term, 41
Pueblo, as Spanish settlement term, 42, 55
Pueblo de visita, 51

Quijada, Diego de, 48, 66, 78, 80, 82, 84, 89, 90, 91, 94, 102, 105, 110, 114–15, 117, 118; cacique opposition to, 91–93; opposition to encomenderos, 105; support of Landa's anti-idolatry campaigns, 106–109

Reducción. See *Congregación*
Regidor, as indigenous office, 79
Repartimiento de indios, 88
Repartimiento de mercancía, 93
República de indios. See *Cabildo* (indigenous)
Roys, Ralph L., interpretation of Maya Lordship, 6, 8
Rueda (labor rotation system). See *Saplam saplam*

Sací. See Valladolid
Santillán, Diego de, 102, 116, 117, 120
Saplam saplam, 18
Señoría. See *Batabil*
Sotuta, 22, 26, 94, 107, 108; as reducción, 65, 73
Spanish conquest, 32–37; first attempt, 40–41; second attempt, 41; and Spanish corporate groups, 39–40; and spatial reorganization, 41–43, 46–48
Sucilá, as reducción, 74
Suyuá, as linguistic court ritual, 31–32; decline of, 112–13, 117

Tahmuy, as reducción, 74
Tasación, 45, 96
Tekax, 71
Teniente de alcaldía, 39, 46–48, 93
Ticul, 87
Tihó. See Mérida
Tihosuco, 35, 78, 107, 114, 115; as reducción, 74
Tizimín, 87, 96, 98, 111; evangelization of, 54; as reducción, 66–70, 71
Tizonot, as reducción, 75
Tlahtoani, 4
Toral, Francisco de, 21; opposition to Diego de Landa, 109
Tupil. See *Alguacil*

Umán, as reducción, 65, 66
Uxmal, 12–13

Valladolid (or Sací), 22, 35, 36, 54, 66, 93, 97; establishment as city, 42, 46–48; evangelization of, 49–50; as reducción, 64, 73
Villa, as Spanish settlement term, 42
Villalpando, Luis de, 56, 103
Virgin of la Purísima Concepción, 52–53
Visitas (Franciscan), 50

Xicalango, 34
Xiu, Francisco de Montejo, 60, 78, 87, 94, 103, 105, 110, 115, 117
Xiu lineage, 12, 18, 22, 24, 38, 100–101, 116
Xoth, labor practice, 18
Xul: and 1546–1547 Maya uprising, 36; as ritual calendar date, 27

www.ingramcontent.com/pod-product-compliance
Lightning Source LLC
Chambersburg PA
CBHW021348230426
43666CB00006B/441